INTERNATIONAL PRAISE FOR

MASAHIKO SHIMADA'S

DREAM MESSENGER

"Shimada may turn out to be one of the major new Japanese voices."
—*New York Times*

"The discovery...is Masahiko Shimada."
—*Times Literary Supplement* (London)

"Tantalizing...provocative...skillfully mixing genres like a
quick shuffle of cards, the young author creates a peculiar
pastiche challenging notions of self and sexuality,
morality, spirituality...."
—*Booklist*

"Shimada captures his characters' imaginations with lavish
imagery that incorporates elements of both
realism and fantasy."
—*Library Journal*

"A haunting, ac

DREAM MESSENGER

DREAM MESSENGER

a novel by

MASAHIKO SHIMADA

translated by
Philip Gabriel

WARNER BOOKS

A Time Warner Company

Translated and adapted by Philip Gabriel with the permission of the author.

Originally published in Japanese under the title *Yumetsukai* by Kodansha Ltd., 1989.

Warner Books Edition
Copyright © 1992 by Kodansha International Ltd.
All rights reserved.

This Warner Books edition is published by arrangement with Kodansha America, Inc., 114 Fifth Avenue, New York, NY 10011.

Warner Books, Inc., 1271 Avenue of the Americas, New York, NY 10020

 A Time Warner Company

Printed in the United States of America
First Warner Books Printing: September 1994
10 9 8 7 6 5 4 3 2 1

Library of Congress Cataloging-in-Publication Data
Shimada, Masahiko, 1961-
 [Yumetsukai. English]
 Dream messenger / Masahiko Shimada ; [translated and adapted by Philip Gabriel] . -- Warner Books edition.
  p.   cm.
 ISBN 0-446-67010-3
 I. Gabriel, J. Philip. II. Title.
PL861.H526Y8613 1994
895.6'35--dc20   94-10174
                                                      CIP

Cover design by Julia Kushnirsky
Cover photograph by Sally Boon

Contents

Part I

1 Maiko's Sense of Smell   3

2 Baby Buggies and Outer Spacemen   20

3 "What Choice Do I Have?":
A Theoretical Approach   29

4 An Orgy a Day   53

Part II

5 A Japanese Rip van Winkle;
A Weird-Looking Dog Eating Pizza   79

6 Orphans of the Storm   90

7 Penelope   131

Part III

8 Primitive Man Arrives in Tokyo   165

9 In Search of Karma   190

10 Raphael   212

11   The Tale of the Heike;
Taro Urashima's View of History   220

12   A Gentle Heretic:
It's No Good to Suffer Alone   228

Part IV

13   Talks with Ghosts   245

14   A Weird Job   255

15   The Desert Troubadour   266

16   Creation   287

PART

I

1

Maiko's Sense of Smell

"Please find my son."

That was the gist of the letter. It arrived entirely without warning, and all Maiko could think was, this person is out to lunch. If it was meant as a prank, it wasn't very funny.

The letter was from Mika Amino, widow of the infamous land speculator Motonobu Amino. Amino was a bloodsucker, people said, but strangely enough after his death Mrs. Amino managed to escape the hatred of the enemies he left behind. If the husband is rotten, people think the wife must be too; even if the woman was unsavory on her own, people think the man made her that way. But when her husband was alive, Mrs. Amino stayed far away from his business affairs. She didn't participate in his foul schemes, and she didn't run around trying to be charitable to make up for them. Then, as now, she was simply a loose cannon, a rich lady who used her fortune in unpredictable ways.

Mika Amino was a second-generation Japanese American. She'd grown up in New York and come to Japan at age twenty-eight. And now, as the benefactor of a real estate fortune, she was spending money like the old-time American nouveau riche.

Mrs. Amino didn't think of herself as either Japanese or American. Living in an age when there was little comfort in being one or the other, she came to think of her identity as part of the space in between. She'd been born on the border between California and Arizona and was now a hermit in the exclusive seaside resort of Kamakura. But the only place she could feel at all at home in was what lay between—the Pacific Ocean. It wasn't so much because of her parents or ancestors, or America or Japan. It was instinct.

Maiko Rokujo had met Mrs. Amino only three times, and obviously they were not close. But suddenly here was this letter almost demanding that Maiko locate Mrs. Amino's son, and on top of that, the phone ringing the instant she finished reading it. It was as if someone had been watching her through a peephole. A man's voice, a vacant-sounding voice with a distinctive rhythm, flowed out the receiver and swirled round Maiko's ear. Bewitched by the rough, working-class intonation, Maiko dropped all her defenses.

The man introduced himself as Mrs. Amino's personal secretary. Maiko's success as a securities analyst was well known to Mrs. Amino, he said, and she wished to avail herself of Maiko's insight and talent. Of course, Maiko had an engaging personality, but it was her intuition that was of paramount interest here. Mrs. Amino would like you to come see her, he said. Name the date and time and we'll send a car around. Think about it as if you're going out for a spin. This guy is a bit forward, was Maiko's reaction.

Just back from a business trip, Maiko hadn't yet shaken the jet lag mist from her brain, and so she did as she was told. She took out her appointment book and told the man when she'd be free.

Exactly one week later, at seven in the evening, Maiko, her mind now clear, found herself en route to Mrs. Amino's Kamakura estate. For some reason the chauffeur's eau de cologne made her hungry, and she felt like she was off to a fancy ball.

Inside the limousine, the strings of Schönberg's "Verklärte Nacht" clashed and coiled round each other. She asked the driv-

er to switch to the FM station where a broadcast of a concert by
the Libido Quartet had just begun at Topica Hall. She wondered
how long it took the sounds in the concert hall to ride the radio
waves and reach her speeding along.

The first time Maiko had been to Mrs. Amino's was at a
party. The terrace of the estate faced the sea, and the crashing
waves played a basso continuo to the strumming of a guitar.
People with identical tans and smiles stood about making cocktail conversation—a dozen mannequins in the swimwear department, others in shorts, white linen suits, muumuus, or the
kind of evening dress that brought to mind a group of backs out
for a stroll. Maiko herself was wearing one of those sexy, high-
cut swimsuits and a pink cape.

The people that night are like invisible men to me now,
Maiko thought, but still she could not forget Mrs. Amino's face.
Maybe it was her makeup—how well she wore it; even the
crow's-feet around her eyes and the double quotation marks at
the sides of her mouth seemed like charming accessories. Maiko
was introduced to everyone as "Maiko Rokujo—Miss Shonan of
1984 and a twenty-year-old girl wonder." It was her first book-
ing as the beauty queen, and she was the entertainment for the
evening. She stood on a makeshift stage on the terrace and answered a series of malicious questions from the guests, who
were a bunch of morons. Are you a virgin? they asked. What
part of a man's body do you like best? What part of your own
body do you like best? What do you want to be in the future?
What sort of man would make the ideal husband? One guy
asked her if she loved him. She threw answers back at them: I'm
not a nun; I like the part women don't have; I like the part I can't
see myself; I want to go back to the land and grow flowers; I
don't think I want to marry an ideal; and, to the last question, I
don't necessarily dislike you.

Anyway, as Miss Shonan, Maiko did little to liven up the
party, but she did arouse the interest of Mrs. Amino, who told
her she'd help find her a job. Still in college, Maiko started work

part-time in the research and planning department at Imperial Securities, at the same time training as an analyst. She ended up making it her career. Despite all this, how much did Mrs. Amino really know about Maiko? In the last two years they hadn't met or spoken, just exchanged the usual greeting cards during the holidays.

So what's the connection between a securities analyst and a tracer of missing persons? Maiko wondered. What does she think I am—a detective? For a second, the image of a senile Mrs. Amino, bizarrely wearing the head of a Buddhist statue, floated through her mind. No, Mrs. Amino had another twenty years before she'd be put out to pasture.

"How old is Mrs. Amino?"

The chauffeur slowed down slightly and made as if he was counting on his fingers.

"I think she's fifty-two. Her skin's so smooth, though, she looks like she's in her thirties."

Aha! thought Maiko. So the juices of a young lover are her beauty secret after all! Wait a second—what if she's a lesbian? What if she's trying to seduce me? I mean, she'd be the perfect queen of a harem of lesbians. She'd make me dress up as a man, wear the same cologne this chauffeur is wearing, . . . Steady now, don't be ridiculous.

"That fragrance smells great."

"Thank you. It goes well with the smell of nicotine. Mrs. Amino likes to buy men cologne."

Maiko recalled that her boyfriend in high school had had no body odor at all. No matter how much he perspired, he had the fragrance of a freshly laundered shirt. Unable to smell his presence, Maiko found something lacking in him, as if he were a doll or a ghost. Her sense of a man's odor was so acute that simply by walking past a man, she could sniff out if he'd just had sex. With her nose, she classified her likes and dislikes on a very physical level. To complicate matters, she was the type who wanted to stick her nose into everything. If she seemed a bit crude at times, you could blame it on her nose. From the nose on, she wasn't much different from a bloodhound.

The Libido Quartet's first piece came to a close, and the second piece of the program, Mozart's String Quintet K. 406 was about half finished when the limousine pulled up to Mrs. Amino's mansion. Maiko got out of the car and felt the sea breeze infusing her hair with the smell and wetness of the ocean.

She remembered the front door with the carved relief of a leaping horse. Once inside, she found herself in a lobby with cathedral ceilings and an antique Turkish carpet spread out before her. At the landing of the stairway, for whatever reason, there was a six-foot-tall Godzilla doll that wreaked of sweat and mold.

Today, as the chauffeur escorted her into the lobby, Maiko was surprised by the rhythm of footfalls. There, on a Persian rug depicting the tree of life, a man was leaping back and forth. Maiko stood there awkwardly, waiting for this odd person to face her.

I know this guy! she realized.

"Maiko Rokujo has arrived," announced the chauffeur.

Nodding like a woodpecker, the man reached out to shake Maiko's hand. His hand was fevered and slimy, and Maiko caught a whiff of a sweet-smelling cologne.

"I am Takehiko Kubi. I'm Mrs. Amino's houseboy, I guess you could say. I'm the one who called the other day."

It can't be, Maiko gulped. That self-styled genius juvenile-fiction writer—here? Was this Mrs. Amino's own little farce? He seemed quite different from the Kubi on the covers of his novels five years before, but there was no mistaking those wild coyote eyes.

Five years before, when she was Miss Shonan, Maiko was a big fan of Kubi's. His juvenile fiction, his characters wired with screwed-up nervous systems, attracted a small but fanatic band of followers. Most used his novels to learn a number of dubious skills: ambushing people, evading questions, and making someone who'd asked a question blush with embarrassment at his own words. At the very least, for the crime of fostering some three thousand obnoxious human beings, Kubi should have been locked up.

"'Seems I've added another thing to my list for Mrs. Amino to explain," Maiko said out loud.

"And what's that?" Kubi asked. "Don't just hold yourself to one—add as many as you like. It doesn't bother me. Anyway, Mrs. Amino's been waiting, so why don't we join her? I'm also her secretary, you see."

For the moment, Maiko decided to say nothing about having been a fan of Kubi's. Just keep smiling, she said to herself, and enjoy his eccentricity.

The room she was led to was the same one she debuted in as Miss Shonan. The huge, terraced room facing the sea made her feel like she was on a gigantic yacht. In the center of the room were a round table and three chairs. Mrs. Amino sat there, sipping an aperitif. Her curves showed clearly through her clinging, white satin dress.

"Thank you for coming," Mrs. Amino began. "It's been such a long time, hasn't it? You've turned out to be quite elegant, though it looks like you've lost a few pounds. Here, please take a seat. What would you like to drink? I must apologize for all this business I've thrown at you. While I've been waiting for you I've been thinking where to begin, and before I knew it, I drank four of these Tio Pepes. What will you have?"

"A Tio Pepe would be fine," Maiko replied. "I'm sorry it's been so long. How have you been?"

"My legs haven't been the best, so it's difficult to travel. If I don't get a massage every three days, I can't even leave the house. Your legs are the first thing that goes, I'm afraid."

"I'm Mrs. Amino's extra leg, you see," Kubi interrupted. "Hey!" he yelled to the maid as he circled the table, "gimme a bourbon! And turn on the Muzak! Mrs. Amino's about to tell her life story, so pick something schmaltzy."

"Be quiet!" Mrs. Amino ordered.

"Excuse me!" Kubi squealed. "One word from you and I'll shut up till I die."

Maiko worried what kind of show this was going to be. She glanced at the irritated Kubi, and froze. Worms that'd been cut in two writhed beneath his eyelids.

"Maiko, isn't it?" Kubi continued, despite his vow of silence. "You know, everytime I meet a beautiful girl like you, so healthy and bright, I feel like I've hit the jackpot. It makes the old juices flow. When I'm free of this, I'm going to kidnap you and demand a ransom from Mrs. Amino."

"Are you drunk?" Mrs. Amino asked angrily.

"I'm sorry, I'll try to cool off. Hot in here, isn't it? Hey, can you step on it with that bourbon!" Kubi yelled to the kitchen, then walked out to the terrace.

Kubi seemed ill. His face was pale, his head filled with a mass of warring thoughts. Had his brain crash-landed in a garbage dump? Though she could feel no sympathy for the former literary genius, Maiko was polite and pretended not to notice anything unusual.

"What can you do with a person like that?" Mrs. Amino said. "I don't mind his selfishness, but I won't tolerate his being rude. My apologies."

"No apologies necessary," Maiko smiled. "What I want to know is, what is Takehiko Kubi doing in your home? He said something about being a houseboy."

A bland-faced Filipino maid brought drinks and hors d'oeuvres to the table. And took a bottle of bourbon to the terrace.

"He's not a houseboy. Or a secretary either. It's something different. You know the system where you can pay to keep your own whiskey bottle at a bar? Well, Kubi's my bottle."

"So he's a gigolo?"

"No, that would be a business arrangement. Kubi doesn't have to sleep with me."

Out on the terrace, a voice cried out, "Stop it, you filthy old man!" followed an instant later by the sharp report of a slap. Unconsciously Maiko tried to hide her own right hand.

"You didn't have to hit me!" Kubi screeched. "All I wanted to do was rub that firm little butt of yours."

In her mind, Maiko slapped Kubi again. Three women's worth. Put a lid on him, was her thought. And as if reading her mind, the maid shut the door to the terrace, locked it, and turned to see Mrs. Amino's reaction. Mrs. Amino nodded, and the maid returned triumphantly to the kitchen, her muscle-bound calves bouncing along. Kubi pressed his nose flat against the glass like a pig. You could hear a tongue clucking faintly.

"To get back to what we were talking about," Maiko said, "how was it that he came to be 'kept' here? It does seem odd."

"You're a securities analyst, so I imagine you have to be pretty good at judging people."

"I try to be."

"What do you make of Kubi?"

"Well, personally I have mixed emotions," Maiko replied. "Until about five years ago I was a fan of his. I liked his novels and all those weird characters. Everything about them was strange—their personalities, the way they talked, their hobbies, likes, looks, even their names. Harlequin romances with weird-os. I thought Kubi was just making up stories, but I can see that his novels were the story of his life. Kubi made fun of his characters, and I have to admit that I was touched by this. I even thought some of his characters resembled me, which is a little embarrassing. Still it wasn't such a bad feeling. But Kubi doesn't tolerate any narcissism on the part of the reader; he grinds *everybody* down. In any case, I did learn about how others might see me."

"A wonderful way of looking at things," Mrs. Amino said. "I'm sure Kubi would choke up if he remembered the author he used to be. I guess that he was so much a part of his novels, so much a part of his own parody, that he lost track of whether he was coming or going. His own words turned on him and backed him into a corner. If you get too self-conscious, you become a robot in someone else's hands. Usually people control themselves, but Kubi's convinced he's under *my* control. He's decided to become my slave."

"Oh, he's not writing anymore?"

"As far as writing's concerned, he's been tossed on the scrap heap," Mrs. Amino said. "That's why I bought him. His body, the copyright to his works—all owned by me. It's one of my little amusements. Like what Japanese men used to do with women in the old days. It takes money to buy out the contract of a geisha. What happened was Kubi stopped writing and got involved in some shady deals. He was way over his head in debt and ran all over Japan trying to escape. He decided to end it all. He chose a building to jump off and was making his way up the fire-escape stairs. Three floors from the top, the idea hit him: 'If I'm going to throw my life away, why not sell it instead?' So he put an ad in the classifieds: 'Pay back my loans and I'll be your slave. You name it, I'll do it. Takehiko Kubi.' Pretty funny, don't you think?"

"It's right out of his books."

"He'll be a novelist till the day he dies, so that's why he could come up with that kind of idea."

"And you saw the ad?" Maiko asked.

"A friend told me about it. We thought it wouldn't be beyond Kubi to run that sort of ad for a joke. I decided to call his bluff. When I met him, he was haggard. He told me his life story. At first I thought it was another joke out of a novel, and I laughed in his face. But then I realized he was serious, and I felt sorry for him. And I could sympathize with his business venture as well. So I bought him."

"May I ask the cost?"

"Forty million yen—and I haven't recovered my investment yet."

Kubi's business venture had involved the purchase of a derelict tanker he was planning to moor in international waters off Tokyo Bay. This was to be a "Movable Stateless City." He printed up pamphlets and handed them out; he met with securities company presidents, bank managers, university presidents, and ambassadors from every country, trying to convert them to his vision. The idea was for the tanker to be the nearest foreign country to Japan. "EXTRATERRITORIALITY PAYS!" was his slogan. On the tanker he planned to have a bank for laundering money and a temporary shelter for the boat people and illegal workers ordered out of Japan. There'd be a bar where people of different countries and languages mixed together, a brothel with white, black, and yellow prostitutes, and a casino that'd rake in money from tourists. He wanted to make it like Kowloon, or the Casbah. Or one of those tax-shelter islands in the Caribbean. Kubi was tired of words; he wanted to use real things to create one huge fiction. When it came to this project, he was completely serious. One person *was* pulled in by Kubi's eloquence and bizarre conviction, a person as eccentric as himself; naturally this would-be investor lost money on the deal. What Kubi raked in were laughs; if you had money to invest, why not put it in Tokyo Disneyland, instead of a mirage that the Self-Defense Forces could sink with a single torpedo?

Maiko looked over at Kubi, cut off from them on the terrace. He steamed up the glass with his breath and was writing something on it with his finger:

YOU SWINDLING ADULTRESS

He was thoughtful enough to write it backwards so it was easy to read. For a man like him, whose soul was mortgaged off, the only freedom left was to swear and say outrageous things.

"If memory serves me right," Maiko continued, "wasn't Kubi put in a mental ward at one time?"

"That's right," Mrs. Amino said. "He stopped writing and had himself hospitalized. He said he was going to commit suicide at the rate he was going, so it was the only way to prevent that from happening. He was out of the hospital pretty soon, though, and that's when he got involved in the tanker project. He'd been thinking about all sorts of business ventures while he was recuperating. I think he felt the project was a fresh start. That tanker, by the way, is still floating off Tokyo Bay. It may prove to be the anchor he needs after all, but right now he's suffering from depression again, the same as when he entered the hospital. Someday I'm sure he'll be able to stand on his own again and come up with an idea no one's ever dreamed about. The man is a genius. That's why I bought him up when the price had hit rock bottom. What do you think? Is Kubi worth investing in?"

"I can't really say," Maiko replied. "He doesn't seem to be as depressed as you make out. In fact, he seems on the road to recovery. Of course, that's just my impression. I'm not a psychiatrist."

The maid approached the table, pushing a serving cart. There was a large dish heaped high with sea bream cut into slices and served in the form of the fish, surrounded by prawns, abalone, oysters—a veritable symphony orchestra. Faced with this bounty of the sea, Maiko's empty stomach felt about to burst into song.

"With all this wonderful food in front of us," Maiko said, "perhaps you could tell me why you asked me here. You mentioned a missing son. I was under the impression that you only had a daughter."

"She's Motonobu's child," Mrs. Amino replied. "Motonobu died without ever knowing I had a son. The only people who knew about him were his father and me. For a long time I didn't even know if the boy was still alive. It's been almost twenty-five years since I've seen him."

"But you're sure he's still alive?" Maiko asked.

"Oh, he's alive all right. He's twenty-eight now. And I'm positive he's in Japan. That's where you come in. I'd like you to find out where."

"But I'm not a detective. There's got to be someone better suited for the job than me."

"I don't know about that," Mrs. Amino said. "I expect you're a good judge of people. I'd like you to be the one who finds him and figures out what kind of man he's grown up to be. Use your charm and lure him back to his mother. He was three when he left my life, so he probably doesn't remember me at all. Maybe he thinks he never even had a mother. You'll have to help him develop a positive image of me. Someone who's grown up without a mother might think there's no need for one. And I'm afraid he might have no appreciation for my feelings as a mother. I tried to forget him, but the pain he's left behind is too great. You're a woman, Maiko, you understand what I mean."

True, Maiko was a woman who had been born from a woman's body, but she had never experienced motherhood. Maybe, she speculated, mothers want their children to repay them for all the suffering they went through giving birth. Or else, even after mothers have passed the childbearing age, their wombs continue to yearn for what's departed?

For a quarter of a century Mrs. Amino had nursed this love for her son, not the son himself. And this illusion of love had created for her a whole new son. Now she had two, like twins whose personalities might be light-years apart.

"You said you haven't seen him for twenty-five years," Maiko said.

"My son was kidnapped by his father when he was three years and five months old," Mrs. Amino said. "His father was the lowest sort you could imagine, many times more bizarre than Kubi. For him, everything, including his son, was something to make money out of. I think I could forgive him for walking out on me, but he stole my rights as a mother. Can you imagine anything worse than that? Then having kidnapped my son, he refuses to be a father to him, so the boy ends up no better than an orphan. I spent a year searching for them all over the U.S., but they'd vanished. I swore I'd get my son back someday. I wanted revenge. I wasn't married, you see. Later I found out he'd deceived several other girls and gotten them pregnant, too."

"So he's a professional cad."

"Specializing in Japanese women. I must have been pretty blind falling for a guy like that. While I was traveling around the States I grew up really fast, I can tell you. I ran into another girl he'd tricked, the daughter of an envoy at the Japanese Embassy in Washington. A sheltered little princess. Lucky for her she didn't end up with a fatherless child, but I don't think she ever realized she'd been had. She was seventeen, and she was positive that he'd come back to her. Her name was Kasumi Tsumori. She wasn't very pretty, but she was a sweet thing, very kind. Meeting her brought me back from the edge. No matter how much of a bastard this Don Juan was, he was her first man, and I'm sure she wanted it all to remain a beautiful memory. Who knows, she may have willingly let herself be taken in. Unlike me, she didn't plan to get revenge; she forgave him right away.

"Anyway, I started to see how stupid it was to keep thinking about getting even. So at age twenty-eight, I cut all my ties with the past, and, like a half amnesiac, I came to Japan. Kasumi returned with me to take her college entrance exams. I was one of the first Japanese-Americans who came to Japan to make a living. At the time the only Americans in Tokyo were people working at military bases or trading companies. Now there're all kinds of Americans here—English teachers, street performers, bums—but back then the Japanese were still yelling 'Yankee, go home!' Of course, I looked just like any other Japanese, but I could never think of Japan as my homeland, the way my parents did. I kept fluttering back and forth between being a Yankee and a Jap. I wanted a place where I could feel comfortable and safe. Kasumi's parents introduced me to a club owner in the Ginza, and I started working there. That's where I met Motonobu. He was from Niigata—a real hayseed, but a go-getter. You could tell right away he was going to make it big. Here's a man who can protect me, I thought, someone I can feel safe with. It was like New York—if you have Mafia protection, you don't have to worry about a thing. Motonobu was the No. 2 man in the *yakuza*, and he had connections with an important politician from his hometown."

"Kakuei Tanaka?"

"I see you've done your homework. After I got to know Motonobu, I forgot my past completely. I was twenty-nine and he was thirty-seven. Tanaka was forty-five."

In her college seminar three years before, Maiko had read a thesis on Tanaka. That a manipulative contractor could rise to become the prime minister of Japan was pretty impressive. In Tanaka's day the country was one big de facto contracting firm, with him as company president. His mode of operation was nicely outlined in a document entitled "Reconstruction of the Japanese Archipelago," according to which Japan Inc. was to become an enormous company-state that the world would revolve around. Four manufacturing regions were to be created, each producing as much as the whole country of China; with these regions as the motivating force, local labor power and public investment would propel industry forward. For this to happen, Japan would need 10,000 kilometers of super highways, 9,000 kilometers of bullet train lines, and a transportation network of 7,500 kilometers for an oil pipeline, through which half the world's supply of oil would rush. Every hour Japanese tankers would greet each other passing the Strait of Hormuz. If the sea lanes were ever cut off, Japanese tankers would form a huge chain, a long and narrow extension of the Japanese archipelago itself.

Tanaka was a megalomaniac, the shaman of Japan's high-speed growth. Everyone believed him. If the Boss says, "Leave it to me," then naturally something good will happen. Because—hey—Japan is one big contracting firm, right? As long as the tunnels and bridges and bullet trains keep coming, the future's rosy, whether anyone lifts a hand or not. Buy land—that's the ticket! Ten kilometers of dirt will turn into ten kilometers of gold!

Motonobu Amino rode this wave for all it was worth. He bought wasteland in Hokkaido and mountain forests in Shikoku at dirt cheap prices, which he then sold and made a killing on; he invested in land downtown in small cities; and finally, he bought up prime property in the heart of Tokyo. Needless to say, he was the real estate mogul who walked away with the biggest windfall from Tanaka's reconstruction program. This made sense, since he was the trusted henchman of the president of the Japan Construction Company—Kakuei Tanaka himself.

Mrs. Amino had a keen eye. If her son hadn't been kidnapped a quarter of a century earlier, she never would have ended up the widow of the biggest landholder in Tokyo. Unwittingly, she'd foreseen it all.

"You know the story," she told Maiko. "How I've had a great time spending Motonobu's money. That was my job. Being a patron of people engaged in offbeat enterprises, people stirring up things in the world. That was my reason for living. Motonobu was a human money factory, but he was strictly an amateur when it came to spending it. I've always liked beautiful things, weird things, big, wild things. But above all I like to waste money. Huge houses, cars, clothes were a child's playthings. *People* interested me. So I opened a salon where anyone was welcome, no matter what their occupation or race. I invited artists in all kinds of fields, and we created wonderful happenings, movies, concerts. Motonobu'd just say, let's buy more land. What a bore."

She let out a high-pitched sigh.

"After a while, though, I got tired of the patron business. It began to seem so pointless. I didn't mind that people saw me as one big walking bank note. No, it was the feeling I had in my heart, that it was a bottomless swamp that everything disappeared into. I went into analysis and discovered that I felt this way because I had lost my child. I started a search for him. Finally I found someone who knew something about my son. Meeting this person will be where you begin."

"Where is this person?" Maiko asked. "In Japan?"

"He's in Tokyo. His name is Ameo Okayama. I wouldn't worry about him running off as he's in prison. Maiko, you will meet him for me, won't you?"

The sound of the word prison filled Maiko's mind with the clanking of the crude plates and utensils that prisoners ate with. Her appetite for the spread before her vanished.

Maiko's next thought was, Mrs. Amino's story might be touching but I could get burned. Hear the lady out, take a few days to think it over, then politely turn her down. Mrs. Amino was a bit eccentric for sure, but getting caught up in her chase could mean the end of a stable lifestyle. Maiko's greatest virtue had always been her ability to keep everything on a strictly business level, her life neatly in order. She was intent on getting ahead, and she calculated every move she made. But she wasn't about to let anyone catch on to that.

Mrs. Amino continued:

"You're a wonderful young woman, Maiko. If you were in the Red Army, you'd have been the prima donna, not Fusako Shigenobu. You're the kind of woman other women trust. Women open up to you, don't they? People tell you their problems. It's a talent you have. Oh, you'll have your fill of cunning, greedy people, but you'll always be on the inside track. You'll always be the star. Did you notice how Kubi was bowled over by you? You have special charm. You ask for something, and people happily place it in your hands. That's why you're perfect for this job."

The flattery was a bit thick, to be sure. Maiko was supposed to be Mrs. Amino's bait. The bait was to be stroked and encouraged, then reeled out and sunk deep. But the bait was to have no will of its own. Even so, it could turn out to be fun, Maiko smiled to herself. It could be a game. Meeting people, gathering information, solving a puzzle. It was a test of how good she really was. Getting there would be half the fun.

Good enough, but it wasn't so easy for a securities analyst to put her job on hold. There was that restless beast called the company to worry about. The company quivers, and you tremble in your boots. Stock prices fall, and you're torn to shreds.

"You'll have to quit your job, but you won't have to worry about money," Mrs. Amino stated. "Naturally I'll pay all your expenses, and I'll guarantee you your current salary. If you're successful, there'll be a bonus of three million yen. And when this is over, I'll find you a new job."

Not such a bad deal, Maiko mused, even though the chances of cashing in on the bonus looked slim. At any rate, she'd take a week to think it over. The business portion of the interview at an end, Maiko found her appetite suddenly returning, and she plunged like a ravenous shark into the school of fish before her.

2

Baby Buggies and Outer Spacemen

Where the hell am I, anyway? Trappings of life, so it's got to be a town. But there's no human smell—like, this might be a hallucination. Hills, far off in the distance with their tops sliced off. As if they were going to make a town over there, too.

There's only the smell of concrete and asphalt, which won't quit. At this rate, my snot's going to coagulate. The sky looks like it was dipped in concrete.

Dragging my blistered feet and my baby carriage, loaded down with everything I need, I am walking on a road, I don't know where. The road connects to a place off the edge of the Tokyo city road map I am carrying, but where? My head aches when I try to figure that out.

I stumble along in a fog, like I've just landed from outer space, a complete blank on why I am here. Should I be doing something else besides walking? I am a horse whipped on by shadows. I am afraid, but of what? The town is flat. It looks like a mistake. Neon motels, gas stations, restaurants, and cemeteries—they line the street like merchandise in a showroom window. They're trying to attract customers. But they don't attract me. I'm not a customer. I'm a lost child. This thought makes me feel better.

And then it comes back to me—I got beaten up! Shattering

glass, a mad dog growling, . . . Those bastards really worked me over.

Mikainaito, man, do memories always have to hurt this much? The back of my head throbs. Blood and memories gush out with each throb.

I thought Tokyo was supposed to be the safest city in the world, but you run out of luck and you get beat up. Where is truth and justice when they're five against one of you? Two had no eyebrows, the hair at the sides of their heads razored off. Another was a tub of lard with rolled-up sleeves—this dreamboy swung a metal bat wrapped in a towel. The other two were girls, hair dyed bright red, wearing tight miniskirts. They zoomed up to that park in Shinjuku and started trashing the phone booth. To me the phone is like my own nervous system, so it's like those guys were trashing me. I yelled at them to stop. They turned their attention to me, and the phone booth and I ended up in the same shape.

When I woke up, the morning sun was gently holding me and I was flying along in the back of a flatbed truck. I had the feeling it wasn't an ambulance going to a hospital, but at least it wasn't a garbage truck or a hearse.

I was covered from head to foot with a pile of the kind of blankets they use to wrap furniture. Pretty much like it is with me on most mornings, so the first thing I did was grope for the clock. What my hands found instead was a soiled stuffed dog. I sat up with a start and—*eeagh!*—a nail gets driven into my skull.

My body went crazy. I was losing my mind. Slowly, I crawled around the truck. I found my baby buggy. I clutched it tight, and I leaped out of the truck the way rats jump out of buildings when they smell an earthquake.

I ran two hundred meters before I fell, gasping for breath. My temples were going *thump-thump thump-thump*, and my head was electric with pain. I tried to keep from panicking. I took my pulse. But things were already out of control. I had to find the emergency exit. I covered my mouth with a handkerchief. Wait a minute, what am I doing? There's no fire. Some lowlifes beat me up is all. I got knocked out, I got a concussion, my head's killing me, and I don't know where I am, but otherwise I'm cool and the baby buggy's fine.

I managed to calm down.

Hey, Mikainaito! Up and at 'em! While we were blacked out, Tokyo disappeared on us.

Mikainaito muttered back: *It's OK. We're still among the living. Put it down as a bad dream.*

Dreams don't hurt this much. Maybe we should call an ambulance, a real ambulance? I could be hemorrhaging. The wind blows and my head hurts.

You were hit with a bat, that's why. But if we take you to the hospital, they'll tie you down for a week running tests. You really didn't do so bad, you know, getting out of the way of those punks. If you feel well enough to call an ambulance, we might as well hitchhike.

Maybe he had a point there.

But where was I before I got beat up? What was I doing?

I belch. Sausage. Sausage? Where did I have sausage? It was late—I was going somewhere. I was alone. Or I was with someone? Who? It was late, so I must have been drinking. In fact, feels like the booze is right under my eyelids.

Mikainaito, help. I'm losing it.

I remember Mariko Fujieda's apartment. I was dressed up like a woman. When was that? Two weeks ago, I think. Some lady, I forget her name, was giving me room and board and she was telling me how she was going back to her old boyfriend, so I wasn't needed anymore. When was that? Figure ten days ago.

I feel dizzy. My hair's a plastered mess. My scalp is itching me to death. But there's no stubble on my chin.

Strange. Ten days ago and last night stitched together with nothing in between. No record of anything. Just files scanning through my brain.

You're usually pretty bad at keeping track of your life. As long as you don't keep a diary, that is. But hell, who cares if you don't know what happened in the last ten days? Obviously nothing worth remembering. Anyway, oblivion's your job, right? Memories dredge up embarrassment, pain, and a bunch of loser relationships—this is the time to make a clean break.

But I can't shake wanting to know what happened the last ten days. Before a remotely glowing vertical-lined background, I pick up a faint sound. I don't know what kind of sound, or if it's a voice. It's like being on the top of a tall building and there's a thick mist and I'm hearing the city stir. Sounds scattered at ground level, but high in the sky the restless city harmonizes. Sounds, a voice, picked up from somewhere—orphaned sounds swirled up by the wind, making this weird harmony. From deep inside me, this weird music swells up.

One swing of the bat—ten days gone. I know I didn't sleep through it all. I had to be doing something. I let myself soak in the music. A woman's face floats before me, a smile through a clouded window. She's giving off a faint light, like a spirit of the dead. An instant later the image comes into focus. It's a face I've never seen before. Boy, is she beautiful.

Suddenly a car horn blares. I move to the side of the road. The woman's face cracks; the music fades farther away.

Having lost my memory like that, I suppose the best thing you could call me is a fallen angel. And that grim town looked like it had amnesia, too. A blank town, with blank spaces everywhere you look. One of those bedroom communities that go well with potato chips and Coca-Cola.

I rummage around in my pockets, but the six one-thousand-yen bills are gone. So the "ambulance ride" set me back six thousand yen. But it'd take more than that to buy back my memory.

I'm scared, Mikainaito. I want to hole up some place and hide.

*No place to hide. There's a motel sign a ways ahead—why don't we stop there? They might have a waterbed—you could have your sweet dreams. Relax. After all you've been through, no way you're going to run into anything worse. I figure something wonderful's just around the corner. *Be cool!* Stick that thumb out! Just two kilometers till that motel. Get us a ride!*

You've got it so easy, man. You never get hurt, you never get tired.

What are you talking about? The only time you ever call me is when you're in a jam. You keep all the fun for yourself.

Don't be paranoid. Not when I'm too beaten down to argue.

I see a phone booth, and I run to it like a long-lost home. I take out my address book and go over the names—maybe three hundred acquaintances, comrades, lovers, and friends—from A to Z. Some I don't remember at all. Who are these people anyway? Every year I get a new address book, and every year I copy all the names from the old address book into the new one. Every person I've ever met is in the book. Even people I've forgotten, and people who've forgotten me. I keep the book in a hidden compartment in my baby buggy. It's the only way I'm able to hold onto the spider web that hangs over New York and Tokyo.

I gaze at the book for five or six minutes, the names giving me a headache in the shape of the letters that spell them. I stuff the book in my pocket, and sigh—lonely, pitiful, in vain. This is the book of my life. If I burned it, I'd be nothing. I have the sudden desire to smash everything I can lay my hands on, sink my teeth into anyone passing by. There's no baggage as rotten as a throbbing head and an aching body. I want to be transformed into something, I want to take possession of a healthy body.

Why can't I be a guardian spirit, clinging on for dear life? Why can't I, Mikainaito?

Human beings are really marvelous structures, he replies. *Makes me jealous. You can have sex, babies, good things to eat, . . .*

Man, gravity's heavy, or haven't you heard?

Yeah, but no gravity's a bore, pal. Everything's so meaningless.

Too bad. Maybe we could start all over from the beginning?

Hmm, blow away the blues with a dream, eh?

*   *   *

Somehow we make it to the motel. It's called the Chinese Palace, and of course it's abandoned. Shit. I am frustrated at every turn. I pick up a ten-kilo lump of concrete on the ground and heave the sonofabitch against a boarded-up window. The boards splinter, the glass breaks. I am able to reach in and open the door. Imagine—a trespasser on the grounds of a Chinese Palace.

All the room doors are open. Mikainaito recommended the water bed, but the one in 205 has a hole in it. I decide to sack out in 209, which has a revolving bed that doesn't revolve. The room has its own bath and toilet, but no water naturally. Huge portions of the floorboards are swollen, and a stain the shape of Australia spreads across the ceiling.

I lock the door and lie down. I close my eyes and find myself in a wartime field hospital. A soldier laid low with a bandaged head dreaming of his nurse. I'm asleep before my next breath.

Like a log in an open car, I was tied down on a moving freight train. I could see only to the right. The train passed through a woods, a tunnel, a small town, on its way to the city. More and more people were coming out to see the train pass by. I didn't have any pants on. My boxer shorts were flapping in the breeze, and my hairy balls were sticking out. I had nothing else on but socks. Come on, I begged, let's blow it by. Instead, the train pulled up to a station.

A bunch of kids came running over to me.

"Leave me alone!" I yelled at them.

It was like they didn't hear me. I tried to speak in Japanese, but the words got stuck in my throat. One kid pulled a ruler out of his backpack. He slipped it inside my shorts and at the same time started to grope me.

"Fuckin' stop!"

Another kid attached a clip to the bottom of my boxer shorts. He attached a length of string to the clip. When the train started moving again, my shorts were pulled down. Stark naked now, except for my socks.

The vibration of the train made my cock stiffen. The train passed into the outskirts of the city. The engineer, figuring he could make a sideshow out of me, made a point of stopping at a platform crammed with people. Soon the crowd grew bigger. Nobody was too ashamed to stare. As a last resort I pretended to be dead, like the body in Delacroix's "Liberty Leading the People." But how could a corpse have a hard-on?

A panting, grossly overweight woman waddled up to me and the next I knew was lifting her skirt and peeling off her panties. She began to fuck me. And other women got the same idea. Housewives out shopping, secretaries, coeds—they all lined up for their fuck. The flesh on their faces sagged, like disembodied heads of criminals standing on poles.

And just then, I felt a sharp burning in my asshole. Behind me a line of men had dropped their pants. No! Maybe nobody had shame anymore, but I wasn't about to lie there like a corpse and take this.

I yelled, "Fuck off!"

Immediately the train pulled away. Where was it going next? Some place where I spoke the language would be nice.

En route Mikainaito returns, and I awake.

The lower half of my body is sleep-heavy.

Mikainaito, it was a nightmare.

Right, he replied, *you look wasted.*

When that fat woman started to hump me, I was thinking, time to wake up. But I thought I'd wait and see what happened, even if it was pretty embarrassing. I guess I'm glad I did.

It was an interesting dream, Matthew. Reminds me of the time right after we landed in Tokyo.

I never did anything that shameless.

I wouldn't say that. You let Tokyo rape you. Why don't you go back to sleep and have another dream.

I look at my watch. Three P.M. Can't stay here forever. Nothing to eat, and that barking dog has me worried. Sounds like a mean one, the kind they keep around abandoned buildings so bums can't camp inside.

I grab my gear, throw on my jacket, and get ready to leave. About the third week I was in Tokyo, hard up for money, I slept under the stars a couple of nights. Boy, those dogs came around fast. They can sniff out the homeless in a second. Only stray dogs like bums. Dogs that have owners got something to protect.

Mikainaito, man, you remember how they kept barking and wouldn't let us alone? I was scared to get near them.

We make our escape from the Chinese Palace, the dog's yapping growing more shrill. Damn, if it's not one thing, it's another. I clutch the baby buggy, trying not to make any noise. When I think I'm far enough away, I start dragging the baby buggy behind me.

Matthew, this really reminds me of when we landed in Tokyo.

Put a lid on it. I'm going to collapse. I just want to get back to the apartment. I don't want to see anyone. I don't want to talk to anyone.

After you get back home and cuddle up under your mosquito net, that's when I have to start running around visiting all these people's dreams.

Don't worry. You're taking tonight off. Let's go get something to eat.

Now you're talking. Let's take three or four days off and get our act together. Maybe I shouldn't say anything, but you know, your life's a mess. Just like—

I know. Just like three years ago, right?

I stop in a drive-in and they call me a cab. While I wait, I dig a few coins out of my pocket and inhale some *ramen* noodles. The pits. The cab comes after twenty-five minutes.

My vision is blurry, everything is foggy. I rub my eyes and look out the window. The cab cuts its way through the mirage. At a construction site, workers vibrate from a giant drilling machine. Their heads attached to helmets, their bodies, their arms and legs all scattering everywhere. The taxi picks up speed, and the billboard-like buildings alongside the road melt into gray. A stream flows down the highway. For a second I think it's the Hudson.

If only that river could wash away everything.

3

"What Choice Do I Have?": A Theoretical Approach

More Inept Than Money, But Worthy of Love

Mrs. Amino could predict the future. In a week's time, she knew, Maiko would accept her request. But what else could she see in that crystal ball of hers? The advent of the King of Fear? The Messiah wandering down a back alley? Or—as she laughed out loud—all the money in the world becoming barely worth the paper it was printed on?

As the stock market betrayed its stability and the yen plunged against the dollar, Maiko worried constantly that the collapse was near. A distrust of money had been smoldering in her mind, and waves of some vague lethargy washed over her until she was numb. What she feared was a return of the nightmare of October 19, 1987.

The panic had left Maiko ravaged. In bed, fevered and exhausted, she neither slept nor rested. Her body was like a city after an air raid, half in ruins. She had tried to calm herself, but no sooner had her thoughts cooled down than they would short out and sparks would fly.

A similar panic had raged through the Japanese financial markets. Frenzy, which was almost normal, turned to hysteria. Only the computers remained aloof and cold-blooded.

Brokers were afraid to act, and the newspaper summary of stock market activity reflected the day's disaster. The horizontal line showing the near-total absence of market transactions was the encephalograph of a brain-dead patient. When trading resumed the day after the crash, the fluctuations were wild, the buying and selling having little to do with worth. This wildness continued for days.

Was this 1929 all over again? people shuddered. To be sure, there were some who saw the panic of 1929 as romantic—not unlike the last gasp of a tragic, tubercular youth. But there was nothing romantic about the panic of 1987. This was rheumatism, where death did not beckon; this was an ongoing agony, a trek across an desert where no end was in sight. Of course, the whole event was an illusion. There was no reason for stock prices to drop, and in time the market recovered. People were left flustered and vacant, wondering what had happened, but business went on as usual.

Money. Wrinkled pieces of paper that make sport of us, Maiko thought. They make us crazy. They are so easily transformed into land, dresses, steaks, drunkenness, sex, but they have no intrinsic value. They're not gold or silver; they're mere pieces of paper or plastic replicas of precious metals. Pieces of paper and plastic chips that find their way into your pocket and make themselves at home in the body heat.

Up until that frightening time, Maiko had willingly given herself over to money and the human relations it formed. She had shelved any doubts and devoted her life to chasing it down. That was her job. In fact, she had for all intents and purposes changed into money herself, her brain in tune with the electronic flow that sent money shooting off at the touch of a computer key. The world, after all, revolved around money. Politics, science, technology, fashion, rumors, human relations—all manifested themselves in this ebb and flow of money. A rumor about the prime minister and his geisha gets out, and a couple hundred million yen change hands. The Old Man living in the heart of Tokyo has a fever, and yet bigger sums are made or lost.

Maiko, eating a two-hundred-forty-yen cheeseburger, scanned the newspaper to find out which stock was on the rise. The purchase of a cheeseburger, the health of the Old Man, and the PM's affairs ending up reasons for speculating—they were all the same. All part of the great flow of money.

But then, what was this lethargy she felt? And why was she so unhappy?

Maiko went to the supermarket and bought some chicken, paying with a thousand-yen note and getting back seven hundred and two yen in change. Suddenly she could *see* the flow of money. The money that she earned had bought a piece of the leg of a chicken that a farmer had raised for several months. Money was exchanged for a value that was the product of time and effort. You could dismiss this as too obvious for words, but suddenly money for Maiko had a reality. And this revelation thrilled her. Of course, the next day she would forget this completely as she moved hundreds of millions of yen around the world at the press of a button.

Ever since the 1987 panic, Maiko had thrown herself into her job. For one thing, she didn't want people saying a woman couldn't handle it. But on a more personal level, she believed that work would make her forget the stifling feelings choking her. Recently, though, she'd begun to feel that the Maiko she was before the crash was nowhere to be found.

When Maiko decided to become a stock analyst, her mother had this to say: "Don't forget to fall in love. Get taken up by work, but work is not love. Go out. Fall in love. If you don't, you'll always regret it."

Now Maiko understood those words to mean this: "Better to trust a man than money."

Have I done it the other way around? Maiko wondered.

Money means deals, making a profit or taking a loss. A man means what? Love? I gave myself to money. And somewhere along the line I'm going to get dumped. Cooly, brazenly—far worse than it would be with a man.

Two years earlier, Maiko *had* fallen in love for the first time. Nijioka was his name. He loved her heart and soul, but she held back. She gave him half her body, a third of her soul. This bothered him, of course, but then his anger turned to gentleness: "Your coldness is nice, actually," he told her. When he proposed, she couldn't bring herself to say yes. She didn't mistrust him—but she couldn't trust him completely. If only Nijioka were to appear before her now, as her faith in money was fading, he'd see a woman transformed.

You're not money, you're a man, Maiko would say to him. More inept than money, but *worthy of love.*

The Monday after she had gone to meet Mrs. Amino, Maiko went to the office. But work was the last thing on her mind. She hadn't been able to eat and had slept only with the help of tranquilizers. She felt nauseous. Would accepting Mrs. Amino's proposition save her from this eternal seasickness? Or would it confuse things even more?

Maiko was torn. Stocks were fluctuating crazily again—almost as if they were afraid that their falseness would be unmasked. Maiko looked at her colleagues: They were all swindlers, except they didn't know it. In the religion that worships at the feet of money, they all were disciples. So she was a swindler, too. She could start yelling about it, but was there another life free of it?

That evening Maiko made the decision to accept Mrs. Amino's offer. Her determination still firm the next morning, she deliberately got to work late and handed in her resignation to her section chief.

Laughing, he told her: "You're just worn out. Don't take things so hard. The drop in stock prices is like a menstrual period that's a little off schedule. There's not going to be a panic. Trust is priority No. 1. If trust falters, then you have yourself a panic. You're in a position that has to maintain trust. You must not waver."

I wish there *was* a huge panic, Maiko thought. Because then the whole word, scared to death as it spins around, would be washed clean, like it was in Noah's flood. Pure, shining, exposed in its nakedness. And then we could tell the beautiful from the ugly .

"TELL ME ABOUT MIKAINAITO!"

So instead of trusting in money, Maiko decided to trust Mrs. Amino.

Maiko had faith in her own good grace and cleverness as well, and once she had made up her mind, she felt no anxiety about her decision. The fact that there were few clues in this search for the missing son ironically made her feel even less apprehension about the whole enterprise. Anyhow, you meet people, you talk with them—wasn't that it? Think of it as a part-time job interviewing people. And besides, you could use the time to find a new boyfriend.

Maiko got to feeling quite good—getting paid as she reassessed what she wanted to do with her life was like playing around on a scholarship. It's not money that makes the world go 'round, she decided, it's human beings. Especially the weird variety.

Maiko's first task was to determine the name Mrs. Amino's son was going by. This was no easy task. The child's name at birth was Masao Fudo, but when he was kidnapped his last name, and maybe his first as well, might have been changed. The son Mrs. Amino knew had blood type O. He was Oriental, so his hair was black and his eyes were brown. He had a line of four moles running vertically from his waist to the crack of his butt.

Mrs. Amino had a photo of Masao at age three; this was all they had to go on as far as what he might look like today. From this photo, a computer had generated an image of what Masao looked like now, at age twenty-eight. It was a refined sort of face, certainly handsome, but sand-dune flat and devoid of expression. If you wanted to be mean about it, you could say he looked a little stupid. But if he let his beard grow, the face might take on some character.

To be sure, environment and attitude could have drastically affected this face, disguising any trace of the three year old. As if it had been washed over by a wave. So, essentially, what you had in the computer-projected image was the face of a man who had no history from age three to age twenty-eight.

Kissing a twenty-eight-year-old guy who drools—good grief. The thought gave Maiko the shivers.

Throughout the years, Mrs. Amino had kept one item that the three-year-old Masao had carried with him everywhere. It wasn't a Linus blanket, but a pillow. The cotton batting was now dust and falling out. The whole thing was pitiful, like a sewer rat run over by a car.

"I haven't washed it at all since Masao was kidnapped. The pillow still has his smell," Mrs. Amino said, pulling it out from a silk bag. "If he remembers this, he'll be in tears. He must have cried and cried for it when he was taken away from me."

Really? mused Maiko. Chances are he made friends with a new pillow and forgot about this pathetic rag.

Mrs. Amino went on with her reminiscences, but for Maiko it was all in one ear and out the other. Save it for Masao, she thought, but even so, Mrs. Amino's tale soon took Maiko back to her own childhood, where memories of life at age three lay like buried fossils. In old photo albums there she was, playing by a pool, then at a shrine for the "Seven-Five-Three" children's holiday—sullen with pouting, lipstick-covered lips, then held by a sumo wrestler, a perplexed look on her face. Slowly she realized what her parents, and she too, had done with these photographs—which was to construct a tale in which Maiko was the heroine. Mrs. Amino was doing the same with Masao.

What Maiko remembered most clearly about childhood was the terrifying grain of the wood ceiling of her room. Whenever she was ill and in bed, she would look up and see the wood grain turn into a river of mud. Then the entire room would get swallowed up in the mud. The joints of the ceiling boards became whirlpools, witches and monsters sticking out of the corners. When she closed her eyes, the river did not stop. Whether the lights were on or off didn't matter; the river of mud was sure to enter into her.

Only Maiko had known this fear. Her parents had no understanding of it. Maiko wondered now if Masao had known this terror, too.

"One word is important," Mrs. Amino was saying. "There's not a chance that Masao will have forgotten it. If he has, he's not Masao."

"What is the word?" Maiko asked.

"*Mikainaito.*"

"Mikainaito? What does it mean? Is it a code?"

"I believe it's a name. But what kind of name, I don't know. Mikainaito. It's what Masao used to call his precious pillow."

Yes, a curious name. Maiko wondered if it was the knight who protects the archangel Michael (which was closer to "Mikhail" in Japanese). Or maybe some kind of a hero based on Mrs. Amino's first name, Mika?

When he was three, Masao apparently spoke three languages. English with his mother, Japanese with his father, Cantonese with his baby-sitter. And he talked to himself in a mixture of all three. But what language, at age three, did he *think* in?

If Mikainaito was a mixed breed, Maiko mused, a blend of heroes in all three languages, he must be an open-minded sort of guy. But also a lonely one.

"My theory," Mrs. Amino continued, "is that it's a name he made up that combined TV heroes and words he might have heard his baby-sitter use. I don't know when it started, but it didn't matter what I'd say, he'd answer back with something about Mikainaito. He'd beg for stories about Mikainaito. I would tell him stories about Jesus and change the name. But then Masao began to change the stories themselves. Mikainaito could turn into Daddy or Mommy, he said. Mikainaito could fly through the air and jump inside the TV. He could get bigger or smaller. I'd ask him what Mikainaito looked like, and Masao would say, a lot of different faces."

Mikainaito was a bond between mother and child, it seemed, and Mrs. Amino had already conceived a plan to find her son based on the very word. All this assumed, of course, that the word still remained in Masao's consciousness.

Earlier, for a year, Mrs. Amino had put out a dragnet in search of her son. Information had been collected by a private investigation firm in New York. The leads were few, so Mrs. Amino took out ads in various media—newspapers and magazines, TV, computer networks, even subway and bus posters. Information poured in from the well-intentioned as well as the merely malicious. (The numbers were evenly divided between the two.) This is how the ads read:

TELL ME ABOUT MIKAINAITO!
THE COMMITTEE ON THE MIKAINAITO LEGEND
Call Toll Free: 1-800-606-7000

And this is what the responses were like:
Mikainaito's a new video game, right? When does it go on sale?
Mikainaito's the code word for a KGB spy.
Mikainaito's a hero in the myths of a tribe deep in the Amazon.
Mikainaito's a new kind of makeup, isn't it?
Stop using my name without permission!
. . . .

Several of the responses were similar, and there were even some who said they'd met a person they thought was Mikainaito. As Mrs. Amino expected, the word had special power. A surprising number of people reported that their own children used the word Mikainaito, but almost none had a clue what it meant. The head of the investigation even searched through library documents for the word Mikainaito; he asked historians, philosophers, and geographers. To no avail.

But just then, the detectives located a man in New York who'd drawn a direct connection between Masao and Mikainaito. The man would disclose nothing about himself other than his name, but he was able to describe a person who in many ways fit the facts known about Masao Fudo. The man was a Japanese gentleman, well over sixty and living on a pension; his name, Yusaku Katagiri.

In Katagiri's account, told in English with hardly a trace of a Japanese accent, the boy was known not as Masao, but Matthew. This Matthew had the same hair color hair as Masao and the same color eyes, and was the right age. More intriguing than these facts, however, was what Katagiri told them about Mikainaito.

All human beings carry around a guardian spirit, Katagiri said. Very few can ever see these spirits; those who can are known as mediums. Although he admitted to not having that power himself, Katagiri spoke with knowledge and confidence. A guardian spirit is like a shadow between yourself and others, he said, between yourself and the world, yourself and the past. And it never stops watching you and watching out for you, even for a second. Matthew called his guardian spirit Mikainaito. Katagiri told him to be friends with it.

But Katagiri hadn't any idea where the name Mikainaito came from.

"Matthew used the word Mikainaito from the beginning when he came to live at my place," Katagiri said. "Maybe he'd felt the presence of his guardian spirit even as a child. Once a long time ago, I asked him about it. Is Mikainaito any different from Christ or Buddha? I said. Matthew just said one thing: 'He's a friend.'"

So was Mikainaito the name of a real friend? The name of his old pillow? Or maybe the name of a superhero like Ultraman? Or, as Katagiri had told them, was it the name of a guardian spirit?

As to the relationship between Katagiri and Matthew, Katagiri's answer was curt: "If you must know, I'm Matthew's foster father. Actually there is a stronger bond between us than that."

Katagiri would not say more. He did not appear interested in the reward money nor in the relationship between Mrs. Amino and Matthew. A foster father didn't have the right to invade Matthew's privacy, he said, but then he went on: "Actually the reason I called you after I saw the ad was that I thought maybe you could tell *me* where Matthew is. This Mrs. Amino and I have the same goal. She's looking for Masao. I'm looking for Matthew. And Masao and Matthew are one through the power of Mikainaito. The Matthew I know went to Japan three years ago. He wrote me that he'd found a job. He's probably still in Tokyo. There is someone who might know, a Japanese man Matthew worked with just before he went over there. He should know where Matthew is. His name is Ameo Okayama; he imports furniture and household goods."

Then Katagiri had a proposal for Mrs. Amino.

"Fortunately both Matthew and this lady who's looking for him are in Japan," he said. "Now wouldn't it be to everyone's advantage for this lady and me to exchange the information we have? I know things the investigation in Japan can't do without."

"But maybe we already have all the information you're holding back on us," the detective said, playing coy.

"Do you know how long Matthew and I were together? I'm sure this Mrs. Amino would like to hear about Matthew's past, seeing she's his natural mother. I'll save the details for another time."

So this Japanese gentleman had a motive, after all. Money. The detective was sure the old man was out to make a few bucks, but since the money was coming from a rich Japanese woman, the detective wasn't worried.

Maiko's task, then, was to fly to New York to purchase the information.

The Japanese man who had worked with Matthew did indeed exist, it was discovered. And Mrs. Amino could forget about having to look all over Japan for him, because, as it turned out, he was in jail.

With Masao now transformed into Matthew, Maiko was eager to move quickly before there was another name change and things got complicated further. In preparation for her trip to New York, she phoned the prison and requested an interview with one Ameo Okayama.

For this interview, Mrs. Amino indicated that Maiko would have a companion, adding that he would be a strong ally but an annoyance, too. As Maiko expected, it was Kubi.

"For the time being, he'll be your driver, and you can do with him as you will," Mrs. Amino said. "Eventually he could be of some use."

How could Maiko say no?

Not Including the Deposit

"I don't get a salary, but if we find this Masao guy I'll be pardoned and let free. Mrs. Amino promised me. Actually I'm the one who asked her to let me do this in the first place. I wanted to be your bodyguard."

Kubi was driving Mrs. Amino's red Jaguar, and Maiko, sitting next to him, was having a hard time relaxing. The two of them must have looked like a gangster's son and a cabaret hostess driving down a side road with electric arrows flashing the way to a papier-mâché castle of love.

"Are you a pretty tough fighter, Kubi?" Maiko asked.

"Well, I can run fast. Did you ever do any sports?"

"I played basketball in high school. And I've skied ever since I was a kid," Maiko said. "What about you?"

"Rock climbing's my game. If anybody tries to chase me, I can climb to some place way high and escape up or down, left or right—any way you like. Anybody who wants to mess with me is going to take a dive."

"You know how to climb up buildings and towers, too?"

"Sure. And just in case I have to, I always wear crater shoes. You know, the kind climbers use."

"So you're always thinking about escape?" Maiko asked.

"No, not really. I just get a kick out of going where other people can't go. About ten years ago I went to Rome. One night I snuck into St. Peter's and climbed up to the highest passageway. I crawled across the wall up to the roof and discovered a getaway route all the way to the Vatican. Someday I'm going to try it."

Weird, Maiko muttered to herself, glancing at Kubi. And what an antsy guy. Maybe it was paranoia that had seeped into the cells of his face and made the skin under his eyes quiver like tiny worms. No, Maiko decided generously, it's just Kubi's artistic temperament trembling.

Why couldn't he have had a girl like Maiko when he was young, Kubi wondered. He might not be so burned out now. As it was, just being alive was bad for his health. He needed something to rejuvenate him, get him back on his feet. He wanted to suck this girl's young blood and feel the rush he'd once known. During his tanker project, he had enough energy to make him leap around like a lobster.

But Maiko had the effect of rendering Kubi impotent. Made him embarrassed, itchy, hesitant. And not terribly thrilled that Maiko had learned about his past from schmaltzy old Mrs. Amino.

Maiko used to love his novels. Great, but there was nothing worse than a fan. How was he supposed to treat her? As an equal? As someone who's saying that he can doing anything he wants with her? Talk about a predicament.

Kubi wasn't a novelist anymore. It was a shabby business he wanted nothing to do with, and to prove it, he burned all his business cards that called him that. Accordingly, Maiko was an ex-reader, an ex-fan.

Hmm, Kubi thought, an ex-novelist and an ex-reader—not a bad combination after all. But there was something wrong about it. If they were like old lovers getting back together again, they would start building things from the ground up. But in this case the ex-novelist ends up with the short end of the stick; he has only the ex-reader's sentimentality and bad taste to fall back upon. Now if he were still writing novels, he'd call the shots— he'd be the master, she'd be his disciple. Obviously this was a different scene.

As a result, Maiko was making Kubi lose his grip. What he needed to do was to rewrite the relationship: an ex-novelist and an ex-Miss Shonan. Read this way, both parties start at zero and one's no better than the other. But Maiko was more woman than Kubi had ever been a man. Name a category—complexion, legs, muscle tone, intuition, purity, simplicity, innocence, upbringing—it'd make more sense for him to run away than to try to compete with her. Like a king running away from a queen. On a chessboard the queen's the one who has the most freedom of movement anyway; the king's the one who's stuck.

Maiko was twenty-five, Kubi thirty-seven. The difference in their ages equaled one complete cycle of the Chinese zodiac. In that interval Kubi had driven himself from society four times, and three times set himself up as the axis around which society revolved. Right now he was adrift from the world once more, but found himself yearning to be at the center again.

"Maiko, how much money do you think I have on me right

now? How much do you think I *should* have?" In other words, she was to judge his worth based on how much money he carried.

Maiko thought for a moment. "Fifty thousand yen," she said.

"You think I have that much? Let me tell you how pleased I am to hear that. But the pitiful truth is, I only have enough money to buy a bottle of milk and a piece of *anpan*."

"Is that all you have? Two hundred yen?"

"A hundred and sixty yen. I wasn't including the deposit on the bottle."

"Did you forget your wallet?"

"How much did Mrs. Amino give you?" Kubi asked.

"Two million yen for expenses. She opened an account in my name."

"How much cash do you have on you?"

"About a hundred thousand."

"Do you think you could split some of that with me? Maybe take it out of expenses? Help me save some face?"

"You mean Mrs. Amino didn't give you any money? Maybe she meant for me to take care of the finances."

"Guess so. You're supposed to be a pro when it comes to money, right?"

Maiko didn't answer. As far as the kind of supercharged money that raced around the world on electronic waves, yes, she was a pro. But when it came to dealing in the one- and ten-yen coins housewives' purses bulged with, Kubi was probably smarter. She dug into her purse and handed him a handful of bills.

Their Jaguar abruptly pulled up to a large pastel mural on a wall high enough and long enough to be a boundary between two countries. Maiko imagined it was the mansion of a rich eccentric like Mrs. Amino. When Kubi said that they'd arrived at the prison, Maiko broke into a smile. So, she thought, prisons are beginning to look like amusement parks.

The World's a Tougher Place Than You Think

Ameo Okayama was in the second year of a five-year sentence for the murder of his wife. The erstwhile Mrs. Okayama had been kidnapped and killed in an apparent case of mistaken identity. Of course, it wasn't a mistake but a scenario calculated to look like one.

First, Okayama needed a woman whom his wife was to be the "double" of. This was the actress Yoshiko Sasaki, the real (but false) target of the kidnapping for whom a large ransom would be demanded.

Next, he needed a killer. Okayama had plenty of candidates from among the South American and Asian laborers in the country—people who'd gotten in on a tourist visa, worked illegally, joined criminal gangs, stole jewelry and electric goods, and smuggled them out. And there were others, too—terrorists and spies who'd slipped into the country posing as Japanese, holding passports cooked up in Hong Kong or Macao. But because somebody like this, let alone a Japanese hit man, would be so easy to trace, Okayama imported his killer from Manila.

According to plan, the killer kidnapped the unwitting Mrs. Okayama, then murdered her. And Okayama collected on the insurance.

The media dubbed the killing "A Tragedy of Mistaken Identity." Everyone felt sorry for the victim, as well as for the bereaved husband. The police thought this "Royally Flubbed Kidnap-Murder" smelled fishy, but the killer was nowhere to be found. He'd been paid off by a third party in Hong Kong and was sitting pretty in Manila. Any suspicions surrounding Okayama melted away. He picked up his insurance money and flew to America, where he invested in real estate and antiques and wooed women with his wad of cash.

Meanwhile, the Manila murderer who'd carried out the "perfect crime" decided to try the same sort of stunt on his own.

When he blew it, Okayama was put on the most wanted list. As soon as he returned to Japan, he was arrested. And this is where Masao/Matthew came in. He'd had some dealings in America with Okayama just before Okayama went home.

In court, Okayama held back nothing. His statement was more like the confessions of a fanatic religious follower. For forty minutes he mumbled about the curse of money, and the curse on himself for having fallen slave to it. Over and over, he begged to be executed. Only death could sever him from the filth of money, he screamed.

What could have brought on this change of heart?

Abhor the crime, but not the criminal.

This was the philosophy that motivated him. If he wanted to win over the judge, the prosecutor, and public opinion, this was the way. 'Cause the world's a tougher place than you think.

The interview with Okayama was to last twenty minutes.

Maiko and Kubi were ushered into the bulletproof-glass–lined visiting area. The musty smell of concrete made Maiko's nose itch.

After a while, Okayama appeared. A fair-complexioned man, straight-backed, around forty-five years old. The moment her eyes met his, Maiko felt as if a warm slug was crawling over her belly.

She started in immediately. Was Okayama familiar with a Masao Fudo, otherwise known as Matthew, whom he should have met in New York three years ago, and was there was anything about him he could tell her?

Okayama scratched his head and replied: "I am a model prisoner now. I am working as a shoemaker, polishing my skills. The past does not interest me. Consider me a priest who has given up the world. I have nothing to say to you. I have no past." His eyes were full of conviction.

"What sort of relationship did you have with Matthew?" Kubi asked, ignoring Okayama's soliloquy.

"Are you familiar with the word *Mikainaito*?" Maiko asked.

"*Mi-kai-nai-to*. You know it, right?" Kubi pressed.

"Think of me as an amnesiac. I remember nothing."

"Arrogant bastard," Kubi clucked.

Maiko restrained Kubi and apologized for his behavior. For at the mention of Mikainaito, she had seen Okayama's face muscles twitch.

"If there's anything you need, we can have it sent here," she told Okayama.

"Send me anything you wish. It will not change my mind."

"That's perfectly all right. Actually the person we're working for is the mother of this person named Masao or Matthew. She's trying to find him after many years. She'd be grateful for any clue you could give us. Even if there's nothing you know, we would like to express our appreciation to people who've helped Masao in the past. So please feel free to ask for anything. Naturally, we don't want to force you to recall something you don't want to. You're in the midst of charting out a new life for yourself. I understand how you feel because I just quit my job myself, and now I'm starting a new life, too."

"It's been so long since I've seen a woman as beautiful as you. You've made me very nervous," Okayama said, transformed back into a normal middle-aged man.

Kubi laughed out loud. "This reminds me of one of those peep shows in Kabuki-cho, Maiko. This guy's a peeper."

Immediately Okayama's expression grew fixed.

"Mr. Okayama, when was the last time you saw Matthew?" Maiko went on, ignoring Kubi's outburst.

"Matthew? Never heard of a Matthew. Can I go back to work now?"

You Have Mean-Looking Eyes

Maiko and Kubi were preparing to send books and food to Okayama before their second meeting with him, when the letter was delivered. They went immediately to see Mrs. Amino, who had repaired to her bedroom since the rain had made her rheumatism act up.

Okayama had scribbled the letter in pencil, going on at length about himself, declaring his one-sided friendship with Matthew. And so, for Mrs. Amino, an image of Matthew began to form. It was painful, she said, for each tiny bit of scrawl was transformed into Matthew's hair, voice, smile.

Maiko tried not to conjure up too much from the letter. Because what you had there wasn't Matthew. It was nothing more than the companion Okayama had concocted to suit himself.

The letter said this:

I've been thinking about Matthew all week long. When I first met him, I misheard his name as Maa-*chan*, not Matthew, and that's what I always called him. "It's funny. It sounds like 'merchant,'" he told me. Yesterday I dreamed of Maa-*chan*. In the dream he scolded me:

"I hope you're not still spending all your time calculating how you can best make out, this what's-in-it-for-me attitude. There comes a time when everyone's face has to turn innocent and childlike and be free from thoughts like that."

When I heard this, I felt enlightened. It was like an oracle and then I found myself writing this letter to you.

As you know, I murdered my wife. I'm what you call a Life Insurance Murderer. Life insurance—it's like gambling—and I'm just a poor bastard who tried to pull a fast one and got caught. The whole scam about life insurance is that the insurance company doesn't want you to die, and the person who takes out the insurance doesn't want to die either. So life insurance is really just a big fraud, like selling property on the moon or on Mars, or like selling stocks. It's a big gamble—some guy makes a bundle, the next guy loses his shirt—that's how it goes. If you don't want to lose out, you've got to deceive people. Well, I didn't want to be a loser. . . .

If you don't mean to kill somebody, they can't call it murder. All you have to do is convince yourself you didn't really want to kill. In the perfect crime you got to make sure you've deceived yourself, or else the whole thing falls apart. When I had my wife killed, I even forgot I was the one who planned the murder I was so busy playing the victimized husband. I hated the sonofabitch who did the dirty work. Everybody felt sorry for *me*. It felt great. Nobody suspected me. I actually started to believe I was innocent. You take some embezzler who rips people off through a computer— he has a different kind of guilt from your regular sort of thief. The guy thinks the computer did it. Me, I blamed the way life insurance works.

Even after I was arrested and tried, I didn't feel guilty. I just thought I had rotten luck. But when I got put in prison, I started to think about the other side of myself. Before that, I never had anything to do with religion, but I began to think I needed something like it. There were lots of inmates who sweated it out when the police were after them, but after they were arrested, they found peace. I wasn't like them, at least not at first. I thought they were stupid, and I laughed in their faces. I thought I was better than them. I didn't want to have anything to do with them.

They put me in solitary. All day long I tried to figure out where my perfect crime failed. But the conclusion was always the same: The plan *was* perfect. Lots of guys manage to carry off the perfect crime. My hit man screwed up—that's where things went wrong.

Before I got caught, the only thing I believed in was

my own smarts. I thought if I could keep cool with my wife dying, I was tough. I thought I had it in me to make it big. But when I got put in prison, my confidence took a dive. I was just another criminal. After I got out of solitary, I started to talk with the other prisoners to see how they felt about being locked up. But for some reason, nobody liked me. "You have mean eyes," one gangster told me flat out. The other cons knew exactly what they did; they were a million times smarter than me.

And then I began to understand what Maa-*chan* had been telling me about—it was like these convicted criminals had this thing about them that didn't have anything to do with the balance sheet always floating around in my head. They weren't always thinking about making it big, or even making it at all. It was a look they had—mostly when we were in the workshop. When they were planing down wood or stitching up shoes, it was like they were almost . . . a part of . . . nature. They were like mountains, rivers, oceans, forests. But if people don't have nature in their hearts, they're stuck, I figured. It's too late for me. I'm stuck for the rest of my life with what I've done. That's what scares me. I wish I could get rid of it—my past, my arrogance, this always being on the lookout for No. 1. If making shoes can make me forget all these things, I can stay sane, I think. I can sell my shoes and somebody will buy them. That could help save me. It could be like my own religion. When I make a pair of shoes, it could be a prayer. Of course, I don't think it's quite that simple.

I realize now that Maa-*chan* told me all about this a long time ago. I met him in New York. After I had my wife killed, I thought I would go play around in a foreign country until the excitement died down. I could

plan my next job. I didn't know any English, so I hired
an interpreter, who turned out to be Maa-*chan*. He was
a good companion, too, especially when I went out for
a night on the town. Maa-*chan* knew everything about
opera, striptease, golf, horse racing, drinking, drugs,
you name it. I thought he was pretty young to have all
that experience. When I asked him about it, he said it
was because he was bored. He didn't really tell me anything about himself, but the way it seemed was like he
had some special education in order to get by in this
world. Like Maa-*chan*'s parents had trained him to pick
up small things about people, as if he was supposed to
be a spy. He was a little embarrassed about it, when I
asked him. He said he got that way because he always
did what his parents told him to, no matter what. When
I found out these people weren't even his real parents,
I was pretty surprised.

After two weeks together, I got pretty attached to
him, or maybe we got on the same wavelength, I don't
know. But once when I was drunk, I started to brag
about my plan for the perfect crime. Naturally I put it
all on a theoretical level, and I didn't tell him I killed
my wife.

That was when he told me:

"In crime, machines, and human relations, whatever's perfect eventually collapses. In nature nothing's
perfect. The complete or the absolute's only in your
head. Go outside your mind and it falls apart."

He was so simple and innocent, I felt jealous. Maybe he disliked me. At any rate, I got the distinct feeling
that he was reading my mind.

Another time, all of a sudden he told me:

"Atheists exhaust themselves, spinning around like
a top, with themselves at the axis. You're just like them.
So was my father. It isn't that god doesn't exist, or that

there's only one. There're tons of gods in the world; you should meet some of them and make friends with them. It's ridiculous to make yourself the one absolute deity and to exclude all the others. To me, you're the god of the perfect crime. You're also the god who's going to lead me to Japan. To you, I'm the interpreter god. And the god of good times."

He said some weird things, all right, but what persuaded me was his smoothness, his personality, I guess. Anyway, I knew he was someone special.

He wanted to go to Tokyo. It was getting hard to bear New York, he said, and he wanted to find a job in Tokyo. Maa-*chan* had three lovers at the time, and he wanted the chance to make a clean break with them. I promised to take him to Tokyo and help him find work.

He was smart, athletic, and funny. He was good in both English and Japanese. He was the type of person people like right away. I told him he could try writing for a magazine, and he said why not. So after we got back to Japan, before I got arrested, a friend of mine introduced him to a magazine editor. Maa-*chan* worked at the magazine for three months, but I don't know what happened after that because, by then, I was thrown in jail. He's probably still wandering around Tokyo. Not too long ago, when I was in the prison rec room, I saw somebody on TV who looked just like him. I forget the name of the program, but it was about things going on in Shibuya. In the middle of the crowd, Maa-*chan* was pulling a small cart that looked like a baby carriage. In fact I'm positive it was him. That's why I think he's still in Tokyo.

I hope this helps. I pray that you find him.

Mrs. Amino asked Maiko to fly to New York right away. "Talk to Katagiri and try to find the missing pieces of Masao's life," she said. "This business of him having some special education in order to get along in this world is very unsettling. His foster father must have been a real scoundrel. Also, please find out all you can about Mikainaito."

"New York, huh? Haven't been there in ages," Kubi interjected. "There are two tickets, I presume." He was stroking Mrs. Amino's legs, his expression serious.

Mrs. Amino replied, as pleasantly as she could: "If you went to New York, too, who would massage my legs? This bad weather really aggravates my rheumatism."

"But I want to go. Don't make a young guy like me spend his days hanging out with rheumatism. My feelings will all turn rheumatic."

"Kubi, I need you to meet the editor at the magazine Masao worked at. I want you to check out lists of English instructors. There are all sorts of tasks for you here. Even as we speak, Masao is walking around, pulling something that looks like a baby carriage. You're the one with the healthy legs, Kubi. Go out and track him down."

"You want me to wait around with a butterfly net? Don't you realize that there's just one Masao in the world? And we don't even know what he really looks like."

"Since there's only one of him," Mrs. Amino responded, "he'll stand out, now won't he? Use your intuition."

"Do you have any idea how big Tokyo is?"

"It's smaller than you think. I'm always running into old friends. All you have to do is stand in a spot where a lot of people walk by."

"People might think I'm a pervert."

"Then wear something shabby."

"They'll think I'm a bum."

"Then be a bum. When Maiko comes back from New York, I'll have her look in on you. Do your best and you can look forward to her visits. Think of it as an exercise in ascetics."

*   *   *

The next day, Kubi hit the streets as a bum. Though for a bum his skin was too fair and his hair too neatly parted. He might talk back to Mrs. Amino, but he did as he was told.

The idea of a stakeout was irritating. But Kubi could only sigh, and reach the stoical Japanese conclusion—*shikata ga nai.* "What choice do I have?"

In the face of all the unknowns in this world, this is a theory that has an answer for everything. Just like the Unified Theory of Physics.

Indeed, what choice *do* I have, Kubi conceded. Mrs. Amino started this search for her son, and he was going to have to see it through to the end. The irony, of course, was that Kubi, the former novelist, was now a character in somebody else's novel, a novel being written by Mrs. Amino.

OK, I'll do what she says, Kubi decided. It's her show. But somebody, please, *CRUSH THIS NOVEL TO BITS!*

He suddenly thought of other novels. He thought of Vladimir and Estragon, those folks still waiting for Godot. He thought of K never making it into the castle. Kubi felt uneasy, exactly as he had when he read those stories. Then this uneasiness changed into a premonition—that they'd never find Masao. He did not say this to Mrs. Amino, but two days into the stakeout this premonition changed into a different sort of conviction:

There is no such person as Masao.

Kubi was looking for someone who didn't exist. And what was worse, he couldn't stop looking for him.

Kubi set up a folding chair in a corner near the west exit of Shinjuku Station. Counter in hand, he clicked off the number of people who passed before him. For the next ten days, this was how he was going to follow Mrs. Amino's orders.

About ten meters away Kubi spotted a Buddhist priest in a sedge hat, ringing a bell and asking for alms. Obviously this priest was not Masao, but Kubi decided to go over and talk to him anyway. If this business was supposed to be an ascetic exercise, who knows, they might even have something in common.

4

An Orgy a Day

Mikainaito's Brain Waves

After I rested and pored over my calendar with all my appointments written in it, I recovered the ten days' worth of memory that'd been stolen from me. I had audiovisual recall of even the smallest detail.

But to be on the safe side, I went to a hospital and had them do a brain scan. The beating hadn't damaged anything, but the doctor kept going on about my brain waves.

"Usually when people are awake," he said, "they emit gamma and beta waves. Only people who have received special spiritual training give off alpha and theta waves. Theta waves in particular are almost exclusive to dreams. Zen monks engaged in za-zen give off theta waves. Za-zen, you know, is done with the eyes open, awake. Unless someone is really relaxed, they won't have these kind of waves. Now, your brain waves have alpha waves mixed in, and theta waves as well. Do you practice some special meditation technique?"

"I'm a psychic," I replied, grinning. Then I went on, "Mikainaito's waves must be mixed in with mine."

"Mikainaito? What's that?"

It would have been too much to explain, and he probably

wouldn't have gotten it anyway, so I just said, "It's my guardian spirit. The guy that's pasted to my back there, dozing."

The doctor and I looked at each other for a while, laughing.

The Amnesiac City

It's been three years since I landed in Tokyo with the help of a Japanese man who's now in prison. Officially I'm an illegal alien, but so far I've managed to make a living without any hassle. Through connections I was able to get a journalist's visa stamped in my passport, a visa that's still valid. The sticking point of course is that I'm not a journalist. But at least the documents are legal.

According to Katagiri, both my parents were of Japanese descent, but I've never been particular about being considered Japanese. In New York I was just an Oriental. It's a question of consciousness. The day I find myself thinking I'm a Japanese is the day I turn into one. I don't hate Japan the way the Boss does, and since I don't have a complicated past all mixed up with Japan, I've never really thought much about the Japanese. When I say "Boss," I mean Katagiri, my foster father, who, if you want to sum him up, is a refugee from Japan. Ever since the Second World War he's been anti-Japan, and after he fled to the U.S., he hasn't once set foot back in his home country.

Growing up, I heard all kinds of things about Japan from him, but the Japan in his imagination is a whole lot different from the country I'm standing in now. He hated everything about Japan—the land, the people, the money, the constitution. And out of this hatred he created his own Japan. The country in his mind, naturally, doesn't have citizens or money. What it does have is a ruler and a constitution whose whole purpose is to see to it that the ruler gets on in the world. And that's it. I came to Japan because I wanted to see what the place was like with my own eyes. That way I could also understand what Katagiri's Japan is all about.

"You'll be disappointed," he told me. "Forget it."

Katagiri was annoyed, and tried to stop me. But I had my own ideas, and since I was already out on my own, I ignored him.

To tell the truth, I didn't really have anything special I wanted to do in Tokyo. I had a vague desire to earn the most powerful currency on the face of the earth and then maybe go live in Southeast Asia or a small town in Europe. Three years ago, for personal reasons, I needed to get out of New York. You say "personal reasons" and it always means something sort of embarrassing. In my case, relationships were getting out of hand.

Before I came to Japan I did all kinds of jobs in New York. By nature, I'm kind of flighty, not the kind to stick to one job for long. I always think of moving on, so I end up doing a lot of crap in between stops. Same thing happened in Tokyo. In New York, right after I finished with the rental child business, I studied sculpture at Columbia—the place offered the biggest scholarship, though actually Columbia's pretty stingy. My grades were OK, and I went on to the M.F.A. program. But I had no desire to be a sculptor, really. Maybe this is pretentious, but I decided sculpting human hearts would be more fun. Later, since I could speak Japanese and was up on the latest art trends, I got a job trying to get young artists into the Japanese art market. I didn't do that very long. Then an artist I knew recommended me for a scholarship, and I played around in Berlin for six months. Back in New York, I became a gofer for artists. If they couldn't make an appointment, I'd fill in for them, I'd assist in production, promote galleries, set up parties, clean up. I even cat-sat. I wanted more money, and so I expanded into the gofer network in TV and movies. Japanese film companies paid the best, but they were also the most boring and the most irritating. We weren't called gofers, we were coordinators, and you had to do the advance work and the negotiation; you had to go pick up stuff and standby as a translator. It was like baby-sitting.

Gofers are busy like you wouldn't believe. Even if you try to be cool about the business end of it, once you try to have normal relations with customers, friends, or lovers, you find yourself spending only a tiny amount of time at your own home. Some mornings you wake up and you don't know where you are. You hop from a friend's place to where they're filming on location. You go from your lover's apartment to some customer's office or art studio, from a restaurant to a hotel, to a bar. Once or twice a week you manage to pick up some groceries from the supermarket and drag your weary body home.

I was wasted. This kind of work never goes according to plan. And you get more worn out than you could ever imagine. New York's the kind of city where anyone can be friends or lovers with anyone else, and after a while the body just can't take it. I had three girlfriends, all named Susan. An Upper East Side Susan, a Soho Susan, and a Brooklyn Susan. I could tell them apart by their voices and jobs. There was NHK Susan, the critic Susan, the actress Susan. I never used their last names. Even so, when I was on the phone with one of them I'd suddenly realize that the conversation had made a wrong turn. Like I'd find myself saying to the actress Susan, "Hey, your new book on AIDS is really great."

Everything became a hassle. I wanted to set my gauge back to zero. That was a reason for coming to Japan, eh? My body and brain were worn out.

More freedom!

For the first month Tokyo dazzled me. I felt like I was seeing the world for the first time after a long illness. But actually as long as it wasn't New York, any place would've been OK.

At any rate, it was my first time in Tokyo. Anyone in an unknown place turns into a kid. I rode the orange Ginza subway line with guidebook in hand. I started from Shibuya and hit all the hot spots—Harajuku, Akasaka-Mitsuke, Ginza, Ueno, Asakusa. Harajuku on holidays was, like, overflowing with junior and senior high school students. They were just hanging out, and they were friendly and told me where I could get things cheap. Uninvited, I slipped into a party at a hotel in Akasaka-Mitsuke. I ate and drank to my heart's content. I practiced the art of making friends, got to know an old woman selling flowers in the Ginza, ended up fighting with the owner of an art gallery. I took naps next to bums and lovers in Ueno Park, and in Asakusa people came up to me thinking I was dealing drugs.

After the orange line I climbed on the red, setting off on the Marunouchi line from Shinjuku. I ate *ramen* and yakitori in Ogikubo, got lost in Nakano, was stopped and questioned about my occupation in Yotsuya, rummaged through old books in Ochanomizu, ate shoulder to shoulder with students at a stand-up *soba* joint. In Ikebukuro I sat in the park with a Filipino girl and exchanged dirty jokes.

All this in the first two weeks in Tokyo. After that a man helped me get work as a special reporter for a weekly magazine, and then I taught at an English conversation school. The result was that, after six months, my ecology in Tokyo wasn't that different from my ecology in New York. But New York and Tokyo are as different as Venus and Mercury.

In New York my life had more adventure than I wanted. I never knew what would happen the next day. One of the Susans might be crazed with jealousy and threaten to hang herself, or I might get into an argument with someone over religion and never talk to the person again. I might get mugged on the way home from a girl's place, or just out of the blue I might find myself on board a ship headed for the South Pole. (I actually *was* asked to work on a tanker as what they call an "attraction boy" once. Sort of a half-companion, half-entertainer.)

Compared to New York, Tokyo is more dense with people, and they're all spaced out. They all have the same black hair (except for the old folks who are bald or have white hair), and the streets and trains are filled with their sleepy, expressionless faces. On the surface, things are buzzing, but strip off one layer and everyone's bored out of their skulls. That's Tokyo. I discovered that if you want to survive here, you got to follow two rules. First you got to find some ups and downs to break up the monotony. In other words, friends or lovers who aren't like everybody else. The second is never ever think Tokyo is boring. If you want to live here, you got to love the place.

"No matter where you go or who you try to be, all you have to do is have a good time. Like Gulliver." That was Mama's advice.

The reason kids like *Gulliver's Travels* so much is because Gulliver is a kid out to have some fun. So in Tokyo, as Mama said, I made out like Gulliver. To survive in an unknown land, Gulliver learned the language and kept his dignity, despite the contempt and curiosity rained down on him. It doesn't matter where—Lilliput, Brobdingnag, Laputa, Japan, or the land of the Houyhnhnms—a Gulliver can get by without becoming a slave precisely because his head is in the right place. He never loses his curiosity—about midgets, giants, people with their head in the clouds, Japanese, or horse people. He never stops being an eccentric playboy. He faces all kinds of dangers, but even after he returns home safe and sound, he's aching to set sail again. The point is that the world isn't here for the sake of some vast thing like the British Empire. It's here for children to play with.

Even in Tokyo people live like they're in little villages. I'm not a Lilliputian or a giant, and on the surface I look like the average Japanese, so I fit into the village well enough. Just like people who'd lived for a long time in Japan, I was lousy at reading Chinese characters and I had no idea why Tokyo was the way it is today. There was one difference between me and everyone else, though: I knew why I was in Tokyo, they didn't.

There's nothing around now that can help you get a handle on the history of Tokyo. If you go in the back alleys where the boutiques and restaurants are, it's all old people and ghosts exhaling their musty breath; they know something about history, but they don't touch anybody, and nobody touches them. Slums are buried one layer underground, with the postmodern structures by Tange and Isozaki pushing down on them like stone weights in tubs of pickling vegetables.

There used to be waterways cutting through Tokyo. Boats loaded with people, goods, and materials plied the rivers; this was one arm of the distribution system. Before long, they were taken over by a highway in the sky; it was a phantom river that spread like a spider web over the city. On that river there are no boats. And nobody swims there. But information goes zipping along.

Tokyo itself is an amnesiac city set in a desert. Things that happened yesterday are already covered with shifting sand. And last month's events are completely hidden. The year before is twenty meters under, and things that happened five years ago you'd have to bore to unearth. Memories of ten years ago are fossils. There *are* people who know the past, but they're illiterate and mute.

Katagiri said: "Like a desert island with no history—that's Japan."

Katagiri, though, had his own history. I knew why he'd ended up in New York. It's what you call historical consciousness. In New York each person has his own history, his own nation, his own god. New York is where all these things bump up against each other, get mixed together like in a stew. In a place like New York, your sense of history gets focused and sharpened. But I wasn't able to organize my own past into a neat mythology the way Katagiri did. 'Cause I wasn't filled with hatred.

If you try to be laid back in Tokyo, you end up with amnesia. And something in me makes me pretty vulnerable to forgetting. I don't know who created me, and I've never been the child of any one particular set of parents for very long. I was always being broken up, the parts presented to a new set of strangers, so arranging my memories into a single personal history isn't so easy. Still, I can't stop trying.

With Mikainaito's help, I try to piece together this jigsaw puzzle of myself. Fragments of memories come together in dreams.

Only dreams will work. Life stories and myths are not enough. Dreams put the past in order, even help me see into the future. Ever since I was little I've polished my skills at dreaming. In dreams I practiced overcoming problems, and I used dreams to get over illness. I had to—it was part of my business. It was also a way to cope with business. In dreams I looked for ways to cope with reality. The hardships I endured in dreams were real. It all came to me naturally.

My own consciousness gets muddied from all this running back and forth between strangers, lovers, brothers, patrons, and acquaintances, digging deep into their inner lives. I have to run my own mind through a filter sometimes, and dreams are the best way of doing that.

After a while, I discovered a new technique: I would send Mikainaito in and out of people's dreams. He becomes a glob of consciousness and shoots off through time and space. He visits lovers that I lost track of. Just as I'm drifting off to sleep, Mikainaito jumps three times on my stomach or back, depending on what position I'm in, and then is off and away.

While Mikainaito's paying a call to someone else's dreams, I invite other people into mine. Dreams are a great way to stay in touch. With just a little bit of training you can send your thoughts flying out like radio waves. There's no need for drugs or incantations. And you don't need to strain yourself till you're red in the face. Just think of the person you want to see, breathe deeply, then fall asleep, and your dream communication begins. The key is to think of events in dreams as if they really happened. The wall separating dream from reality isn't all that strong. It's easy to cut a hole in it and go back and forth as you like. And in the end the two worlds end up as one. Well, not completely one. Dreams are one part of reality, reality one part of dreams. The point is to live traveling back and forth between the two. That's the morality Mikainaito and I share.

For the time being, if I continue to make an effort, I can stay the way I've always been—like Gulliver, a kid out to have some fun. Surrounded by giants, I still can keep from becoming a giant myself.

Mikainaito, here I am! *It's me—Matthew.* *Don't mistake me for someone else!*

It's scary trying to get along with total strangers, people you don't know from Adam. Things you say or do without thinking might end up insulting them. A while back I got beat up by a Muslim. He asked me what kind of god my god was, and I said, "There're more gods than there are people. Every day the gods fight each other, hate each other, love, deceive each other, and play. I'm a god myself, and so are you."

This guy blew his stack and yelled, "There is only one God!"

I should've kept quiet, but I made the mistake of trying to explain. "Why can't there be a lot of gods?" I asked him. "Allah and Christ are gods, but there're plenty more where they came from."

He punched me in the jaw, and I bit my tongue. You think someone's your friend and life's a ball, but it doesn't work out that way most of the time. You can't judge others by your own standards.

I try to be modest and humble. During the past year I've added 108 people to my address book. So maybe modesty works, who knows? The number of people I keep in touch with regularly, including those in New York, comes to 290. Here's the breakdown:

Acquaintances (friends): 179
Friends (closer than acquaintances): 30
Lovers: 23
Customers: 18
Brothers and sisters: 8
Younger sisters: 1
Elves: 1
Enemies: 27

Foster parents: 2
Other: 1

Right now I feel about the same way that I felt three years ago when I was in New York and thought I wanted to start all over from scratch. The gravity of Tokyo is starting to get to me; it's cramping my carefree lifestyle. But even if I make plans to escape, it'll take me another six months to get out. My friends in New York were always pushing me out toward a gravity-free zone, but half my friends in Tokyo pin me down and won't let me fly.

Matthew, it's time. Forget about all that pointless stuff and get ready.

Urged on by Mikainaito, I started to shave. I wouldn't be back in my place for the next four days.

Itinerary:
SUNDAY: Date with Pooh.
MONDAY: Have a ball with Mariko Fujieda.
TUESDAY: Birthday party at the Unos' for their dead child.
WEDNESDAY: Baby-sitting ex-actress and her daughter.
THURSDAY: Professor Yamaga's lecture. Return home.

Elisabeth and Venus

It's hard to believe that Pooh and Mariko are both Japanese. If I had to make a choice I'd opt for Mariko, I guess, but I like Pooh, too. In Mariko's eyes everything is wonderful; in Pooh's eyes everything is unhappy as can be. I don't think people should generalize too much about Japanese. Before you can do that, you need to prove these two girls were the same species.

Pooh was a virgin when she started going with me. I don't think she'd ever even gone on a date. If you told her she was pretty, she'd feel hurt. That's the way she was. She liked opera, and most of her ideas about what goes on between men and women seem to come from the stage. Behind those silver-framed glasses, her eyes (which I was never sure were focused on me or on some mosquito buzzing around me) overflowed with infatuation from this made-up world of love.

A long time ago, in order to get Penelope to pay me some attention, I learned to sing the "Deserto sulla terra" from Verdi's *Il Trovatore*. This is the aria sung by Manrico backstage as a kind of prayer for Leonora's love. When I sang this aria for Pooh, she loved it so much her lips quivered. Actually I'm not that great a singer. My voice has its good points—I can hit the high notes—but this was the first time my singing ever moved anyone.

Pooh really likes Wagner's *Tannhäuser*, and even though she's not much to look at, she wants to be like the character Elisabeth. She's crazy about the kind of woman who educates men and is a symbol of self-sacrifice. Pooh lives a single, solitary life, a lot like a nun.

After she graduated from junior college, she got a job selling tickets at a concert hall and spent half her salary on tickets; the other half she stashed away in savings. She got to know about me through a friend. She called me up and said she'd like to hire me: she wanted someone to talk to. Imagine how much courage it took her to call. The first time we met she didn't look me in the eyes once, and she didn't touch her tea. It seemed like she regretted the whole thing. When she told me she was an opera fan, she began to loosen up a bit. *Mikainaito, I understood what was going on—Pooh felt guilty for buying a guy's companionship this way.* But a professional boyfriend like myself doesn't make a client feel guilty. 'Cause my job was to help her get rid of the guilt, get to know a man's body, get to feel with her own body the love she saw in the opera. Once she got to that point, my job was over.

The third time we got together, Pooh had her first sexual experience. If you say a woman in love with love is someone like Mimi in *La Bohème*, then Pooh was a woman trying her best to change from a woman in love with love to a woman who *loves*. I wanted her to be more confident, to become even more like an operatic heroine.

I was really looking forward to our fourth date. I'd been really busy, and hadn't been able to see her for two months. Roses cost too much, so I bought a bouquet of carnations and went over to her place. Dinner was already on the table. I was surprised to find her wearing makeup and perfume. On the stereo, volume turned down, Leonora sang her aria from *Trovatore*.

"I've been waiting for such a long time." Pooh's eyes behind silver-framed glasses looked straight at me.

"I'm sorry, Pooh. I just had a lot of things to clear up."

"That's what I figured."

She sat down beside me and poured me a beer. Rising leisurely, she walked to her chest of drawers, took out an envelope, and handed it to me. Inside was money, about a hundred thousand yen from the feel of it.

"Please take it," she said.

My standard fee for one night was twenty thousand yen, so this was way too much. "The La Scala company's coming to Japan soon," I said. "Why don't you use the money for that."

"But I want to help you," she whispered, then stuck the envelope in my pant's pocket.

At first I didn't know what she meant. Maybe she wanted me to come see her more often—or maybe she wanted to keep me from falling for some other girl. *No, Mikainaito, Pooh's words had no double meaning.* Her love was pure, like Elisabeth's. Her heart hadn't been gnawed away by jealousy or possessiveness yet. I promised her I'd put the money to good use.

That night, she held me close, crying out how happy she was.

If you're all tired out, don't even think about paying Mariko a visit. She'll wear you to a frazzle. Mariko works at a travel agency and goes abroad a lot as an escort on package tours. Her souvenir to herself is to sleep with a man in each place she visits.

After she'd done this a number of times, what you had was one lewd lady.

The woman is crazy about sex. She even bragged to me about bedding five guys at once.

But you wouldn't know it to look at her. Her face isn't man-hungry, and she doesn't have the kind of body that oozes sex. She isn't really that well built either, and she doesn't wear much lipstick or makeup. She reminds you of those stretched-out Modigliani women. If you saw her sitting quietly, you'd never in a million years imagine that she was the kind of woman who could say quite calmly, "Semen is one of my main sources of protein."

When I met her the first time, she looked me straight in the face and asked very businesslike, "Do you think you're in pretty good shape?"

"I guess so," I replied.

"I've got a couple of boyfriends," she said, "but I'm sick of their jealousy and the way they get after me all the time. That's why I asked for you."

We had Seven-and-Sevens, which put Mariko in the mood. This is how things always work out with her. Her body gets all flushed and she takes off her clothes. And laughs uproariously. Then she lets it all hang out, as it were, telling me about things that happened on her trips, rumors about her boyfriends, stories about her family.

"The first time I did it was a gang bang. I was sixteen, and it was in the pumphouse at school. Ever since then my body hasn't been the same. When our class went on an overnight excursion, I went to one of the rooms the boys were staying in and took them on in the closet. I charged the other boys five hundred yen a peek."

"How many men have you slept with?"

"Hmm. Maybe thirty different nationalities."

A tough case, I thought. That night we got undressed and

she brought out wet towels. Whip me this way, I'll do the same to you, she said; it'll get us worked up. Sure enough, I felt this glow where I got whipped.

After we had sex, she pulled out a ceramic pig about the size of a rice cooker from under her bed and asked me for a five-hundred-yen coin. Why? I asked. She said she was saving money. Every time she slept with a guy she put five hundred yen in the piggy bank. When it was full, she'd have five hundred thousand yen. In other words, she was working toward a thousand acts of love. She was going to use the money for a trip to Africa.

She paid me for my services only once. But I've visited her a half dozen times. Before I realized it, her venom had gotten into me and I, too, started to crave the kind of wild sex she was into.

The sex where we switch roles is my favorite. As soon as we strip, I start talking like a demure young girl, and Mariko acts like a guy real horny for a fuck. I put on all the clothes she's just taken off, even her panties, and she slips on my still-warm underwear and pants.

She sticks her hand under her skirt, which I'm wearing, and says, "Come on, baby."

And I, like a woman in a soap opera, say, "Stop it or I'll scream!"

"Quit bitching!" she yells. She takes off my belt, which she's been wearing, and whips me.

"All right, all right! I'll do what you say!"

"Take off your skirt."

I do as I'm told. My cock, half erect, sticks out of her panties.

"Lick me!" she commands.

I get down on all fours. Mariko pulls down my pants and stands in front of me, her legs spread wide.

"No, you bitch! Stick your tongue out more! Ye-es—that's the way. I'm gonna stick it in. OK, lie down on your back!"

Drenched in icy pleasure and burning embarrassment, I am content. Sex with switched roles—it's like a metaphor for my life. Mariko's like me, another child at play. When it comes to sex, we're pretty equal.

A Smear of Paint

A friend of a friend once asked me to take on the job of being the adviser to a seventy-eight-year-old man. The man used to be the president of a medium-sized company, but had handed over the reins to his son. He seemed to be living a life of ease, but because work had been his whole life, his relatives were afraid that without stimulation he'd become senile. It was the son who hired me to find a hobby for this man who had none.

Sure enough, all he talked about were the hard times he had running his company and how proud he was of his good health. The man's son and grandchildren had heard these stories hundreds of times, and were probably sick to death of them. The old man's speeches had the ring of a priest chanting sutras.

The idea struck me that maybe painting would get him to knock off all the talking.

"Forget that you're even painting," I explained. "Smear paint on the paper. Make the smears as complicated or as weird as you like. And try to plan out ahead of time the best place to put them."

I'd laid in a supply of sketchbooks and acrylics. The old man complained at first, but when I told him his finished product was pretty good, he was pleased.

"People who set out to paint," I told him, "never have a clue what painting is all about. Just think of the surface and smear on the paint. That's the only real form of pure expression."

After repeating this a number of times, one day the old man said he wanted to try oil paints, too.

*   *   *

Love's Not Easy

Another client was a well-known former actress. She'd retired four years earlier and was living well in a rent-free apartment she'd gotten from her husband as a divorce settlement.

She started off by showing me videos of all the films she starred in, keeping up a running commentary as we watched. I suppose I should have been flattered, but I knew there were other reasons for this special screening. A part of her seemed to think she was still the youthful star on the screen, and she didn't want to be the only one deceived.

"You haven't changed a bit," I told her, even as I found it thrilling to see where her former beauty had faded.

She had a twenty-year-old daughter, who looked a lot like the younger woman on the screen. Their bodies, though, were completely different. The mother was built along Japanese lines, while the daughter was of more Western proportions, with long legs, a fuller waist, and ample breasts.

The daughter was as outgoing as her mother and never hurt for boyfriends. She brought each one home to meet her mother. She wasn't showing off, but the mother couldn't bear it. There are a lot of mothers who get jealous of their own daughters, but for this former actress, her daughter was a rival in love. Often, when the mother had finally gotten a man to show interest in her, he'd take one look at the daughter and jump ship. The daughter wasn't bothered by going out with her mother's boyfriends, and didn't mind ditching them, either. Naturally, this hurt her mother's pride, and she wanted revenge. My job was to be a partner in her vendetta.

"I want you to play the sort of man attractive enough to make my daughter jealous," she told me.

The actress added: "My daughter doesn't have a clue how rough love can get. She thinks love means having guys fall all over themselves for you. If this keeps up, she'll never amount to anything. I'm her mother and I've got to make sure she learns the facts of life. But I don't want people saying she learned everything from me. So *you*'ll be the one who teaches her the lesson."

I thought the best plan of attack would be for me to start off as the daughter's boyfriend and then fall in love with the mother. I'd be a double agent. But the mother hated the idea. I was to be *her* boyfriend, visit her regularly, and try to develop a love triangle so the daughter would learn the harsh realities of love.

There were several conditions attached to the job. First, I was not, under any circumstance, to grow fond of the daughter. Second, I was to earn the daughter's respect. Third, I was not to try to bring them together. And fourth, as the mother's lover, I was to keep a steady stream of compliments going her way.

But if I did all of the above, the plan seemed doomed to failure. I decided to relax and let the chips fall where they may. No need to do a thing, I figured. This thing between mother and daughter is going to come to a head by itself.

And sure enough, in the second week of this arrangement, their maneuvering was out in the open. The daughter began to show interest in me, and her mother tried to put a halt to it. Once, in front of her mother, the daughter said to me, "You're my mother's boyfriend, right? Well, you sure don't act like it."

The mother shot back: "There you go again—trying to snap up my boyfriend."

"No, I'm not."

"Yes, you are."

Their conversation was playful, but beneath it was a mutual distrust. I stayed neutral so I wouldn't get roped into their drama. Later, my employer, irritated, told me, "You're acting too wishy-washy. She's taking advantage of you. She's a flirt through and through."

But now I had my doubts. The more hysterical the mother became, the more the facts seemed to take on a different color.

On one occasion I gave the actress the slip and spoke to the daughter alone. I told her the reason I was there. The daughter could hardly believe her ears.

"She's incredible," she said. "I don't know what to say. But she's been that way ever since she and my father split up. She forgets how old she is; she's always trying to compete with me."

"Aren't you always stealing her boyfriends?"

"That's not true. I just don't want strangers taking advantage of her. One look at a handsome man and she gets all hot and bothered. Then she goes out and spends gobs of money on them. I try to get rid of those worms. No way I'm going to let some jerk eat up my inheritance."

Now it all fell into place. But where did that put me? I stayed neutral, seeing both sides to every story. A friend to man and beast.

After this, the mother and the daughter both seemed to like me, and I continued to drop by their place. Not as the mother's lover, though, but as a neutral agent who swept away suspicion. Sometimes the daughter asked my advice about love, and sometimes the mother tried to lure me into her bed.

Of course I obliged them both. I'm a professional, after all.

A Sigh

Matthew, your life's like one big orgy, isn't it? Mikainaito said.

What do you mean?

I don't mean just sex. You don't care who you get mixed up with.

It's my job, there's nothing I can do about it.

Such stamina.

Yeah. In this line of work, your body's your working capital.

I'm worn out flying all over Tokyo.

It's like Tokyo's fucked us, isn't it?

Discarding the World

The lectures always began exactly at nine A.M.

Professor Yamaga, my most depressing client of all, was an economics scholar who'd given up his position at the university and now lived holed up like a larva.

When I arrived, he was putting the coffee on. He was the meticulous sort who reset the second hand on his watch each morning. Today I was twenty seconds early.

"Good morning," he said.

I was sick of this greeting. It was less a greeting than three dead syllables. For him everything in the world was dark and dismal: sex, study, health, heaven, daytime, the sun. My job was to teach him that for a person whose body was fulfilled the whole world was bright. Crime, hell, sickness, insanity, night, death—even these had a cheerful side to them.

I'm not a doctor, but to me Professor Yamaga was deep in depression. He knew this himself, I think, because the first time we met he launched into this harangue about psychiatry.

"It's a lot better to be friends with a young healthy person," he told me, "than to let some idiot doctor analyze you. Right, Matthew?"

He grasped this much, but he ignored anything I said. He was more concerned about working out his analysis of the state of the world.

I got ten thousand yen a shot to be an audience for his lectures.

Even if the network of friends and acquaintances I'd laid over Tokyo was unresponsive, I still managed to attract strangers in need of friendship and affection. And this guy was one of them. His younger sister had asked me to take on the job, and she was footing the bill. She was worried about his mental state and had heard about Matthew the Dream Messenger from a friend. The thing was, though, I'd never met the person who gave her my name. I'd never even heard of him. People, it seemed, were starting to hear about me.

Professor Yamaga may have taken out his anger on psychiatry, but to people who would listen to his lectures he was the perfect gentleman. I knew I shouldn't hurt his pride or his condition would get worse. But if you were too obvious with the flattery, he'd see through it and get upset. That particular day he lectured me on "The Fall of Japan."

"Matthew," he began, "with my own body I can feel the gradual disintegration of Japan. And who is destroying the country? You know who it is, don't you?"

I don't know, I told him. I'm not a prophet. I'm not a historian. But actually I did know the answer. Everybody does—they just don't talk about it. Professor Yamaga, out of spite, chose to put it into words.

"Japan is destroying *itself*," he exploded. "It is the Japanese themselves who are wrecking this country. People are always trying to shift the blame. They say it's not their responsibility—the boss is a charlatan, politics has gone downhill, it's a Jewish plot, et cetera. But it's the Japanese themselves who are rotten to the core. I can feel a colony inside my body with anti-Japanese riots breaking out. Yet I have this Japanese face pasted on my outside. So I suppose it's my fate to be a Japanese orphan."

I know I'd heard these words before. Professor, I thought, orphans are freer than you think. Orphans have to be children at play. And you don't know the first thing about playing. How many times have you had sex? I bet I've done it a hundred times as much as you.

"Professor," I asked him, "wouldn't it be better if you destroyed Japan yourself?"

"Matthew, you know why I left the university, don't you?"

"Because the students and other professors were idiots, right?"

"Precisely. I discarded the world so I could watch from my own deathbed the future of Japan. I'm pretty old. It would bring me great joy to see this country disappear while I am still alive. I wrote an essay about it last night. Here—I'll give you a copy."

Strangely, the essay brought on a wave of nostalgia. When I was in high school, Katagiri made me listen to his old stories as part of my Japanese lessons. The professor's essay fit almost perfectly with what Katagiri used to tell me.

This is what the essay said:

To all you a century late in becoming Caucasian! Toss off your Christian morality. Until a century ago—no, even now—Christians have programmed the control of the world with their god. Everywhere their hatred of other races and other religions has become the fountainhead of their energy. They are masters at cloaking their feelings, showing their true colors only to others of their kind. The dichotomy of *tatemae* and *honne* —outer appearance and inner reality—is not the reserve of the Japanese alone. No, it is the forte of all for whom Christ is God. It is the scam of Catholics and Protestants.

To all you nouveau Caucasian chameleons! Cast aside your Christian shell! Fling it back in their faces! Inherit the will of those puerile chameleons who plunged our homeland into World War II. Do as you will and ignore the future. Rid yourself of shame! Forget such pettiness as the security of Japan which the United States has nurtured since the war. Destroy that Japan utterly! Rip it apart with your bare hands! Become a race of exiles. If but a few outstanding Japanese survive, they will be enough!

If Japan really was destroyed, people like Professor Yamaga would be among the first to go, you could count on it. Just like him, Katagiri was always running off at the mouth about Japan after the end of history. And he was one of the exiles. But there was a world of difference between him and the Professor. One was a crybaby out to commit suicide, the other a man trying to declare himself God. In terms of physical strength, too, it'd be hard to imagine two men more unalike. If Yamaga was a wimpy squirrel, Katagiri was an aggressive hyena. And when you get down to it, strength is what counts.

I never asked the Professor about his dreams. I didn't feel like trying to interpret his dreams, and besides, he hated people poking around in his unconscious.

What he needed more than anything else was to have a good time. But if I took him out to play around he'd probably spend his time coming up with some theory about "The Meaning of 'Play' in Human Culture." It'd be impossible to drag him out for a night on the town.

One day a flash of inspiration hit me. Even though it was my own idea, I had to admit it was pretty amazing. And I had the perfect partner to help me put it into practice: Mariko, the nymphomaniac. As always, she had to hesitate for a second before she leaped at the chance.

I arrived as usual at nine A.M. for my private lesson. It was Sunday, and Mariko was with me, wearing glasses and a navy blue suit. I'd told the Professor before that I'd be bringing an auditor along.

The five-part lecture series on "The Fall of Japan" was over, and the schedule called for a new lecture, "The New Yellow Peril," on the evil influence of the Chinese in the twenty-first century.

"As you are well aware," he began, "China is in the process of becoming more democratic and open. But I would be very cautious about this, since Chinese continue to flood into foreign countries. The narrow passage into Japan will definitely widen to allow entrance to more Chinese—as the power of Chinese in America surges inevitably upward. All advanced capitalist states will, in part, be Sino-fied. Everywhere there will be racial and religious strife, not to mention dislocations in local economies.

When that occurs, there is a real danger that a new Yellow Peril theory will spring up in the West. And that will come down just as hard on the Japanese, because in Caucasian eyes we are the same."

"Is this guy worried about something?" Mariko asked, stroking my thigh.

"He doesn't want to be mistaken for a Chinese," I told her.

"That isn't what I said!" Professor Yamaga blurted out.

Ignoring him, Mariko began unbuttoning my shirt. I reached for her breasts.

"What do you think you're doing!?" the Professor demanded.

"We thought we'd put on a show for you."

Mariko took off her jacket and unbuttoned her blouse. I reached under her skirt and started to feel her up.

"Both of you, leave at once!" Professor Yamaga was livid.

But Mariko played the tease and blew him a kiss. "Professor," she said coyly, "it doesn't cost a single yen to watch. Is this making you hard?"

"Professor," I added, "I want your cock to come alive, to be potent again. How about sleeping with Mariko? I don't think she'd mind."

"Professor Yamaga, hold me!" Mariko implored.

Professor Yamaga stayed with Mariko in his bedroom for quite some time. The door was locked. No matter how many times I knocked, he wouldn't answer. I felt a little sorry for him, but if I'd let his condition get any worse he would have been beyond hope. I guess you got to be cool and businesslike about things.

The next day, the Professor called and proposed that we continue the "New Yellow Peril" lecture series the following Sunday. His voice had a cheerful ring to it. The treatment seemed to have done the trick.

A Week's Worth of Work

MONDAY: Dinner with the ex-company president, me playing the court jester. The prez thinks he's a poetic genius.

TUESDAY: Tutoring a junior high school boy who refuses to go to school. His English is excellent, thanks to me. In the evening, analyzing the dreams of a young girl who wants to be a writer. I've been trying to persuade her to create her own alter ego. Something along the lines of Mikainaito.

WEDNESDAY: Took it easy. Read at home during the day. Slept. In the evening a party given by Raphael. Partied till dawn.

THURSDAY: Listening to Mrs. Miura's complaints. Seems she's caught her husband sleeping around.

FRIDAY: More lessons with the junior high school boy. The reason he doesn't want to go to school is because he's so fat. The other kids have nicknamed him "Sumo-*san*." I suggested he go to study in the U.S. The place is crawling with kids twice as fat as him.

SATURDAY: Hanging out. No plans.

SUNDAY: Invited to a reading circle of writers and critics. One novelist named Masahiko Shimada told me he's seriously thinking of making me the main character in his next novel. He'll come to interview me soon. I made it clear to him that I don't come cheap. I asked the budding girl novelist what she thinks of Shimada's work, and she said, "It's too sentimental. He needs to live a more demanding life, like yours."

MONDAY: Rested. Wrote a letter to Penelope.

PART
II

5

A Japanese Rip van Winkle; A Worried-Looking Dog Eating Pizza

The plaza in front of Shibuya Station is a lake at the bottom of a valley where several rivers meet. When the sluice gates fly open, hordes of people flood into the intersection from all directions and whirlpools start to swirl. So on rainy days like today it's a sea of different-colored umbrellas bouncing and knocking around for space. Made me imagine some bizarre machine with a lot of gears going round and round for no good reason.

For twenty minutes, I stood there, staring down at this machine from the passageway to the Inokashira line. Next to me, I noticed a bum staring vacantly at something in the square. As far as the other passersby were concerned, this guy was invisible. What caught my attention? I looked down where he was looking and saw, right below the rump of Hachiko, the faithful dog memorialized in bronze, another bum in the pouring rain, sitting on the pavement and eating his lunch. Chicken nuggets, maybe. Beside him sat a wet dog, which the bum was sharing his meal with. Nobody paid them any attention. Only me and this dark, seedy man beside me.

Mikainaito, it's like I've seen this scene before. Where? Manhattan! Right—Seventh Avenue and 14th Street. It was raining then, too, sprinkling, really. Some guy was squatting in the road, wearing a coat stained with ketchup and a Yankees cap. Remember? He was eating pizza and giving some to the dog. A mongrel, black and white spots, that had these worried, funny eyebrows, as if the bum had used a magic marker on them. The eyebrows looked like this:

"A worried-looking dog eating pizza," I muttered to this guy in Spanish. I'd been studying it for three months and was beginning to get the hang of it. Still it surprised me how easily this sentence leaped to my lips.

"The dog supports me," the bum explained. "I call him Flipper. Hey, can you spare some change?" The man turned up the visor of his cap. He looked just like the dog—wasted eyes, mouth hanging stupidly open.

They hung out between 14th and 17th. The man slept under the scaffoldings of buildings under construction. In the summer, he lay quietly in the shade under the scaffolding, naked, too hot to move. In the winter, he made his home out of cardboard boxes; his body heat was the only thing between him and the cold. The main trick to survival, he said, was to preserve your strength.

The man and dog ate nothing but pizza. Who knows why. Maybe it was their thing, or maybe it was a cheap way to fill up. At any rate, pizza kept man and dog together. The dog looked cute, and people threw coins into a paper cup. The man bought the pizza, and the two of them ate it.

I wonder, could Flipper still be eating pizza with that worried look on his face? Maybe he found a more affluent master. Or maybe Flipper is dead. If Flipper died, the bum wouldn't be able to live. Guess it'd be the same with me. If Mikainaito died, it'd be all over.

"Got a light?"

It was the bum next to me, a Hi-lite dangling from his lips. Actually, the cigarette was wedged in a gap between his front teeth, so it didn't fall even when his mouth was open. This guy didn't look Japanese. Maybe he was from Southeast Asia?

I held my lighter out for him. And just then our eyes met. His were dark brown, walleyed. I had the unnerving feeling that it was Mikainaito himself, staring right into me. I stiffened.

"So you were you watching them, too?" he asked.

"Watching who?" I answered.

"You know who I mean. *Them.*" He pointed to the dog and bum.

I didn't like the way this conversation was going. Here I am, sober, in broad daylight, and I bump into a guy with eyes that read my mind. Not a good sign.

I closed my eyes, exhaled loudly three times, and called for Mikainaito. *Hey! This guy gives me the creeps. What should I do?*

"Well, take it easy," I said, and started toward the stairs. Mustn't forget I got to get to a job. Grab a cab and hightail it to Aoyama.

"Wait a second, please."

The bum was following me, weaving a path through the crowd of people. Nope, he wasn't your run-of-the-mill Tokyo vagrant who couldn't care less about anything. He was more like the homeless in New York who collar you and won't let go. I slowed down. If he puts a spell on me, I'm in deep shit. Give him fifty yen and split. I groped in my pocket for a coin.

"You're not so uptight like other people," the bum started saying. "I bet you're not Japanese, are you? You're pretty strange, you know."

"Do you speak English?" I asked him.

"A little. Please follow me."

The guy walked down to the Ginza line platform, me right behind. The passageway turned out to be a high-class condo for bums; it was clean, they could bed down, it didn't have a whole lot of traffic. We stopped where another bum sat, hands around his raised knee, deep in thought. Beside him was a family-sized barrel of Kentucky Fried Chicken.

"Master, I've brought you a man of leisure," the walleyed bum reported in.

Somehow I got the feeling that Master was a rather complex sort of vagrant. I brought my hand, still clutching the fifty-yen coin, out of my pocket and scratched my nose.

"Help yourself," Master said, acknowledging me by holding up the barrel of chicken. "I just bought it, so it's still warm."

I looked back at the walleyed bum and said, "What do you want?" The real question, though, was why the hell I followed him here.

"I'm sure you'll like my Master," he answered.

I turned to Master, who apparently was Japanese. "Who are you?" I asked.

"Won't you have some fried chicken?" he offered again.

"Thanks, but I just ate. What do you want?" I asked again.

"This fellow's name is Swami," he said, pointing to the walleyed one. "He's a friend of mine from India who's come to work in Japan. He's not really a bum."

Oh yeah? The two of them were now sitting on a sheet of cardboard, peering up at me, smiling. I quit asking my silly questions and joined them. Master passed me the barrel and Swami handed me a paper napkin. Why not. After all, when I was a kid, I thought Colonel Sanders was greater than the president of the United States. We'd go for a drive to Westchester County, and there he was, decked out in his white suit waiting for you. I stole his glasses once, I remember. Watching me eat, Swami and Master shook hands and grinned.

"My name is Matthew," I said. I gave my real name, or at least the name I'd grown used to. It was best to be honest in the face of uncertainty. Otherwise you end up cursed.

"I am Taro Miyashita," Master said. "It's short for Taro Urashima of Miyashita Park. I spend most of my time there, but today it's raining so I'm here instead. This is my living room, and you are my guest."

Taro Urashima laughed, and I laughed, too, like a bumbling owl. It was then I noticed the string of prayer beads in his right hand. He was methodically moving his fingers along the beads, one by one.

"Is that some sort of meditation?" I asked him, though I knew full well that it was. Under Katagiri's instruction, I'd done the same thing. In fact, I now suspected that this Taro Urashima really *was* a Master.

"This string of beads is called *mara*. Yogi always carry *mara* with them. You count the 108 beads as you chant a mantra. You breathe down your spine and hum *om*."

"And then what happens?"

"You feel good."

The sight of Taro Urashima mouthing *om* was like a baby sucking his teething ring. Here, in the middle of all these tired people bumping into each other and clucking their tongues and hurrying off in every direction, Taro Urashima had the nerve to sit still, concentrating on breathing in the protection of his guardian spirit.

"Do you always feel good?" I asked.

"At the present moment, I've just finished my meditation and am eating some chicken," he answered.

But wasn't eating meat harmful to meditation?

Swami smiled, teeth showing, chicken in hand. "Do you want to feel good, too?" he asked.

"Not right now. Maybe some other time," I said.

Neither Master nor pupil responded to this; it seemed they were waiting for my curiosity, like mist, to gather. One thing was certain: these two meant me no harm.

"The beads of the *mara* are the seeds of a fruit tree called *rudraksha,*" Taro Urashima began. "The only people who can carry it are those who have left the world behind."

"Master's left the world behind," Swami interjected, "but not me."

Swami laughed like he was chomping the air. What a pair these two were. Made me think they really were brothers—just like Mikainaito and I were twins.

Besides, that used to be my job, being friends with people who'd left the world behind, that is. Very few of these folks had thrown the world away on their own. Most lived in the past, or they had been discarded by the world. They were up to their necks in the bottomless swamp of stagnant time.

Mikainaito, you remember that old lady Sayo? When she rented me, she said: "Matthew, you're the spitting image of Koichi."

My job was to let her catch a glimpse of her dead grandson. I had to eat Koichi's favorite bonito until I got heartburn and pretend to play the trumpet, even if I couldn't play a note. Poor old Sayo. I heard she died of a stroke seven years ago, without seeing her hometown again. She's probably a ghost now, hovering over the Pacific Ocean, looking out for a porpoise that reminds her of Koichi. When she finds one, you can be sure she'll tell it all the tales of Tosa, the place where she was born. The porpoise might even take her back to Tosa, who knows, but if it made a wrong turn and they ended up in Australia, Sayo'd begin to search for Koichi there.

Mikainaito, that apartment super, Jack—remember him? He was another one who'd left the world behind.

"Yo, Matthew!" was how Jack used to greet me. "Using your brain? After you're twenty-five, you lose a hundred thousand brain cells at a shot. Better store up knowledge while you can." It was the kind of greeting you'd expect from a former teacher.

When Jack was twelve, he won first place in a national math contest. He was supposed to be able to solve any cubic equation, bingo, all in his head. But people who can calculate a bunch of numbers in their head aren't necessarily mathematical geniuses. This was way before the age of the pocket calculator, so people who had trouble with simple arithmetic thought Jack was a genius. A gold mine, like a piano prodigy or a boy chess whiz.

"When I was a kid, they called me Boy Euclid," Jack said. "I'd look at equations on a piece of paper, and the answer would flash into my head. I barely had to think. God just put the answer in my head. I think God gave me a lifetime's worth of love right off the bat."

Jack told me this, too: "When I was fourteen, there was this girl I liked. She'd heard I was this math genius and that I liked her, so I guess maybe she wanted to tease me a little. She said, you might be a genius at math, but if you can't do anything else, you're no good. I can too do other things, I told her. I can swim and play baseball as well as anybody else. OK, she said, if you want me to like you, jump off the high diving board. I went to the pool with her, humming as I climbed up the ten-meter diving platform. But from there the pool looked a hundred meters away. I was scared to death. I stood there for about five minutes, frozen. I could hear her voice: You going to jump or what? Well, here goes, I said. I took a deep breath and leaped. The next thing I remember was waking up in the nurse's office. I don't know how I hit the water, but I got a concussion. The girl was sitting next to me, sobbing as she held my hand. She's mine now, I thought.

"But the real tragic part came later. I was studying Newton's law of gravitation—you know, the forces that affect the earth as seen through mathematics. But now this equation looked completely different from what I could remember. The numbers hadn't changed; my brain had. Before I could solve problems automatically, just like a calculator. But after I hit my head, I had to write things down on paper in the middle of my calculations or else I couldn't come up with the answer. The connections in my brain that made me such a genius had been cut. Matthew, you know what I mean? Mathematics was my native language, then all of a sudden I couldn't speak. Talk about a wipeout. Everything went black before me. The earth's gravity was suddenly out of whack, and everything was floating up in the air.

"But I didn't give up that easy. For a while I thought I could be a math genius again, and I used to have these face-offs with the equations. But I could never do them in my head again. I didn't speak the language anymore. At least one good thing came out of it, though—I know how to dive now."

At age thirteen, listening to Jack Brown's tale with my Linus-like face, I didn't have the talent to comfort this disheartened former boy genius. But then Jack didn't expect me to. He wasn't really talking to me—he was talking to himself. The child prodigy he used to be. The Jack Brown who died at fourteen.

Who knows. Maybe Jack's sitting at his desk in the super's office right now, toying with useless equations.

People who've thrown away the world have minds like black holes: once time's sucked in there, it can never move again.

"Why did you turn your back on the world?" I asked Taro Urashima.

Embarrassed perhaps, Taro Urashima tapped the back of his head with his left hand. His short hair was fluffy, as if he'd just washed it. "I didn't turn my back on the world," he said. "I'm living off in one corner of it, see?" With this sibilant "see," his spit hit my cheekbones.

"And where's this corner?" I felt like pouncing on his words and harassing him. I wanted to drag it out of him, to make him confess that it was the world that had cast *him* aside.

"Where I am right now. You think we're at the center of the world? No way—it's the corner."

"What's so good about being in the corner?"

"You can see things clearly."

"Friends—friends—you and Master—you're friends, right?" Swami interrupted, tapping me on the shoulder.

"What can you see so clearly?" I went on.

"Lots of things," Taro Urashima replied. "I see people naked, without the clothes that hide the truth. I see what they're searching for. I see people die—and my own body going to pieces. I see ghosts roaming around."

"I don't know yoga too well, but what Master says is true," Swami added. "After I came to Tokyo, I started to study yoga. I can see all kinds of things, too. But it's a little scary."

"You mean when you meditate you have hallucinations?" I asked.

"Yes. When you perfect yoga, you see a dark world, even during the day," Taro answered.

Swami laughed. And for some reason, mixed in with his laughter I could hear a siren wailing. I was hearing things. The sound was in my ears, deep within my ears. The pitch started to change. Like the Doppler effect.

"I can't see the universe yet," Taro Urashima said. "My master could see everything. I came back to Tokyo before my training was complete."

I exhaled three times through my nose, and summoned Mikainaito again. *What do you make of this guy named Taro Urashima?*

Nothing out of the ordinary, Mikainaito replied.

I doubt that. How could there be people like this in Tokyo? Did I get lost somewhere along the line? Did part of Shibuya open up? Have I wandered into a time tunnel?

Tokyo's pretty big, Mikainaito said. *There're plenty of places like that. A wall in an alleyway falls over—wham!—on the other side is India.*

But Tokyo's too boring for that. It's the amnesiac's capital. People can't remember what happened the day before yesterday. In a place like this, how can there be a person who can see eternity?

Taro Urashima's in Tokyo all right, but he's living in a different time zone from the rest of the city. That's all it is.

Just a second ago I heard a siren. With the Doppler effect thrown in. What was that? Another memory?

Goddamn nuisance, a siren from the past. Ears aren't working right.

Mikainaito, is your watch set correctly? Somehow time feels like it's standing still.

My watch doesn't have any hands. You must have met this kind of guy before. Try to remember. And don't lose your cool.

Taro Urashima offered me more fried chicken. The piece in my hand still had some meat on it, so I said no thanks.

What kind of god does this guy believe in? He must have been living among the gods for a long, long time. Don't you think so, Mikainaito?

"And where is it you come from?" It was the first time Taro Urashima made any of the small talk you'd expect from a host. "You must have come from very far away."

For a second, I was stuck. I'd come from New York. I was sure of that. But it was like I'd gotten on the subway at Times Square and gotten off at Shibuya.

"Ah—New York," Swami said. "I have a lot of friends there. It is a nice place."

"I was in New York once, too," Taro Urashima said. "For about three years. I was thinking about becoming an artist. I like to have a wild time, and New York was like one big contest to pick the biggest weirdo."

"Weirdo, weirdo, I am a weirdo *gaijin*," Swami chanted.

"Weird people are all *gaijin*, you know," Taro Urashima said. "That's why there're lots of weirdos in New York. Swami's a Tokyo weirdo. When he's not working on road construction, he stays with me. Swami, you don't have any home, do you?"

"Right. But in India I have a wife and several children."

"In Tokyo weirdos can't really make a living," Taro Urashima continued. "But in New York, they have a whole weirdo industry. I wasn't the kind who could make any money at it, so I gave up and came back to Shibuya, my hometown. When my mother died, I had nobody, so I went to India and studied yoga for ten years. A man of leisure. For the past six years I have been

Taro Urashima of Shibuya—Shibuya's own Rip van Winkle. The place changes every day, so it's not bad being Taro Urashima."

"*Taro-ura Shima! Ta Ro-urashima!*"

Swami, his face covered with bits of fried chicken, let out a laugh. Was the Japanese language, which he was just a beginner at, really so funny? Taro Urashima was certainly a good teacher for him. When you're learning a foreign language, it's erotic. It was for me, at least. Japanese assaulted me. At first all I could do was string together a bunch of broken words. It was like wandering around without clothes, totally defenseless. And then a native speaker comes along. Fully clothed, he speaks to the naked virgin. After the opening remarks, the opening act starts. What do you say? The native speaker speaks normally; the virgin doesn't understand. The native speaker tries another tack.

Not to worry, the native speaker says. As long as our hearts can communicate, that's enough. Don't use your head—use your body. Rub your body up against mine. We're thinking the very same thing. Is there still something you don't understand? Don't think in your own language. Think in Japanese. Dream my dreams. Let me enter you. You can't live without me. . . .

Surely Taro Urashima understood this experience. Japanese was his native tongue, but he'd been away from it for so long, it was only now oozing back inside him. And he was enjoying the feeling. I felt the same way, and suddenly I liked the guy. I felt lighter. When you become friends with someone, something about him seeps into your body, but you feel lighter. I don't know why, but it's true.

"Come see me anytime," Taro Urashima told me as I headed off to my appointment. "If it's sunny, I'm always at Miyashita Park. Next time I'll show you something you'll like. How to have sex with the city. You'll love it!"

6

Orphans of the Storm

Five Hundred Bucks a Throw

The hotel soap smelled vaguely animal-like. Maiko didn't think she could bear it for an entire week and decided to buy another brand. But would one week be long enough to dig up the information on Masao that she needed? She'd have to begin with his childhood, after all. And if she didn't stay an extra week, she'd have no time for fun—or to see an old high school friend.

Her body felt heavy. After a long flight, her feet had swollen and she was flatulent. A good thing the bathroom has a window, she mused. If she took drugs, maybe she could rid herself of this weight and fly out like a pigeon over Central Park. A police siren wailed. Her alarm clock ticked. Whenever she was alone in a room, time seemed to stretch. It took three seconds for one second to transpire. She hated feeling this way. She thought of slipping into something sexy and hanging out in the hotel lobby. She'd pretend to look for a trick. Maybe she wouldn't pretend but actually score and charge the sucker five hundred bucks. If she had the courage to do that, she could live in New York without a cent to her name.

Maiko had visited New York as a college student, and at a disco one night her handbag—with her passport in it—was

stolen. After frantically hunting around for it, she leaned back
in a daze. Just then a man—middle-aged, blond, with the air of
a former prince of the night—approached her. Her only identification gone, Maiko was rendered so vulnerable that she went
home with him. His name was Brian. It seemed in retrospect
that he'd understood the circumstances immediately and made
his move at the right moment.

At his apartment, Maiko got drunk on champagne. Her body
was like a sponge. She figured what the hell. When she returned
to her hotel, her handbag was waiting at the front desk, passport
safe inside. Was it all a bad dream?

Something in Maiko had gotten dislodged that night. She felt
violated, torn open like a vacuum pack, her insides exposed,
people breathing on it. But she accepted that feeling. Actually
her body and the city fit, though she had in effect been raped by
New York. She never saw Brian again and could not recall his
face or his voice. The ghost of the city had come to her in the
guise of this slightly tired, middle-aged man.

The Orphans and the Boss

Panhandlers come in all shapes and sizes.

Shaking a paper cup, an old black man with a cane passed
by, shouting, "Jesus is here! Repent! Repent before the Lord
Jesus Christ!" And then he asked for some spare change.

Said another, sidling up close: "Give me a quarter. I'll pay
you back tomorrow." Charming.

Someone else complained about being hungry.

How much do they make doing this? Maiko wondered. If
they spent all day in the streets, could they afford a slice of
pizza? She could never tire of looking at all the faces and clothes
of the people, even if it did cost her a pile of change.

Katagiri's apartment was in the Village, on Fifth Avenue between 11th and 12th. Maiko rode the No. 6 subway and got off

at Union Square. She ran up the stairs to escape the urine stench and found herself at an outdoor market. Men and women from the country, their faces not quite that of your average New Yorker's, were selling fresh vegetables and fish. Surely they must wonder why anyone would want to live in this crazy, mixed-up city.

At two minutes after three in the afternoon, Maiko entered the cathedral-ceilinged lobby of the eleven-story building. She walked past the thigh-shaped pillars to the doorman, asked to see a Mr. Katagiri, and was escorted to the elevators.

"He's in Penthouse K," the doorman said.

As she exited the elevator, Maiko was met by an old man with thick, frameless glasses waiting before an open door.

"Miss Rokujo?"

His voice was high and raspy. Dry, white hair covered his balding head like pampas grass. He had a large wart on his temple, out of which grew a single, scraggly hair. Perhaps because of his glasses, Maiko could not really get a sense of his face. When she shook his hands, they felt like crumpled paper.

"You look so young," Katagiri said. "I was expecting an older woman."

The hall, bathed in the same kind of light as the lobby downstairs, led to a living room which was flooded with sunlight from the west. Next to the door was a full-length mirror with an arabesque frame. Books were stacked high on shelves against the walls. Fortunately, Maiko smiled, no danger of them falling over. Nobody in Tokyo would have bookshelves like that; earthquakes make you lay low.

Mrs. Katagiri seemed quite charming. She had a broad forehead, wore bright red lipstick, and was a little stoop-shouldered. Tilting her head slightly, she shook Maiko's hand, then showed her to the sofa.

"Would you like something to drink?" she asked. "Coffee? Or tea, perhaps? We have soda, too."

Maiko asked for coffee, black. As Mrs. Katagiri left the room, her husband settled into a rattan chair and lit his pipe. Glancing about, Maiko couldn't help but see the photos of the twenty-some children that hung on the wall.

I don't like the looks of this, she thought. It's like all those children are dead. All this scene needs is some burning incense, she thought, bringing on memories of her grandmother's house. The ring of the bell at the family Buddhist altar, the mushroom smell of old people wafting up from her grandmother's clothes. It was the same smell she noticed when she shook hands with Katagiri in the hall. What is the connection between Katagiri and the kids in the photos anyway? Is Matthew among them? The sweet, thick smell of pipe tobacco filled the room.

"Well, where should I begin?" Katagiri now spoke in Japanese. "There are many things we can talk about. But it's going to be tough on you, having to sit still with a talkative old man. Please be patient with me."

Patience was Maiko's job. It was one way to get information. She knew very little about Katagiri, and the little she knew made her suspicious of the man.

His full name was Yusaku Katagiri; he was sixty-eight, Japanese American, fairly well off. He'd emigrated to the United States forty years ago. He taught child psychology at a community college, and was the former director of an institute for research on child psychology. It was an institute in name only; in fact, it was an orphanage set up by Katagiri expressly to put his theories into practice.

The word orphanage usually conjured up images of philanthropy and charity. And what a pain it was to listen to people who ran orphanages—you always had to pretend you were filled with love for mankind. But here, Katagiri and orphanages seemed like worlds apart. Christians and orphanages—now *they* went together. Why was that? . . . Whoa, better keep an open mind.

Mrs. Katagiri was the former Barbara Hopper. At sixty-five, she was a retired social worker who'd concentrated her efforts on children—kids beaten by their parents, kids orphaned through traffic accidents, kids who refused to go to school, kids emotionally disturbed. Yet, what was it about the children that led the Katagiris to set up an orphanage? One thing Maiko knew for certain: They had no children of their own.

Maiko rose to take a better look at the photos on the wall. Assuming these orphan children were still alive, she wondered what they were doing now.

A skinny Caucasian boy in one photo stood on a forest path, arms behind him, head turned up, smiling. In another photo, a young girl clutched her hands to her chest, as if she were singing an aria. In another, a black boy in shorts sat with his legs spread wide, hands resting inside his thighs; he was smiling so broadly his gums showed. There were two Oriental children: one leaned against a window and stared at the sky, while the other was on a staircase, on all fours, with slippers on her hands. Another Caucasian boy lay on a sofa, staring at the camera. One red-haired girl, resembling Anne of Green Gables, clumsily held a cat; both cat and girl stared off in the same direction. What were they looking at? Below the photo was a date: September 15, 1973.

"That girl could speak with cats," Katagiri said.

A cat girl, eh? Maiko mused. When the girl started to speak human language, had she lost the art of communicating with cats? Maiko recalled how she herself, until she was eight, had had a private language adults couldn't fathom. What language might this cat girl speak now?

"Her name is Helen. Greek ancestry," Katagiri went on as he came up next to Maiko. "Now take a look at this boy. Pitiful looking, isn't he?"

He sure was. Next to the cat girl was a thin little boy, slightly cross-eyed, who tried his best to look straight into the camera. A woman who must have been Barbara in her younger days held him. The boy seemed frightened. The photo was dated July 29, 1960.

"He was emotionally disturbed," Katagiri explained. "Poor

child was beaten by his parents, and couldn't trust adults. I took this photo just after we started to take care of him. Looks scared to death, doesn't he? It wasn't easy to get him to trust us. We're the ones who did the learning, really. How to get along with kids. He's a pediatrician now. Goes by the name of Samuel Blue. Sam was my first pupil. He also became the older brother of all these kids who followed."

"Who's the perky one pretending to be an opera star?" Maiko asked.

"That's Penelope. A very bright girl. She lost her parents in an airplane crash when she was twelve. Her father was a good friend of mine; we were on the same wavelength, you could say. Before her parents died, she often came to our apartment to play, and it was she who decided to live with us instead of relatives far away. At that age she was already grown up. The photo was taken when she was fifteen. She was over the shock of the plane crash by then. A little ball of talent, I can tell you. It was hard to find something she wasn't good at. She was a born rental child. She did her part, more than her part really, in putting my ideas into practice. In college she majored in philosophy, but she already knew *physically* what her professors were trying to teach her. Education comes through actual experiences.

"Now the Matthew you're hunting for was very fond of Penelope, and she thought of him as a younger brother. He wasn't as cheerful or as bright as she was, but he was a sweet boy, sentimental, and easily moved to tears. That's Matthew right next to Penelope."

Startled, Maiko looked closely at the adjacent photo. A young boy was sitting sideways on a chair, his face stuck out one side of a double window, gazing up. He seemed to be sighing; his expression was worried. Maybe he was lovesick? Or feeling abandoned? The date: October 30, 1973. This boy in the photo didn't fit Maiko's image of Matthew at all. She'd imagined an expression more piercing; instead he seemed quite gentle—and bored. She'd pictured a sullen, immature nihilist; instead he was the younger brother she always wanted.

"I taught Matthew Japanese," Katagiri began. "I didn't teach Japanese to any of the other kids since Matthew was the only rental child who was Japanese. To tell you the truth, I needed to speak to someone in my native language and Matthew was the likely one. If you have a language, you should use it, right? I wanted to turn Matthew into a real Japanese. When I say Japanese, I don't mean your unremarkable, run-of-the-mill Japanese. The kind of Japanese I mean is a crane—the kind that fly high above the Pacific Ocean."

"A crane?" Maiko asked.

"Correct. A migratory bird."

"Migratory bird?"

"Exactly. My children are all migratory birds. Penelope and Matthew, Helen, Jess, Sam. They don't stay in one place for long."

Katagiri plucked out a few eyebrow hairs with his left thumb and forefinger. He examined each hair before discarding it in the ashtray. Having done that, he passed his pipe from one hand to the other and sniffed his fingers. It was then that Maiko noticed: Katagiri's eyes did not blink simultaneously. There was an infinitesimal period of time between the blink of one eye and the blink of the other.

"Where's Penelope?" Maiko asked, partly to keep from concentrating on Katagiri's face.

"She went with her boyfriend to Thailand and came back to New York not too long ago. I understand she has a new boyfriend now. She and Matthew see each other every three years. The next time will be next year. I'm sure you'll have met Matthew yourself by then. How are things in Japan, by the way? What was it you said you did there?"

Maiko recounted a brief history of herself, allowing that she'd resigned her job in the financial industry. She desperately wanted to come to grips with something *tangible* in life, she concluded.

Smoke trickled up out of the left side of Katagiri's mouth,

which was raised in a smile. It was like a smoke signal from his throat sending out this message: Oh, to be young again!

This job won't get off the ground, Maiko thought, unless Katagiri trusted her. But Katagiri's eyes behind his glasses frightened her. They were eyes facing a past they'd rather not remember.

As Barbara Katagiri brought out coffee from the kitchen, her husband turned and said to her in English, "This Japanese beauty is a bit different. She's young, but she's able to understand."

No, Maiko thought, I *don't* understand. That's why I'm here.

Smiling, Mrs. Katagiri served the coffee and left the room.

"So you're searching for Matthew?" Katagiri began again, switching back to Japanese. "This Mrs. Amino is his real mother, is she? Very interesting. People have come by claiming to be the real parents of our children before. Unless they have proof, we ask them to leave. Matthew's completely on his own now, so I have no say in this particular matter. I have no reason to doubt Mrs. Amino is his real mother. All I can do is tell you what I know. Because it's the child's right to pick his parents."

"Mr. Katagiri," Maiko asked, "do you know where Matthew is?"

Katagiri was silent.

You sly fox, Maiko thought, we're not playing poker here. "Matthew hasn't gotten in touch with you?" she tried again.

"I can't say he's been out of touch entirely. I've had several letters from him. Two years ago he was back in New York for a time. He looked fine. I believe he's working at a variety of jobs in Tokyo now. A little translation, a little English teaching, private secretary to some rich person, lover to someone else. He told me he's not in the business of being a *son* anymore; he's in the *friend* business."

"Do you know how I might reach him?"

"He has several addresses," Katagiri said. "He's not the type to stay put in one place too long. He likes to keep on the move. He might not be at any of the addresses I know."

A temporary dead end. Mustn't try too hard all at once, Maiko thought. "I understand you've been away from Japan for forty years now. In all that time you've never gone back?"

"This is the only place I have to come home to. And it isn't forty years, by the way, but forty-five. I don't have any relatives left in Japan. Ever since I was taken prisoner by the U.S. Army on Leyte, I've considered myself an American. I couldn't wait to be taken prisoner, because going back to Japan would have gotten me nowhere. Even then I believed that the history of Japan was over. There's nothing left. Japan may be an economic giant, and it can internationalize all it wants. I didn't give a damn what happened to Japan, and I still don't."

Katagiri's feelings about Japan were certainly complex. He was a type of ex-Japanese soldier you'd never run across in Japan.

"But Japan today," Maiko said, "isn't the country you used to know."

"It's only changed on the surface," Katagiri replied. "The yen's gotten stronger, the way of life's gotten Americanized. That's all. But Japanese can never be as independent as Americans are. The Japanese are like aborigines who've convinced themselves they're intellectuals. They still have an emperor, right? During the war, he stood aside and let the military, a bunch of nuts to begin with, act like spoiled brats in a losing battle. Then after the war he turned around and gave the go-ahead to MacArthur and GHQ to do what *they* wanted. So how's the old barbarian chief doing these days? Anyone around to take over after he goes?"

Katagiri might have been half joking, but his expression was firm. It occurred to Maiko that here was a very lonely man.

"Earthquakes come and go, planes crash," Maiko said. "Even if the emperor dies, everybody carries on."

"Glad to hear it. Let's change the subject. What about you? Is there a man in your life?"

"Not right now," Maiko said. "Though I always keep my eyes open."

"Love is a form of energy," Katagiri said. "Stronger than the power of the yen. In the case of women, I mean. I was positive that when the war ended the Japanese would become slaves, that Japan would vanish. I figured that the emperor would be executed and all the men sent off in chain gangs. If they were lucky, Japanese intellectuals might become English teachers or servants to the wives of American officers. Or maybe they'd become homosexual, get all dolled up and hire themselves out as page boys. But women would be different. They'd marry Americans, or they'd become their lovers or wives. There would be the slogan again: 'Multiply! Be plentiful!' The kids born after the war would be half-breeds, and they'd be superior to any pure Japanese. A new country would be born. Radical change was needed, after all. Not just a superficial Americanization, but a fundamental change across the board. People, language, food, customs, culture, whatever—all would change, and the power of the Japanese women to love would be the driving force. They'd fight over their foreign lovers, and they'd give birth to a new generation of superior half-Japanese. The Japanese men would work until they sweat blood. If they didn't like it, they could, like I said, become homosexual, or they could flee Japan. When I was escaping the battlefield in Leyte, all I could dream of was becoming a prisoner of the Americans. Instinctively I knew this was the right thing. If I returned to Japan, I wouldn't have been able to stand it. I would have had to run away again."

Katagiri's words were like a curse on every living Japanese. At the same time, that Japan, some forty years later, should have been transformed into such an economic superpower, throwing its weight around, was a hard fact for him to accept. In the small world of Katagiri's mind, the history of Japan was supposed to have ended.

"After the war the Japanese had their chance to become a society of lone wolves," Katagiri continued. "They could have done some soul-searching and learned to face non-Japanese as equals.

Do you understand what I mean?"

Maiko shook her head. She hadn't a clue. "Perhaps you were too self-centered then," she hazarded. "You decided on your own how things should be after the war. But everyone did the same—soldiers, women, intellectuals, kids. And before anyone knew it, Japan had risen again. Everyone rolled with the punches. Even the emperor."

Katagiri's eyes behind his glasses glistened. Maybe she'd been a bit too forthright. The cloying, stifling aroma of pipe smoke filled the room. Katagiri laughed in his raspy voice.

"On the battlefield everybody's an egotist," he said. "You have to be. Otherwise you die. It was the same in World War II, Vietnam, all wars. Everybody looking out for No. 1. In Japan the worst of the egotists were running the show—the generals and politicians—and it's because of them that Japan suffered the shame they deserved. But after the war, did they change? No! They were still the same egotists, this time with a big, strong American daddy to protect them and a Japanese mother to cuddle up to. Worthless bunch of fools.

"When the war was over, I said no more of that for me. I decided to become an orphan. The war between Japan and America may be over today, but my personal war with Japan will never end. Sure the peace treaty was signed, but I haven't signed a thing. You think economic growth will make Japan change? A ridiculous notion! Japanese corporations are utterly irresponsible—they're no better than the Imperial Army. Do you think there's even one orphan among the soldiers of Japan Inc.? I'm talking about individuals who flee from corporations to make it on their own. You're left with these huge corporations full of just a different sort of soldier in a new Imperial Army. Look at you. You chose to become an orphan yourself, right, when you quit your company?"

"I just . . . ," Maiko began.

"I hated the military," Katagiri went on. "I was always looking for a chance to escape, and when the war ended I got my wish. I was lucky. I was sent to America. I lived in camps for two years. I lived all over the place. I got rocks thrown at me, I got beat up, but I made it through. You've heard about the Japanese Americans and how they were treated as the enemy? They lost everything they owned; they were herded into detention camps. They were orphans whether they wanted to be or not. They're the ones who know how hard it is to be an American. I suffered like they did, but I was different in one respect: I was a former soldier of the Imperial Japanese Army. I decided on my own to cut the cord, and as long as I live, I will bear responsibility for the war. My war responsibility will last as long as my private war continues."

"What did you do in Japan before the war?" Maiko asked.

"In my previous incarnation, you mean? I was a fugitive Heike warrior. I was fated to always be on the run. Heike descendants have to travel light. They have to be quick-change artists, too. My father was an English teacher in Aizu, and during the war I was a medical student, slated to be an army physician. I was pretty radical. Maybe somebody had it in for me, or maybe my grades weren't good enough. At any rate, I ended up a medic, but I shouldn't complain because that's how I got to be a prisoner of the U.S. Army.

"I didn't have a license to practice medicine, but still I didn't do badly with the Japanese American community in L.A. But the problem is, if you're an unlicensed doctor, you can't get hold of any decent medicine and you end up doing abortions all day. Ironic, since what I wanted to be was a pediatrician. Anyway, I needed a change of pace. I was still young, so I decided to come to New York. A Japanese American friend came up with this great idea to popularize shiatsu massage. Now everyone knows what shiatsu is—it's even in the dictionary—but back then it was absolutely new and this friend of mine was a real pioneer. He started out treating judo-related injuries and was going to open a shiatsu clinic, but things didn't work out as planned. Sometimes you can be too far ahead of your time. Back then,

Japanese things weren't household names like they are now. Nobody ate sushi, you never saw any Japanese cars on the road, and being Japanese was something you were ashamed of. I washed dishes and worked construction to put myself through medical school. I had some help from a patron of mine. I never actually used my doctor's license, but it gave me the mental boost I needed to succeed as an orphan. As a matter of fact, being an orphan gave me the strength to wade through all the garbage about patriotism, peace, love for mankind. You see, I wanted, more than anything else, to create my own country. An Orphan Republic. *I* was going to live out the history of Japan after it was destroyed."

Maiko sensed someone behind her and turned around. It was Barbara Katagiri, who looked into her eyes and smiled. "Not many people will listen all the way to the end to what Yusaku has to say," she said. "You must be tired. Here, have something to eat." She held out a tray of cookies.

Katagiri seemed ready to go off on another tangent but sighed and broke off. There would be time for more later. Thanks to his wife, the mood in the room had lightened.

"How long have you been married?" Maiko ventured.

Katagiri was quiet as Barbara sat down beside him and answered: "Six years."

"Six years?"

"Yes, six years, although we've lived together since 1959," Barbara said. "Yusaku hired me as an alternative wife. He wanted to remain single."

Goodness, how much does a hired wife earn? Maiko wondered. Would the working hours and number of times you have sex be figured in? In Japan there were lovers for rent, but *wives*?

"Why didn't you get married when you fell in love?" Maiko blurted out before she could stop herself.

"Why don't you answer that one, Yusaku?" Barbara said teasingly and laughed.

"Well," Katagiri started, "you see, I wanted to get American citizenship so I paid someone to marry me. There are American women who make a living that way. As soon as it was official, we got divorced. No sex involved. After that, the whole institution of marriage seemed like a business to me; it was hard to see it any other way."

Barbara caught Maiko's eye and they shared a wry look.

"I met Barbara in a bookstore," he continued. "By chance I happened to be holding the book she wanted. I was a medical student at NYU, and my luck was beginning to turn, finally. I'd met a scholar of Buddhism and I became his disciple. He was like a father to me. For orphans, you see, parents are interchangeable. The man's name was Ludwig Pennman. He was the master who showed me the course my future would take. So when I was at NYU I met the two most important people in my life: One was Ludwig Pennman, and the other—" He pointed to his wife.

It was getting dark outside, and still Matthew's name had not come up.

"Pennman paid for my tuition," Katagiri said. "By then I was thinking maybe I wouldn't be a physician. Pennman's influence was beginning to rub off on me and I began to think about creating an entirely new kind of orphanage. So I studied child psychology. That gave Barbara and me more to talk about, too. I told her about my dream of an Orphan Republic. And she liked the idea."

"This Pennman—?"

"—was the orphans' grandfather. We're the ones who put his ideas into practice. Pennman was Jewish, Barbara's Irish, I'm an ex-Japanese soldier, and the kids were all sorts. Like angels, our children didn't need a family name or a nationality. They were all free."

At that point, Barbara interrupted and suggested that talk of the Orphan Republic be continued over dinner the next night. Maiko was pleased to agree. Her objective the first day, after all, was to get Katagiri to let down his guard. It seemed he had.

Leaving the apartment, Maiko didn't jump into a cab right away. She strolled along 14th Street instead, wandering among the crowds of blacks and Hispanics loaded down with shopping bags from the discount shops lining the boulevard. Suddenly a vision of Penelope came to her: What kind of woman must she be if Matthew is so attached to her? Is she like me? Or quite the opposite?

For a moment she choked on the cloud of foot odor that enveloped her, and then she was hit by a strong blast of sweat. It reminded her that she'd wanted to pick up some new soap. In her photo, Penelope looked like a nice kid. What sort of scent would *she* like? There were kids like Penelope in Japan, too. Kids who'd lost their parents in airplane accidents. Little girls forced to watch their parents die in the pitch black of a mountain recess and then have to go on living. Katagiri took these orphans in and cared for them, but he certainly wasn't the kind of person you'd expect to run an orphanage. How was he different, really? Maiko didn't know yet. She did know that he was a little bit crazy. But, to her, that was a definite plus.

We Have No Secrets between Us

"Josephine Baker tried to build an Orphan Republic, too," Katagiri started the next evening saying. "I wanted to see what kind of person she was so I went to meet her. She was a dancer and chanson singer who used her body as working capital. Women can't help but do that. They use their bodies, like money, to buy status, fame, fortune. You understand that, don't you? In that sense, all women are prostitutes. But that doesn't mean they have to be lewd. What I mean by prostitute is someone who exchanges herself for something else. You could say that women are walking bank notes. Not just actresses and singers. All great women have to be that way if they want to get to the top. Maria Callas, Anaïs Nin, Elizabeth Taylor, Lou Andreas Salome. You name it. Of course, women aren't the only ones. Gay men have to do the same thing. If you want to be a world-class dancer, you'd better be gay, and being Jewish doesn't hurt either. Nothing is more beautiful than men and women who put their bodies on the line."

"Do you feel the same way about your wife?" Maiko asked.

"Barbara's different," Katagiri answered. "She did everything she could for me. As a Christian. She worked hard for the orphans. We're not young any more. Despite all this talk about laying your body on the line, our own bodies just couldn't take it anymore. Six years ago we got married and closed the institute. The youngest of our children was eighteen and could make it on his own. It was a turning point for us."

Katagiri smiled embarrassedly at his wife, and reached for more pasta. They were at an Italian restaurant, at Barbara's recommendation. Katagiri helped himself to the part without cheese.

"It wasn't easy at first," he continued. "We weren't just some asylum taking in orphans, abandoned kids, or problem children. We didn't want them to suffer. We spent as much as we could on their education, and in return we sent them out to work. Our institute was a kind of employment agency, I guess you'd say, finding places for the kids to work."

"What do you mean, exactly?" Maiko asked. Her head was woozy with the wine, and the word "child prostitution" sloshed to the fore. No, it can't be, she thought, but her mind sped off in that direction anyway. In fact, Maiko realized, her mind still speeding, it'd been a long time since she'd slept with someone. Juvenile prostitution? What's the matter with me?

"If you think about it," Katagiri said, "it's not just kids that are orphaned, but parents as well. Parents whose kids died in an accident, or from some illness."

"*Orpharents*, we call them," Barbara interrupted. She only knew a few words of Japanese, so it was uncanny how she managed to follow what Katagiri had been saying. Something close to telepathy was at work here.

"Orphans and orpharents are both looking for someone," Katagiri went on.

"And you rented out the orphans to the orphaned parents, I take it," Maiko asked.

Gazing steadily at Maiko, Katagiri spoke softly in English to Barbara. "It's clever of her to understand, isn't it?"

Barbara nodded and said something in reply. Maiko could catch only the name Penelope. So they *are* comparing me to her, she thought. There was something she didn't like here. She'd definitely have to find out more about this Penelope.

"Everyone thinks you can't barter over children," Katagiri said, "the way you can over cats or dogs. Well, we're the ones who stood this bit of common sense on its head. You guessed right—we rented children out to other people's homes. As rental children."

"Borrowed cats, as meek as lambs at first." The old saying suddenly popped into Maiko's head. Along with the wall in Katagiri's apartment lined with the photos of children. When she first saw these photos, she was reminded of something. And now she finally knew what. A theatrical agency, or maybe a theater troupe. Call it what you will—child psychology research institute, orphanage, whatever—Katagiri's business was like a theatrical agency. Maiko nodded to herself as if that explained everything.

"For orphans to survive, they have to learn how to get along in the world," Katagiri explained. "Have you ever seen the Chaplin movie *The Kid*? How about *Paper Moon* by Bogdanovich? That kid helping the guy selling window panes, or the one working with the con artist—they're all rental children. A rental child is no one's child, and at the same time everyone's child. My dream was to raise children like that who could make it without parents, without God, even. I wanted to raise kids who were free, who could fit in no matter what kind of home they lived in, no matter what the family looked like. Kids who can fit in, but who don't belong to anybody. All children should by nature be free orphans. Of course people everywhere love their own children, but parents end up laying something else on them, without realizing that's what they're doing. They use parental love as an excuse for shoving things down the kids' throats—patriotism, rules of the group, or something like that. I had the same thing done to me growing up in Japan. The war made me an orphan, and as I was telling you after that I became the ward of this offbeat character named Pennman. He was homosexual, and he had this thing about Orientals. It's all in the past so I don't mind talking it about it, you understand. My foster father and I were lovers. Sleeping with him made me absorb everything he had to offer—his philosophy, his way of life. Pennman lives again, here inside my body. He's the guardian spirit I carry around on my back. You can see him, can't you?"

Maiko adroitly broke eye contact with Katagiri and was going to wait until the topic changed. But she couldn't swallow back the question that rose in her throat. I can't, she thought, I *can't* ask him. Nothing good will come of it.

"Why do a father and an adopted child have to sleep together?" There, she'd done it—she'd gone ahead and asked the question. Dumb Maiko, she thought. Katagiri had used his body to get in good with Pennman. That was clear. That was all there was to it.

"I've wondered the same thing," Katagiri said. "Well, we didn't have father-child ties, so I guess we needed to build some other bonds."

"You don't mean . . ."

Maiko was left speechless, and stole a glance at Barbara. Could Barbara possibly understand this?

"Maiko," Katagiri went on, unabashed, "karmic relations are things you can always add on to. Pennman and I were bound together sexually. That's all. America was still in the Victorian era as far as sex was concerned. Homosexuals were like ex-Japanese soldiers—they had to be content with staying in the shadows. I wasn't homosexual myself, but I wasn't about to uphold

any stupid sexual morality. Just by chance Pennman and I found
our relationship mutually beneficial. In the personal war I was
fighting I found a rich ally. All the better for me. And he got a
lover, in addition to an adopted son. Pennman died of cancer in
1959 and left me his estate. With that money and Barbara's help,
I created our Orphan Republic. Things take their course. When
I was young, I was a walking bank note, too, I guess."

What about Matthew? Had he had a sexual relationship with
his foster father also? Was this what Katagiri was hinting at
with all this talk about Pennman?

But what continued to gnaw at Maiko was this thing about a
husband or a lover turning out to be gay. Trying to calm herself,
she turned to Barbara. "How did you feel about the relationship
between Mr. Katagiri and his foster father, Mr. Pennman? Did
you understand what we were talking about in Japanese?"

Barbara didn't bat an eye. "We have no secrets between us,"
she replied. "He had no choice. I mean, . . . Well, I can guarantee he never harmed the orphans. He was only a dealer of orphans. He never had sexual relations with the children."

Maiko filled her wine glass and downed it in one gulp. She
wasn't prepared to hear anything else. It was like a ball of wool
was knotted up inside her. Don't worry about it, she told herself. It's not your problem.

"What's wrong?" Barbara exclaimed, surprised to see tears
welling up in Maiko's eyes. Maiko was just as surprised to find
herself so affected. She felt sorry that Barbara had known about
her husband and Pennman. She no longer wondered why it'd
taken them so long to marry. She didn't want to think. Her
heart ached with a discontent that only drunkenness could wash
away, and she quickly downed another glass of wine.

A Breather

A high school classmate of Maiko's was now a dancer with
the Martha Graham Troupe in New York. Her name was Miki

and the two hadn't seen each other in five years. Their reunion was filled with laughter as they leafed through old photo albums and talked about the old days.

You haven't changed a bit, Maiko said to Miki; neither have you, Miki replied, still no boyfriend yet?

They chatted on, clowning around as they used to. But after a lull in their reminiscences, they began to talk about more recent happenings in their lives.

"Maiko," Miki said, "I think maybe it's time for me to go back to Japan. Everybody at work is gay. Of course, the manager is gay, too, and as far as he's concerned, I can't do anything right. I think I'm as good as anyone else in the troupe, but he complains about everything I do and won't give me a decent part. And he's so sarcastic. My breasts are too big, he says, my expression isn't cool enough. But I'm worried that even if I go back home I'll be left hanging. The guy I wanted to marry told me he wants to wait and think things over."

Now it was Maiko's turn. She told her friend that the Japanese men she'd met were tedious worms—she wanted to sleep with men of different races. And then she related the unsettling story of the ex-Japanese soldier she'd just met.

After all this, Maiko found she was starving. She and Miki headed down to Chinatown for a big meal.

Huge platters of food were placed before them—crabs, frog legs smothered in green peppers, halibut in a luscious sauce— and the two women dove into the food. Maiko's stomach bloated as if she were pregnant, and then they took a leisurely post-dinner stroll in the darkness. Just the thing to melt away her discontent.

1,024 Different Personalities

Maiko visited Katagiri again the following afternoon. The plan was to see the former residence of the rental children, which was the apartment next door to Katagiri's. Up until six years earlier, he had rented two extra apartments on the same floor. Both were airy, well-lit penthouses. Both had since been rented to other people, but luckily one was now vacant. A new tenant was scheduled to move in the next day.

On the balcony there was space enough to sunbathe, barbecue, even play basketball. The largest number of rental children to stay there at any one time was eleven; they must have kept the orphaned ex-Japanese soldier too busy to dredge up memories of the past. The apartment had been divided into six smaller rooms, where Matthew and other rental children slept and ate together. Matthew had been able to walk down the corridor to visit Penelope.

Suddenly Katagiri began to laugh so hard he was nearly choked. "One time Matthew spilled oil all over the floor in the hallway. The place was as slippery as an ice rink. The kids all stripped down and pretended they were playing football."

His laughter sounded like crying. There are a lot of people who cry when they're happy, but very few who can't stop laughing when they're sad. Katagiri was one of the rare ones.

Showing Maiko into the room nearest the front door, Katagiri scrutinized the wall. After a short time, he turned to Maiko. "Can you read this?" he asked, as he traced some writing with his fingers.

The wall had been painted over many times, but a vague outline of letters remained:

M I K A I N A I T O

Mikainaito! Maiko could barely contain her excitement.

"You can still just make it out," Katagiri said. "This is the room where Matthew came to deal with his loneliness. And where he and Mikainaito, his guardian spirit, got close. Matthew could make his consciousness fly. Mikainaito assumed Matthew's role and could fly anywhere in the world, like electric waves."

Katagiri's words reminded Maiko of how, when she was a teenager, she was positive she had a twin somewhere on earth. If only she could float her spirit out on the radio waves, it would lead her to her twin. But she also worried that her twin might speak a foreign language. Like Russian.

The rental children who had lived in this apartment learned to cope with their loneliness, but they were still out there, somewhere. Had they found *their* twins? Wasn't that the fate Katagiri placed on their shoulders?

The great gift that Katagiri had received from Pennman, his foster father, was a wide circle of contacts. Even while Pennman was alive, Katagiri knew these scholars and business entrepreneurs would be perfect patrons of his Orphan Republic, and he lobbied them accordingly.

On Barbara's side, many of her parents' friends were Christian philanthropists. The founding of an orphanage appealed to their urge to do good deeds, and they gave generously. Barbara after all was the kind of person older people responded to. Of course, money isn't everything, she'd say. Kindness is important, too, isn't it? From her mouth, the words had substance, and people dug deep into their pocketbooks.

Katagiri spent most of his time visiting orphanages and acquaintances, scouting out promising young orphans. His job was no different from any Edo-period bathhouse pimp who kept on the lookout for apple-cheeked girls who could turn tricks. The rental child idea was a business, not a charity.

To be a rental child, you had to meet several conditions. First, you couldn't be sickly. Here Katagiri's medical background came in handy during the screening process. Second, you couldn't be shy. Lonely people wanted kids who were cheerful and outgoing. Looks and IQ weren't so critical. Kids who were ever so slightly on the dull side were preferable to ones who would put adults to shame. And if too much of their real parents' education had rubbed off on them, the kids were that much harder to train as rental children. Instead of kids who were already completely formed, Katagiri picked those who were still malleable, still in-between. Because that's where rental children would spend the rest of their lives. In-between.

Katagiri made a thorough survey of the needs of prospective orpharents as well: how much they'd be willing to pay to rent a child, what they planned to do with the children, how they'd use them. And he learned how to raise children who would listen to the whims of their parents.

He gathered four children: Samuel, age nine, Nick and Miriam, age seven, Yen Yen, age five. They were the first class of the Orphan Republic. The children had to turn their backs on their past and set out on a new life. To them, Katagiri was Boss, Barbara was Mama, and the other children were their brothers and sisters.

The children's discipline was a first priority for the Boss and Mama. Barbara taught them social graces so that their upbringing would never be questioned. And the Boss taught them pride in themselves. Work hard, he said, and you won't need to flatter people to get them to like you.

The children took Barbara's maiden name, Hopper, and attended public school, all the while busy with extracurricular studies. Those that had musical talent learned piano or violin, and those who showed skill at languages were tutored to be bilingual, even trilingual. Athletic children were sent to ballet or acting class. There was little free time to be had during the day, especially for talented children like Penelope.

At night, the Boss sermonized:

"Orphans are a ray of light in this rotten world."

"All gods in the world are on the side of the orphans. Respect the gods. But rely only on yourself."

"Orphans are no one's children. They are also everyone's children."

Hear something repeated often enough, you memorize it like the lines of a play. It was a liturgy that turned out to have practical uses, too—more than the kids had thought. When they got into an argument, verses from Katagiri's catechism served as a nice opening volley, and when they mumbled it to themselves, it gave them confidence.

The Boss also taught the children consciousness control. It was a form of meditation, a mix of yoga, zen, and hypnosis that he had developed to help the children relax. According to specialists, Katagiri Meditation was half-baked, even dangerous for youngsters, but Katagiri insisted that experimental results showed it worked. Even so, the idea of children meditating unsettled more than a few people.

"Matthew mastered this meditation," Katagiri said to Maiko. "It took him ten years but he was able to control his consciousness."

"Do you think I could learn to do that?" Maiko asked.

"I can show you how it's done, and then you can try it anywhere you are. The main thing is to relax. Here, let's try it."

Katagiri had Maiko sit down on the floor. She thought the whole thing smacked of one of those new Japanese religions, but she went along anyway.

"Close your eyes," Katagiri went on. "Concentrate on the space between your eyebrows. Breathe slowly. In. Out. Listen to the sound of your heartbeat. Now send your consciousness out over your whole body. Start with the little finger of your right hand, then the ring finger, the middle finger, the index finger, the thumb. Now slowly let your consciousness spread to your palm. Next, from your wrist to your elbow, from your elbow to your shoulder. How do you feel? Does it feel like your right arm's gotten bigger, like it's a crab claw? Now for balance, do the same thing on the left side, from finger to shoulder. After the arms come the legs. From your toes to the sole of your foot, ankle, calf, and upward to the knee, thigh. Then feel the swell of your buttocks. Do that on both the right and left sides. Next, send your consciousness up your backbone. To both shoulder blades, the back of your neck, your ribs. Feel your left and right collarbones, your left and right breasts. All the way to the tips of your nipples. Feel the pit of your stomach? Your navel? Let your mind work its way down below your belly to your groin. Feel your pelvis. Now go inside your vagina."

Maiko had the uncomfortable feeling that some pervert was ogling her. But when she opened her eyes, her body felt aglow.

"Well," said Katagiri, "that's how you start. You trace the outline of your body. Next you learn to project yourself into all kinds of situations: You're walking in a desert in a sandstorm and can't see anything ahead of you, you're crossing a bridge of clouds to a nearby mountain, you're burning bright red, you're flying across the darkened universe at incredible speed. Before too long you're able to make your consciousness take leave of your body and fly off. Your guardian spirit can straddle your back or appear right in front of you.

"That's how Mikainaito was born, you see. Ever since Matthew was little, he would exhale through his nose three times to call him up. When Penelope wanted to call her guard-ian spirit she used to press her nipples like they were buzzers. Yen Yen used to say her spirit came out of her mouth when she yawned. Each child had their own way of summoning up their spirit."

It seemed that Katagiri had deliberately tried to make the children develop split personalities. But he was very confident about his methods and results. "Imbecilic monotheists" was his term for the doctors and academics who tried to cure split-personality disorders with psychoanalysis. Whether you have two personalities, or three, or ten, or a hundred, wasn't the point, he said. What was important was how you used them. To the rental children, getting rid of the alter ego through psychoanalysis was nothing less than a nightmare, because without it what you have left is incurable loneliness.

"Curing" yourself of a split personality was the same as killing a friend you lived with, the person who shared your illnesses, injuries, and misery. You helped each other, argued and laughed together, made fun of each other—and now you were supposed to kill him?

But an alter ego is still a stranger. You might share the same communal space—your body—but you seek out different lovers, friends, teachers. And that's how what starts out as a double personality becomes a four-part personality, then eight, sixteen, . . . a hundred twenty-eight. Two to the tenth power is 1,024. But one to the tenth power is still only one.

Loneliness is bad for your health, Katagiri taught the children. An alter ego isn't that heavy, and carrying one around isn't so much trouble. Actually, that's what most religions do— provide an alter ego with the name of god that guarantees the safety of your personality. Why deal with god with a capital "G" when a portable lowercase one is much more convenient? God's nothing more than a friend, anyway.

Elves Keep Busy

The first class of children in the Orphan Republic were the guinea pigs of the great Katagiri experiment. "It was harder for the parents than the children," Katagiri conceded. "The kids waited around for us to blunder. I thought I should be strict with them, before they started to get a complex about being abandoned. But it was hard going in the beginning. Barbara almost had a nervous breakdown and had to be hospitalized. She couldn't accept the way they were being raised. She was too naive."

Naturally Katagiri had great expectations for this first group of children. He watched the subtle workings of each child's psychology, though Matthew complained later that Katagiri treated all the kids the same, and tried to help them adjust to the business. He used the stick-and-carrot method, like with animals in a circus.

Barbara's role was to comfort the children, which also helped her forget her own past. A past Katagiri couldn't help her overcome. When Barbara was twenty-three, before she teamed up with Katagiri, she'd been married and had had a son. About the time the baby started to call everything around him "mama," he died from a pneumonia that she hadn't noticed until it was too late. A gurgled "abuabu" was his last word. Barbara blamed herself, then refused to sleep with her husband for fear that she'd get pregnant. This might not have been the entire reason, but after three years she and her husband divorced and she never had another child. She was convinced she wasn't qualified to be a mother, but she still wanted to be around children. Becoming a child psychologist was one way. When she met Katagiri, through some sort of karma, she ended up the mother to the orphans.

"I was pretty serious about the first group of kids," Katagiri continued. "I trained them nonstop for seven months before I started renting them out. At first I'd rent them out for just two or three days, gradually working up to a week, ten days. Sometimes even two days in a stranger's home was too much for them and they'd come back in tears. The clients and the kids didn't always get on. That's where Barbara came in. She'd sleep alongside the children, take baths with them, take them to amusement parks. The whole time she tried to convince them that being a rental child could be fun. She showed them *The Kid* and *Paper Moon* over and over so they would know how they should be. She made up dozens of stories for them about a child who sets out in search of treasure and, after many hardships, becomes an adult. The Orphan Republic is a base for heroes, she told them, it's where you hone your skills before setting off for adventure again. Can't have a hero who's a wimp, can you? That sort of thing."

"It must have been pretty hard on Barbara," Maiko said.

"When the kids cried," Katagiri said, "she took it personally. There were no blood ties to fall back on, no ready-made trust. Often she broke down in tears herself. She was supposed to play teacher and mother at the same time, while I had it easier. My role was clear."

It seemed the children could all be lumped together as rental children, but they were still individuals who happened to be living under the same roof. Everything about them was different—their personalities, their looks, their abilities, their likes and dislikes.

Sometimes Katagiri missed things when he was sizing up potential candidates, and then he'd find himself with unexpected illnesses or emotional problems. The eldest boy, Sam, for instance, was bright, but around age ten he suddenly stopped talking. Katagiri and Barbara were at a loss as to what to do. No matter what they did or said, only three phrases would leave Sam's lips: "Yes," "No," and "I don't know." As a last resort, they sent him to a psychiatrist, but this only added two phrases to his vocabulary: "I'm OK" and "Leave me alone!" At this rate, it'd be impossible to rent him out. Even if you put him in with a family that was depressing to begin with, with only five phrases to his vocabulary, the kid could turn the place into a ghost house.

Wracking his brains, Katagiri decided to try hypnotism. It was hypnotism off-the-cuff, but it worked—enough for Sam to up his vocabulary ten phrases.

Katagiri went on to master hypnotism more fully, then he combined it with yoga, which he'd begun to practice, and Zen, which he'd studied in his youth. The result was Katagiri Meditation. And with Sam as his subject, Katagiri was able to polish his technique. Sam was exceedingly tense about being a rental child. He kept his distance from his orpharents and wound up unable to speak. Sam was too proud—that was his problem. What he needed was to relax, and Katagiri Meditation helped him do it.

Miriam, a Mexican girl whose parents died in a traffic accident, had a different kind of problem. She had a hot temper. In the evening, especially when the moon was full, she went crazy. Katagiri and Barbara were ready to give up on her, but since there were customers eager for a child to quarrel with, Katagiri had the perfect sales pitch. You name it, he said, she'll pick a quarrel with it. Today Miriam was a police officer.

Another problem was Helen, the girl who spoke cat. At some point, you began to wonder if she really wasn't half cat. New York can be a dangerous place, and Helen would sometimes behave as if she wanted to be kidnapped. On one occasion she didn't return home for a whole day, worrying the Boss and Mama sick. The next morning a self-styled hippie poet brought her back, having gotten her address off the ID card Helen had hanging around her neck. It seems Helen had been attending a conference of stray cats and made a few remarks as a representative of human children. Helen's guardian spirit was named Stevie, and he was half-human/half-cat, too. Where Helen was now nobody knew. There'd been no word from her in five years.

"I have the feeling, " Katagiri said, "one of these days she'll drop in on us with five kids of her own." In his mind Helen had no doubt turned into a cat.

Yen Yen, the Chinese orphan, now worked to introduce Asian movies into the U.S. She'd married a Hong Kong–born film director, and had herself appeared in some films. In fact, this was what brought about a reunion with her real parents. It turned out Yen Yen was the second daughter of a family that ran a restaurant in Hong Kong. When her real parents saw her on screen—a Chinese American woman who couldn't speak Chinese—they were stunned. The actress looked almost exactly like their oldest daughter, Yen Yen's sister. They checked into the actress's background and discovered that indeed she was the daughter kidnapped from home before she was old enough to talk, then abandoned in Chinatown in New York.

Yen Yen had almost no memories of her parents. They'd given her the Chinese name Lin Ho and the English name Tracy. Fortunately her parents remembered she had a triangular birthmark on her back, and blood tests didn't rule out the possibility that she was their own flesh and blood.

"Yen Yen was the only case we had of a rental child meeting his or her real parents again," Katagiri said. "So if Matthew meets his, it'll be case No. 2." Katagiri's eyes blinked, their timing out of synch as usual, and he laughed through his nose.

"Does Matthew's mother know if *he* has any birthmarks?" he asked. It was obvious from his tone that Katagiri did not welcome this reuniting of child and parent. Blood ties, he seemed to be saying, ought not to be valued more than bonds one forges in life. Blood is just red water. The relationship between parent and child is but a contract, one you could rewrite anytime.

Maiko was supposed to be on Mrs. Amino's side, of course, but for a long time she'd been thinking the same thing—that blood ties were not all they were cracked up to be. The only way to resolve that question would be to ask Matthew. As for the birthmarks, she knew that Matthew had a line of four moles on his buttocks. The only way to check *that* would be to pull down his shorts.

"What kind of child was Matthew?" Maiko asked. "That's what I'd like to know."

"I loved Matthew the most," Katagiri replied. "He was the only child I could talk to in Japanese. He's the sole citizen of the Japan I carry around in my mind."

In the hallway a man could be heard, humming in a discordant falsetto what sounded like a Hong Kong pop song.

"There are lots more Chinese in this apartment these days. Dancers, singers, movie directors, playwrights. In China they must all have been top artists. The Chinese have a sense of solidarity; it doesn't matter where they come from—the PRC, Taiwan, Hong Kong. Even if they speak different dialects and can't understand each other, the Chinese immigrant network runs deep. The Koreans, too, have a strong network, but the Japanese—forget it. The Japanese have money, but they keep to themselves. The future is pretty bleak for them. People who carry around Japanese spirits on their backs are bound to have a hard time. Well, that doesn't have anything to do with me or Matthew. But what about you?"

Katagiri said it as a joke, but Maiko thought the problem deserved more thought. She flashed Katagiri the loveliest smile she could and said, "What I really want is a man I can love with my heart and soul. Once I find the right guy, Japan can turn into a desert for all I care."

Katagiri slapped his knee and laughed so hard he started coughing again.

"You should have been a rental child," he said. "You remind me of Penelope."

Maiko wasn't too upset about the comparison. She wanted to meet Penelope and ask her about Matthew. But more than that, the woman in her wanted to check out Penelope with a critical eye to see what sort of woman she was now. Katagiri dialed Penelope's number, but no luck.

"Seems she's on a trip," he said. "Elves keep busy, you know."

Looking for a Lover

Maiko had been in New York for ten days, but still hadn't gotten the information on Matthew she needed. Katagiri was holding something back, it seemed. He was interesting to talk with, so much so that Maiko had allowed their conversations to get sidetracked.

There was one bright spot, though. Katagiri had promised a copy of the file he'd kept on Matthew over the years. He'd kept notes on all the rental children and a running chart on their lives. Once he passed Matthew's file on to her, Maiko's job in New York would be finished.

But now was time to enjoy the city. She'd done almost nothing for herself. She wanted to go shopping, go to a new disco, and maybe, if she got lucky, find a man to spend the night with. She might take a tour of Wall Street, see the stock exchange, ... Nope. Forget the stock exchange. It made her sick to think of it.

So Maiko, fitted out in new shoes, walked all over Midtown in the morning. After brunch she toured boutiques on the Upper East Side, and in the evening she and Miki, with a friend who was gay as a bodyguard, set off for the East Village to a bar between Avenues A and B. There they drank their fill and then some. The bar had a show: a rock singer who thought he was the devil incarnate, shrieking in the darkness, a comedian whose outrageous jokes almost caused the audience to go for his throat, and a down-and-out duo who belted out old-time blues numbers and made everyone laugh. Maiko and company kept throwing down their drinks. Drug dealers made their rounds through the bar, pushing cheap marijuana and diluted cocaine mixed with laxative. Fluorescent skeletons painted on the walls flickered in the candlelight, ready to break into a wild dance.

A Mike Tyson look-alike, eyes crazed, stared at a miniskirted woman standing at the counter. From the line of her sensuous hips, she couldn't have had any panties on. In fact, the steamy atmosphere of the bar seemed already to have found its way under her skirt: She moaned with the music.

The noise of the bar was so loud it was like Maiko had earplugs on. And for a second Maiko had the illusion that the drug dealer across the table from her was Matthew. The image evaporated in the next instant as Miki, breaking the stagnant silence between the three of them, sighed:

"Oh god—I need a man."

"Me, too," Maiko sighed back.

Suddenly everyone at the bar was sighing.

A Child from Outer Space

The next time Maiko visited Katagiri's apartment, he invited her out for a walk through the neighborhood around West 8th Street.

"Matthew loved Ray's pizza," he explained. "He got up early and the first thing he'd do was go to Gray's Papaya and have a thirty-cent hot dog. He said they tasted best in the early morning or late at night, after they'd been cooked a long time. Then he'd go to Balducci's and get some free samples of mozzarella and pain au chocalate. After a while the people in the store could recognize him and he wasn't able to help himself to the free snack anymore. So the rascal wrote them a thank you note, can you believe that? It went something like this:

> To the kind clerks at Balducci's:
> My deepest appreciation for the free samples of cheese and pastry—also for teaching me the meaning of the word "delicious."
>
> > Yours truly,
> > Matthew

"What a guy," Katagiri chuckled.

Katagiri then took Maiko to the Cafe Figaro, a place he'd gone to for twenty years. He ordered cappuccino for them, and slowly brought out a few letters and placed them on the stone tabletop before her. They were from Matthew—in very charming handwriting, like a mouse running loose, and terribly hard to read. The first letter was in English.

> Dearest Mama and Boss,
> I thought my Japanese was fluent, but when I get together with friends here I can't follow them. I can only get about a third of what's said on TV dramas and variety shows. I can't read a newspaper, either. Too many unknown Chinese characters. It's been a real shock. I figure the best thing is to get a Japanese girlfriend and brush up my Japanese. The Japanese you taught me, Boss, is too logical; it gets me nowhere. And these Chinese characters—now that's some weird kind of writing. They're like hieroglyphics because they don't just spell out words, but have their own meaning.

Seems to me the characters must have sprung up naturally, in the forests, the hills, the towns, in the things
people said to each other.

                                Matthew

This was Matthew's first letter from Tokyo, written two
weeks after he'd arrived.

The second letter had arrived about half a year later. It was a
postcard with a photo of the Metropolitan Expressway, the
Akasaka Prince Hotel, and the Hotel New Otani. This time Matthew's message was scrawled in Japanese.

Boss and Madam,
    How have you been?
    I think I've succeeded in becoming an average Jap-
anese. But only on the outside. The Japanese have
been trying their best to change into Caucasians, but
they can't seem to get it right. They're like those foxes
in fairy tales who change into humans but still have an
ugly tail sticking out. Actually, I think they're kind of
cute.

                                Matthew

A month after this, another letter arrived for Barbara. Katagiri had written Matthew that she'd gone into the hospital for an
operation on her duodenum. This letter was in English.

Dear Mama,
    I didn't know you were ill. Are you OK now?
Please have a good long rest and don't let little things
worry you. I'm doing fine. No need to worry about
me. I get at least six hours of sleep every night, and I
eat three meals a day. Speaking of food, right now I'm
crazy about barbecued eel. There's a bar I go to that

serves eel head and liver roasted on a skewer. Just the thing to recharge my batteries. I've got a new girlfriend. Her name's Kumiko, and she's the personal secretary of the president of an insurance company. She's a little too serious at times, but reminds me of Penelope. If you know Penelope's address, please let me know.

Love,
Matthew

Penelope had also gone to Tokyo, a year after Matthew. Like him, she was always on the move and hard to track down. Even when she wrote to Katagiri with her address, his letters back to her would be returned to him, addressee unknown. To be sure, the same thing often happened with Matthew.

After another six-month blank, another letter from Matthew arrived, this time in flawless Japanese:

My college degree has turned out to be more helpful than I ever imagined it would be. Thanks to those years at Columbia, I've been able to avoid wasting time doing manual labor. The job as a magazine reporter was a bore so I quit. Made me sick having to follow those brainless entertainers wherever they went. I'm teaching English now and working as an interpreter. I earn about $3,000 a month. They say the Japanese, Americans, and Russians are terrible at foreign languages, but the Japanese have got to be the worst. There can't be many countries like this where English is such a booming business. But for me teaching English conversation is just a sideline. Boss, you invented the rental child business, but we rental kids can't stay children forever. So now I'm a professional friend and lover. Just like in the past when you made us into everyone's son or daughter, except with a difference.

Profession: Lover. Profession: Friend.

This seems a natural step for a rental child. But not
to worry. Being a friend or lover is an honest business,
selling friendship and love. And at $3,000 a month it
might even be better than being a son. At least there's
no Boss taking a cut.

Behind his salt-and-pepper moustache, Katagiri clicked his
tongue and chuckled as he pointed to the last sentence in the
letter.

"'Taking a cut'—that's a little hard. But it's the truth. Three
thousand bucks a month, not bad at all. A tiring business, I'm
sure, being a professional friend or lover. If you try to be everybody's friend, you're bound to pick up a few enemies along the
way. But I'm sure Matthew's good at what he's doing. He's not
that handsome, and not that great a conversationalist, either. In
other words, he doesn't stand out, doesn't give off a scent. But
what he does have going for him is this uncanny ability to make
people feel safe just by being beside them. It might sound a little
weird, but there's one thing I'm convinced of—Matthew can go
in and out of people's dreams freely. In their dreams he doesn't
do anything. He doesn't fulfill their desires or get in their way
or play the villain. He just stands next to the hero of the dream
and smiles. That's all. When you meet Matthew, you'll understand what I'm talking about. One day he'll appear in your
dreams, too. For him it's like opening a door and entering a
room. It's probably a talent he was born with."

Entering other people's dreams. What a pleasantly erotic
idea, Maiko thought. Not a bad ability to have herself.

Matthew had first met Katagiri at age five. A friend of Katagiri's from his days as an unlicensed doctor in L.A. had brought
Matthew all the way to New York to see him.

Matthew had been left with this friend—for three days and
ninety dollars—by a young Japanese American who said he was
the boy's father. Two weeks passed and this self-styled father

still hadn't retrieved his son. Katagiri's friend notified the police, and it turned out that the man had been stabbed to death five days after dropping Matthew off. Suddenly finding himself with an orphan on his hands, the friend thought that better than leaving this boy with the police, he'd take him to his friend Katagiri, who ran an orphanage.

At first glance, Katagiri thought Matthew a bit dull, perhaps because of his close-cropped hair. He had a habit of whispering to himself as if he were talking with someone. But the boy's eyes were alert. Whatever his background, he seemed calm. The death of his father didn't seem to faze him. Maybe it wasn't his real father; if so, where was his real father? And mother? When you asked him, he answered, "I don't know" or "They went away some place." He was like some extraterrestrial, a child from outer space, trying his best to lie. Did this mean he didn't care who his parents were? One thing was for sure—he wasn't shy. After three days, he looked like he'd been living with Katagiri for three years. Perfect rental child material.

So, at age five, Matthew began a new life with Katagiri and Barbara, his earlier life sealed away. For Matthew, Katagiri's orphanage was more than he could have hoped for. In fact, it was the only place he could have survived. Coming there was the luckiest thing that had ever happened to him.

"How much did you make in this rental child business?" Maiko asked. She wanted to know the actual figures involved. How much renting a ten-year-old girl brought in, for instance.

"The first five years we were in the red," Katagiri replied. "We managed to get by on loans and contributions. Even if we tried to take a cut, as Matthew put it, money flowed out, not in. Say you were going to rent Matthew at age twelve for a week. The basic charge would be seven hundred dollars. A hundred dollars a day. On top of this there were extra fees, depending on the special requests of the client. So it's about the same as a child actor's fee. Or maybe a bit less, considering that rental children were expected to live in a stranger's house twenty-four hours a day. If the child was younger, the fee was higher. If the child was under seven, we didn't rent them out for more than a day—too many clients were ready to adopt them. We sent the children out to work, but we weren't about to sell them. We were their real foster parents, after all. We planned on raising them according to our ideas on education; we've never thought that growing up in a wealthy family was preferable for children.

"Take a four-year-old away from his parents for ten days and see what happens. He gets standoffish. We were always afraid that the children would get that way with us. At any rate, there were all kinds of rental children. If we hadn't had them earn money, the orphanage would have had to shut down. Private orphanages don't have it easy. But you can be sure that for the children's safety, we made certain that the clients were reliable; we couldn't just rent them out to anyone. And no matter how much money they could make, if the kids didn't want to go to somebody's home, we turned the job down."

In other words, Katagiri did not make the kids work against their will. Even in the middle of a contract, if a child didn't like the place, Katagiri would bring him home. If the client's home was in New York City, Katagiri would go once a day to see how the child was getting along. If the client's home was in the suburbs, he called and talked to the child.

People seeking to rent a child came to the office carrying their own special mix of hopes, guilt, and curiosity. Katagiri and Barbara took turns with the initial interview. The first order of business was selecting trustworthy clients, so the first visit was like an oral examination. Prospective clients with letters of introduction from patrons of the orphanage were the most reliable. In every case, however, some kind of identification was required, even though neither Katagiri nor Barbara put much stock in them.

There was good reason for their caution, for there are people who get their kicks by mistreating children or having sex with them. Kidnapped children often ended up in porno movies. Fortunately nothing of this sort ever happened to any of Katagiri's children, but whenever they chose a new client, Barbara's nerves were on edge. At times she even lashed out at Katagiri for not being rigorous enough in his interviews.

Their clientele was not limited to childless couples. There were single men (whom Barbara was most wary of), young women about to marry, old widows, even gay and lesbian couples. And there were quite a few clients looking for a sibling for their own kids.

After a client passed the first interview, Katagiri and Barbara got down to business. "What sort of child would you like to be the parent of?" Katagiri would ask, showing them his rental child catalogue. "And what length of time were you considering? Right now we have the following children on hand."

While the client looked through the photos of the rental children, Barbara talked about each child's personality, special talents, and language abilities. Next came a meeting between the client and the child selected. Trying to cover his or her shyness with a smile, the child would make a simple self-introduction. A little unsure of himself, the client would clumsily try to win over the child by asking such questions as: "What kind of things do you like to eat?" "What kind of sports do you play?" "We have three dogs. Do you like dogs?"

By the second day in a client's house, the rental child felt at home. They had their pride as a professional; they had to be outgoing no matter what. When a client told a child to make himself at home, that's exactly what they did. For the Boss, the orpharents who came to rent a child were customers, even as the clients treated the child as important guests. And the rental children themselves understood what was involved. Of course they could act as guests only for a couple of days; after that their task was to ingratiate themselves with the client. Occasionally this meant comforting orpharents who'd lost their own child through accident or illness.

Invariably, orpharents would come to see their own children in the rental child. After a pleasant evening, the orpharent often couldn't keep from taking one last look at the rental child's sleepy face and the much-suppressed thought—"if only my child had lived . . ."—would surface. At times like this, the rental child would whisper, "Things will get better soon. If there's anything I can do to help, just tell me."

Katagiri hadn't taught the children how to be sensitive to adults' moods; they learned this through experience.

"There was a time," Katagiri said, "when Matthew was rented out to a family in Boston for two months. He was to be the older brother of this only child of a Japanese American mother and an Italian American father. The poor child was only nine and had leukemia, with not much longer to live. Matthew was twelve and did his best to fulfill the contract and comfort the child. When the boy died, Matthew was as sad as if his real brother had passed away. Matthew was a kind-hearted boy. Actually, come to think of it, he was rented out less as a rental child than as a rental *brother*. He knew how to be a good brother, whether older or younger. But Penelope was probably the best at comforting the clients. She was our most popular child."

"How would you rate Matthew?" Maiko asked.

"Fair to middlin'. There wasn't much demand for Orientals then. But Matthew had a lot going for him—he was straightforward, bilingual in English and Japanese. Even knew some Spanish. If I were still running the orphanage, I think there'd be much more of a demand for Oriental children. Train them to speak Cantonese, pass them off as Chinese. It'd be pretty convenient. At any rate, it's time to pass the torch. Barbara and I are just an average old couple now. She wants to live in New Zealand. If we put our money in a bank there, we'd be able to live off the interest—16 percent. Of course they don't let you take any of it out of the country."

Katagiri sipped his cappuccino and wiped his mouth with a napkin.

"Well, I've probably spouted off a little too much. If you want to know more about Matthew's past, everything's here. It took me a while to copy it all. I imagine this should be enough to satisfy Mrs. Amino."

He plunked down a thick sheaf of papers the size of the Yellow Pages. Within its sturdy binding and black cover was crammed the history of Matthew: the record of Matthew's development which Katagiri and Barbara had taken turns keeping, a diary Matthew had kept once he'd gotten old enough to analyze his own problems, plus a copy of Matthew's work as a rental child.

Maiko couldn't wait to start poring over it. If no one turned up to look for him, she thought, this accumulation of Matthew's past would have ended up yellowing and falling apart like a book sequestered away deep in some library stack. With the help of these documents tracing his past, she'd be able to meet up with the Matthew of the present. She'd see his smile and hear his voice. Maiko was sure of it.

There was one more thing she was sure of. Matthew was going to show up in her dreams.

7

Penelope

I Gotta Be Free!

My job is to be a friend, a lover, so that's how I make my living. But this whole business of earning a living can be a real drag. Whenever I'm alone I mumble to Mikainaito, "I gotta be free!" Sayaka's older brother used to say the same thing. Sayaka, by the way, is my sweet little sister who helped me remember something I'd forgotten for a long time.

The first time I met her she was all alone at the mini-amusement park at a department store rooftop. I was enjoying a soft ice cream, killing time between jobs. She sat staring at me in a strange kind of contemptuous way.

"You want something?" I asked. "You're kind of cute. What's your name?"

But she wasn't about to be taken in by this hackneyed small talk.

"My name's Sayaka Hiraoka," she replied. "I don't want anything."

"How old are you? Wait a sec—let me guess."

I looked at the swell of her chest. Those deep-sea fish eyes of hers weren't the kind you'd expect to find in a straightforward, well-behaved girl. But they weren't the eyes of a rebellious teenager either. She was twelve, I figured, a twelve-year-old girl who had grown up a little fast. Once kids turn thirteen, any trust in adults drains away. But a twelve-year-old's view of adults is unclouded, though just barely. They're still curious about how strange adults are. At least that's the way I was. But my guess was off. The girl was eleven.

"Where're you from?" she asked.

"Hmm, good question. Where *am* I from? Do I look like a suspicious character to you? I'm not, you know. One look at my face should tell you that."

"But suspicious-looking characters are interesting," she said.

"Wait a minute! It's OK to act innocent, but you could get yourself kidnapped talking to strangers like this." I thought I'd tease her a little. It bothered me the way she despised adults.

"I don't mind," she said. "You're skipping out on work, aren't you?"

"Mind your own business," I said. "If you don't go straight home, your mother's going to be angry."

"My mother's busy. Besides, I don't have anything to do right now. So I thought I'd talk to you."

If you closed your eyes, you'd swear it was a housewife talking. I didn't have anything to do either, so I thought, what the heck, walk her home.

When I looked into Sayaka's eyes, I was struck by the thought that I might have had the same look when I was her age. I started to feel a closeness to her. The thought even crossed my mind that I wouldn't mind hiring her as my own rental child.

"What're you doing here on the roof?" I asked.

"Nothing."

"Do you always have fun all by yourself?"

"Umm, maybe," she said.

"How come? Don't you have any friends?"

"I do, but we don't get along sometimes. I'm too moody."

"Something must be bothering you."

She pursed her lips and nodded. She had a straightforward side to her after all. I put my arm around her, and we went into a coffee shop. A piece of cake might cheer her up.

Sayaka was even more complex than I'd imagined. She was pretty precocious for eleven. She told me everything about her family and school. I had the feeling this wasn't the first time she'd gone to the department store roof in search of people to talk to.

Sayaka's older brother had died in a traffic accident the year before. He was just fourteen. Sayaka liked her brother more than anyone else in the world. She believed what he knew more than her teachers or parents, and he was the only one who would sit down and explain things to her. As long as she was with her brother, she always had a good time, no matter where they went or what they did. He was *cool*. He was a good swimmer, could run fast, was popular with girls, and you should have seen him bone a fish before he ate it. But if Sayaka wasn't with him, he had to struggle with the things he was normally good at. She had to be there if he wanted to get things done right.

Her brother liked high places, so he slept on the top of their bunk bed. At bedtime he always talked with her; otherwise he couldn't fall asleep. Sayaka hated to go to the bathroom by herself in the middle of the night, so she always woke him up. He'd grumble, but he always went with her.

Once Sayaka's brother saved her from drowning in a swimming pool. When she sprained her ankle at school, he carried her home on his back. When her homeroom teacher yelled at her, her brother reassured her. School's just one big contradiction, he'd tell her.

Another thing he used to say was this: "I gotta be free!" At the time he'd just entered junior high school and couldn't do whatever he wanted anymore and the world looked pretty bleak.

After her brother was killed, her parents shut themselves up in the house and didn't move an inch. When Sayaka went off to school, there they were, staring into space, and when she came back, there they were, no change. They left her brother's desk and book bag untouched. Sometimes Sayaka slept on the top of the bunk bed. Her brother wasn't there to talk with her before she went to sleep, and when she woke up in the middle of the night she had to go to the bathroom alone. But she could still hear his voice saying "I gotta be free!" When she slept in her own bottom bunk bed, she could hear him roll over in bed above her. She could hear him talk in his sleep. When she took a bath, she felt him peeking in.

Her father didn't want his wife to be alone in the house, brooding about her son, so he quit his job and started a small sandwich shop with his savings and retirement money. Every morning started with their getting up early to make sandwiches. They were busy every day. Keeping busy kept them from thinking about their dead son.

With her brother's death, Sayaka thought her family was finished. Nothing was fun anymore. It was like her own life was over, too. She couldn't bear to think that she was about to embark on the same cramped, gloomy life he hadn't wanted to live.

The world around her filled with doubt. She didn't believe her teachers, and her friends said she worried too much. The entire time, her parents' minds remained a blank as they slapped together one sandwich after another. Sayaka was alone.

Her story touched me. With the death of her brother, Sayaka's whole world had changed, and the weight of absurdity beared down brutally on her tiny body. There are kids like Sayaka who, even before the tender age when they awaken sexually, are already precocious about what life has in store. Innocence has come to an early end. And on top of that is dropped the panic of adolescence and puberty. I had to go through the same experience. Unlike Sayaka, though, I had brothers and sisters to help me through it. I was lucky to have plenty of tutors in the art of living. And that's why it hurt to see Sayaka suffer.

"Sayaka, let's be friends," I told her. "My name's Matthew. If you ever have any problems, call me at this number, OK? And don't you dare think of ending it all. You keep talking about life—well, life isn't like some miniature garden. It'll take in as much as you put in."

"I wouldn't kill myself," she said. "I'd feel worse if my parents couldn't make sandwiches anymore. Matthew, I gotta go. See you sometime."

We were in the middle of a shopping district. Sayaka waved her hand and ran off. Twenty yards ahead a tiny sandwich shop lay plunked down between two large buildings.

Jesters and Elves

Sayaka took me up on my offer and called a number of times. If she left a message on my answering machine saying she wanted to meet me the next day at the department store roof, I'd cancel my appointments and go to see her. I was at an age when it wasn't strange for a former rental child to consider becoming a parent. I wondered what it felt like on the other side of the equation. Of course that wasn't all there was to it—being with Sayaka made me nostalgic for my own youth. What her older brother was for her, my older sister Penelope was for me. The death of Sayaka's brother had been a rite of passage; in a similar way, my situation with Penelope took me from rental child to professional friend.

I remembered my own youth well, and I had to teach Sayaka that there was no time for despair. She had to find her freedom herself.

From age twelve to seventeen, I experienced a terrible confusion. But a loss of innocence and the love of Penelope gave birth to a new me.

*   *   *

I could never be the hero in a tale that normal people would find moving. I am quite capable of putting bad things completely out of my mind—not the sort of character people get all worked up about. When a new job came up and we rental kids went off into a new family, we had to erase from our minds all experiences with families we'd known before. Each family had its own ways, and if we wanted to fit in, we had to wipe our slates clean. It was as if nothing at all had happened, and a new story could begin.

Child actors couldn't hold a candle to us rental children when it came to role playing. We *had* to be good. Ever since we were kids, we'd been forced to examine what being a child was all about.

We were children at play. Nothing more, nothing less. Children minus the parents. If you wanted to know what being a child meant, you could do no better than to take a look at the rental children.

Every time a new job began we wove a new tale, a tale that began with a self-introduction, set in the home that rented us.

With a woman grieving over a lost child, I would say, "Mom, I can't even imagine how much you suffered," and hold her hand, trying to conjure up a mental picture of the now-dead child.

With a childless couple, I would talk about TV shows, deliberately break a window and apologize, then sit hunched up in the garden, sighing.

With a man uncertain of his role as a father, I would tell him about my infatuation with a girl. If he asked me more about the girl, I was halfway home and the man was on his way to being a father.

Some of the clients were strict about manners and language, and I did as I was told. I was a child worth teaching, and by the time we said goodbye they were pleased with what they'd accomplished. "You're like our own son," they'd tell me.

I was pretty clever as far as rental children went, and I did my best to make the clients like me. I tried too hard, in fact, and early on I began to view the whole business as pointless. By the age of twelve, I was a nihilist who thought that life meant trying to deceive people. I was pretty naive, too. I let a lot of mental and physical stress build up trying to guess what the clients wanted. At times like that, the worst thing was to be alone. I knew the clients were supposed to be like my parents, but that didn't keep me from feeling lonely. Depression and fatigue took over. When I couldn't take it any longer, I'd ask for some time off and head back to the apartment where the other rental children were. And then we'd have some fun. Partying it up was just the thing to clear out my depression and paranoia and nihilism. We were, in the end, children who *had* to have our fun.

Each rental child had his own private room, however small. Each room had a single bed, a desk and chair, and was carpeted so you could sit on the floor. Every night somebody had a party. We visited each other all the time. We wanted to know as much about each other as possible.

Each child had his own style of entertaining the other kids.

In Helen the cat girl's room you could play with her cats, and she'd teach you how to say hello in cat language. At Yen Yen's you could snack on sweet Chinese pastries and sunflower seeds. If you wanted a book, Eric's was the place, since he was a real reader. He told these great ghost stories, too. In my room you could flip through the porno mags I kept under the bed. I was a champ at swiping them.

Pattie was a walking P.A. system, and everybody kept her at arm's length. She'd rat on everybody and everything. She was the one who told Mama and the Boss that I had a thing for Penelope. She also gossiped about Penelope's foster father in Chelsea giving her an amethyst ring, that Eric was masturbating over some porn he'd borrowed from me, that Helen ate cat food with her cats, that Yen Yen hadn't washed her hair in a week, et cetera. Pattie's eyes and ears were almost part of the walls of the apartment.

The Boss and Mama never said a word when it came to relations between us rental children. They just left us alone. They let us stay up late and make as much of a racket as we wanted. But skip your homework, or oversleep, and there was hell to pay. You'd have to scrub the whole bathroom, listen to one of the Boss's long-winded sermons; you'd be grounded and you wouldn't get any snacks.

Penelope never once got in trouble. Funny thing, though, since she was one of the biggest party girls of all time.

On nights after I visited Penelope in her room, I always had a wonderful dream. I felt like I was being caressed by her words and voice. When she was in a good mood, she'd sing for me, in the most graceful voice I'd ever heard. My mind would grow as light and fluffy as a feather; I thought I was going to float away.

She loved the opera, and would sing arias for me with these great exaggerated movements, and end up giving my cheek a pinch. Sometimes she'd take me by the hand and we'd dance. Through the warmth of her fingertips, the rhythm of her body flowed inside me. She was music come alive. I was supposed to be mired in depression, but suddenly my feet moved in time to her steps, like a puppet blown to life by the breath of an elfin fairy.

Looking back on that period now, I realize I was thoroughly dismal as a court jester. People in this business are doomed to be either fools or elves. In Penelope's case she was born with a fountain of vitality in her body, so she was one of the elves. She almost never fell victim to nihilism or paranoia like me. Her energy replenished me, made me able to go on. It's been that way ever since I've known her.

Penelope liked to tell me the stories of the movies and operas she'd seen. As she talked she always played the part of the heroine. It wasn't a case of imitating movie stars. Penelope *became* the heroine.

One evening I knocked on her door around nine.

"It's open," she said. She was sitting on the bed, dressed only in a slip and holding one knee up as she gave herself a pedicure. Balls of cotton were between her toes.

"Matthew, how you doing? You know, the other day I went to see *Salome* with this doctor and his wife. God, I wish I were Salome, deep in love with a prophet. Know any handsome prophets?"

"Put some clothes on," I said. "It's going to wear out, you keep flashing it like that."

Her legs formed an L; what was within her thighs lay open for the world to see. She was challenging me, yet keeping her distance. Even wolves have to wait quietly until the nail polish dries. After she took a shower, she wrapped a towel around her head in a turban. When she took the towel off, her soft blonde hair hid the left half of her face. She pushed her hair back, as if brushing back the hand of a guardian spirit, and sighed. What a waste, I thought, for that sigh to escape into the dirty air. In that sigh are the elements that make Penelope Penelope. With a little luck, and timing, I could breathe it all in.

Penelope did things at her own pace. She played, talked, sang as she pleased. She created a whirlpool around her, which I was always being sucked into.

"Herod, king of Judea, wanted the head of John the Baptist because he was stirring up trouble," Penelope started in. "But Salome couldn't care less. The world was a mess anyway. Love was what she wanted. All she could think about was John the Baptist. She danced a striptease for her father Herod, begging for John the Baptist's life, but he was already dead. Salome kissed John's head. Matthew, give me your head! You can be my John the Baptist."

I set my chin down on the back of a chair and closed my eyes. But instead of kissing me, Penelope bit my nose.

Penelope did get very depressed once. She came to my room and made some bizarre confessions. She wanted to be a nun, she said. She wouldn't say why. She just said she wanted to be a nun. Anemic girls would make good nuns, but Penelope was hardly anemic. If she became a nun, her blood would reverse course and she'd end up a whore.

Another time she announced she wanted to be a vampire and tried to take a bite out of my neck. The bruises lasted a week. I played a boy scout wandering through the woods, and Penelope was the vampire in the woods who turned the boy scout into her servant. I certainly didn't mind this charade. I followed after her, became her shadow, followed her everywhere. She made a much better vampire than nun. Funny that the person whose blood was sucked out should get so energetic, though.

When she walked, Penelope kicked her feet out, fell into a rhythm, and bounded along, but smoothly, like gentle waves breaking on a beach. When she trotted, she was even more flamboyant—like a Mozart trill. I can still picture her singing out my name as she ran up the stairs at the city library. She had jeans and sneakers on, her eyes were big and bright, and her smile spilled over her slightly oversize mouth. Up the steps one at a time, as if they were so many one-sixteenth notes, and up the last three steps in a single bound.

I was in low spirits, worried about finishing my schoolwork and the assignments the Boss had laid on me.

"Hey, I'll buy you a hot dog," Penelope said to me. "Here, carry this."

She handed me a paper sack heavy with books. Penelope loved literature, among other things. With the exception of Penelope, I didn't know a single literary-minded young girl who was cute, good at sports, or pleasant to be around. And what an exception!

To be sure, it wasn't like she was learning the things literature is supposed to teach you—like how to love, how to laugh at convention, how to be more narcissistic. As long as she just knew who wrote what novel, she could pass herself off as a young girl in love with books. Old, rich couples really got off on this. If you told them, for instance, that you'd read all of Salinger's works, they'd be impressed. And if you told them you loved opera and could even sing some, getting along with them would be a snap.

She was so good at acting her rental child roles I teased her and called her goody-two-shoes. Whereupon Penelope'd show off her biceps and tell me that it's your "reflexes that count." She was right, of course. Children who use their heads aren't anything special. Take me. Used my brain too much and ended up neurotic. Penelope didn't get upset and confused, and that was the key to her success. She was the No. 1 rental child. Getting ahead in the world is a kind of sport. The most important thing is your health. As long as you're healthy—and Penelope was almost never ill—confidence and luck will follow. If you've also got rhythm, then you've got an unbeatable combination. The rhythm of Penelope's body was so strong it infected those around her.

At age twelve, I had a revelation about being a rental child. The whole thing was nihilistic, about people only too happy to lie to each other. So sometimes, when I couldn't bear the deception any longer, I would leave the client's home and go back to my room and mope. The only thing to do, I thought, was to quit the business.

How could Penelope always seem so happy?

I started to get an inferiority complex and decided to go talk things over with Katagiri. I'd had enough. No more child actor in soap opera for me, I told him.

"I've always tried to be like Penelope," I said, "and party away my blues. I didn't do badly, but I can't take it any more. I'm not cut out for this line of work."

Katagiri told me one thing: "If you quit being a rental child, you'll feel even worse." After that, he wouldn't listen to me.

I took the same complaints to Mama. She was more patient than the Boss. "Everyone hates this job at one time or another," she said.

I wasn't convinced. Because I knew the exception—Penelope.

If Penelope liked this soap opera of deception, I told Mama, then she was stupid.

"No one else thinks that rental children are frauds," Mama countered. "Matthew, you're too uptight. Loosen up. You don't have to change. Just be yourself. Totally yourself. I think you're trying too hard. Compared to you, Penelope knows how to *play* better. She can play with anyone. If you want to be a rental child, you have to know how to play. Don't worry so much— just *enjoy* yourself."

I thought I understood what Mama meant, but probably I didn't. In order for her words to make sense, I had to die first. Then be resurrected.

Ten Times Dead

Whenever any of us got sick, everyone in the apartment would stop by the kid's room to see how he or she was doing. Unless the illness was contagious, that is, in which case the child wasn't allowed visitors.

Stephan, one of my younger brothers, was small and sickly. Once when he was put in isolation, an ominous silence descended over us all. The rumors were rampant: "Stephan's dying," "His tongue is as red as a strawberry," "They've sent for an exorcist tomorrow." It was Pattie's rumormongering, of course. On occasions like this, we thanked our lucky stars we were healthy.

A week later I was sick with pneumonia.

I was thirteen, alone in my room, floating on a fever. Suddenly, it was like the wall between dream and reality melted down, and death in a dream became death in reality.

The shadow of the lampshade writhed like a reptile on the ceiling. Ambulance sirens screaming. Trucks roaring down the street. They head straight for me. I hop into the ambulance and ride with the trucks to some place on the other side of the border. Fear becomes a terrible chill, and overwhelms me.

I lose sight of Penelope in the field of grass.
A plain with reeds taller than me.
I push them aside, seeking Penelope.
Someone looks for me.
Mixed in with the parting reeds,
a grinding of metal against metal,
the grinding closes in.
Suddenly my feet feel nothing.
A trap!
Nothing to hold—
I tumble further and further,
so fast I can't breathe,
further and further
And still I fall.

Darkness.
So dark none could be deeper.
Darkness wet,
stifling.
It parts as I start forward—
forward, I think—
because my feet precede me.
Darkness grows dense.
My feet heavy,
I wade through mud.
Stickiness against my arms,
my shoulders, in my crotch.
I lose my footing, tumble,
struggle to stand upright,
but in mud and dark
I can't tell front from back,
left from right, down from up.
The blackness weights,
thickens,
crushes.

I cannot breathe.
Here I am. Or am I?
Darkness leaves me no
certainty.

On the banks of a stream sparkling
I wade, water to my waist,
scooping up jewels of light.
Upstream, a man's voice, low.
What does he say?
Does he call to me?
I turn, and the voice evaporates—
I begin again to gather jewels.
A while, then a voice—
High-pitched—a young boy?
Again I turn, and the voice stills.
Perhaps the sun slides behind a cloud,
the light sighs, grows faint,
no longer do the jewels sparkle.
Upstream, a woman's voice.
Matthew! Matthew!
A voice as joyful as I am!
Penelope!
I turn
ready to call out,
When water rushes toward me, a wall of water,
before I—

I climb upward.
Upward to the diving board.
Someone has talked me into
taking a dive.
Each step up
increases my fear.
At the top,

my fear is like this:
𝍠 𝍠 𝍠 𝍠 𝍠 𝍠 II
It's time to dive.
Rigid,
I stand on the edge of the board,
peering down.
Can the pool be that small?
No way, I think, and I
start to edge back.
My feet touch softness, and
like ice cream, the diving board melts, and I
tumble, head over heels—
if I knew this was going to happen,
I would have jumped—
the concrete slab rushing up to me . . .

OK, I think midway, wake up.
Four times dead already.
Longer in this dream, I will not survive.
On the count of three I open my eyes.
A huge shadow, on the ceiling, of a person
brandishing a scimitar
aimed at me . . .
I'm going to be killed!
I shut my eyes again.

A dune on an overcast day.
No one is here.
Not even me.
A strong wind blows,
and swirls up the sand.
Hey—something's buried here.
A scrap of cloth—no, a shirt.
White, with an Italian collar.
Beside the second button, a ketchup stain,

and out of the sand a face appears.
Mine.

Zocalo Square, Mexico City.
In the breeze, a Mexican flag,
an assembly begins.
Mixed in with speeches, in Spanish,
a chorus of "La Bamba."
The chorus falls apart, voices panic.
People look at the sky and weep.
Somebody is dead.
It is a memorial service.
I can't find myself anywhere.
From the dome of an abbey,
A bell tolls.
With the sound, I remember:
The one who died was me.

I sit on stone steps.
The Met, perhaps?
No one is near, but I'm muttering to someone.
So it s'posed to be? . . . Might as well die.
'Cause I'll only live to die again.
Doesn't scare me.
Not a bit, I say, showing off.
Not scared, uh-uh,
I swear, and yawn,
but get no reply.
It'll come, all of a sudden, I know.
I brace myself,
but nothing happens.
I strain my ears, but hear nothing.
It's over! I shout,
and stand up
right before a firing squad.

Cut! Start again!
I return to the stone steps of the Met.
To be safe, I look
more carefully this time,
everywhere around me,
and stand without saying a word.
I start down the stairs.
But—
each step chokes me.
I bring my hands to my throat
and find a thick rope wound 'round.
Instantly, the rope is tightened,
with a snap,
and my body hangs in the air.
Help! I yell, soundlessly.
Matthew, hanging by his neck, a pendulum
    swinging.
Matthew, hanging by his neck, and Matthew,
    lying in bed—
Which is me?
Two Matthews gamble with paper-scissors-stone.
Matthew in bed wins.
Hanging Matthew vanishes.

And I found myself looking at a familiar lampshade and ceiling, back in my own room.
  Matthew—you still alive?
  As I lay there, he was standing on my stomach. Mikainaito. It was the first time I'd seen him face-to-face. He was like a shadow in a fog.
  Matthew, you about finished?
  Yeah, guess I'm still alive.
  Glad to hear it. If you croaked, I'd be lost.
  With that, Mikainaito was sucked back into my body.
  I had continued to die for three days. If Mikainaito hadn't

been there, it could have gone on for a week, or a month. Mikainaito led me out of my dreams, so I only died ten times.

This was my day of resurrection.

I needed to see someone, to talk with someone, to make sure I was really alive. I hadn't eaten for two days and my body was stiff. My throat was raspy, and little sound came out. Then my door opened and a sweet smell filled the room. Melon. A melon's come into my room.

"How are you feeling, Matthew? Can you eat anything?"

It was Penelope.

I stuck out my tongue and panted. I begged her to feed me. She scooped out pieces of honeydew melon she'd brought and put them in my mouth. I was like a dry sponge soaking up the sweet juice. I finished off the melon, and scraped my teeth over what was left on the rind. My taste buds were coming alive again, but my sight was still foggy; Penelope had smoke coming out of her body.

She lay on my wasted tabletop thin body. Sixteen-year-old Penelope. Elves were heavier than I imagined. From the valley between her breasts I could smell the faint fragrance of lilies of the valley and butter. When she moved, a hint of lemon was mixed in. Her marble-cool cheeks brushed against mine, which were flushed, and I caught a whiff of omelette. All these smells were part of the essence of Penelope's body—a real live woman, I thought. I was grinning from ear to ear.

Each time I visited Penelope in her room after this, I took along my pillow. I'd deliberately leave it behind so I could retrieve it the next morning. Harvesting Penelope's fragrance became part of my daily routine. To me, her smell was life itself.

With my allowance I bought an expensive down pillow and used that as collateral to borrow Penelope's pillow. I wasn't brave enough to steal her underwear, though.

When I got over my pneumonia and returned to working as a rental child, at last I could understand what Mama tried to make me understand. Life was no longer a matter of people fooling each other. I stopped feeling inferior to Penelope, and I became a first-class child at play.

Instead of worrying about pleasing people, I discovered the fun of playing with them. I rediscovered what I'd been doing unconsciously at age seven.

The world was filled with light. Colors were brighter, pleasure more intense, and people's faces refreshed, like they'd just gotten out of a bath. My mind became a part of this glowing world. And Penelope was more beautiful than ever.

Visiting Dreams

After dying ten times, I found I had gained a strange power. It took another year before I realized it, by which time the ability was fully developed.

Mikainaito, do you remember when Mama had her nervous breakdown and was hospitalized? I was fourteen; Penelope was eighteen. All the troubles Mama carried around with her—worries about the children's health, anxieties that people thought they mistreated the children, troubles with clients—all of it came to a head. Katagiri couldn't handle the office work alone, and the rental child office shut down for a while. For the first time we rental children understood who the real boss of the operation was: Mama.

It's true that I mastered Katagiri's rental child instructions and his technique of dreaming and making friends with your alter ego. But his way of teaching was too theoretical and hard to remember. He led us by the hand each step of the way, but I couldn't help thinking that it was all pretty dumb. He never adjusted his teaching to fit the child. Mama treated us as individuals, coming up with training that fit our different personalities. Mama was the real rental child coach. Katagiri, at best, was the rule book.

Mama's nervous breakdown, it seemed, was triggered by the pigeons and swallows that used to fly up to our balcony. She hated birds. When she was little she had a Hitchcock experience. One very mean crow had it in for her and attacked her every chance it could. It shit on her and dropped stones on her. If that was all, maybe she could have handled it, but early one evening the crow came and dive bombed her and tried to peck at her face. Mama raised her arm to protect herself and ended up having to get several stitches. The crow must have done its job because it never showed up again, but of course Mama had never done anything to deserve being attacked like that.

So how was her nervous breakdown related to her phobia about birds? For some reason, Mama started to think that the birds which flew around the balcony were spreading malicious gossip about the rental children. Ordinarily Mama was a very rational person, but I guess the trauma she'd had as a young girl turned into a persecution complex she couldn't shake off. Every day while Mama was resting in the hospital, Katagiri, his expression entirely serious, chased the birds off the balcony. With my effeminate face, I sat and watched him do it.

"There's a saying," Katagiri said, "that illness comes from a disturbance in a person's *ki*, a person's life force. Remember that. Oriental medicine is the art of curing *ki* that's gotten sick. Western medicine forgets about *ki* and just cures the illness. So chasing away these birds is an Oriental cure. Do you understand?"

But Penelope knew a better cure. And that night all us brothers and sisters put the Penelope Therapy into practice. Each of us returned to his or her room, went to sleep, and willed our individual guardian spirits—Mikainaito for me, Pinopino for Penelope—to fly off toward Mama's hospital room. The plan was to enter Mama's dreams, interrupt her nightmare, and sweep away the things that upset her. Things like darkness and storms, floods, centipedes and cockroaches, reptiles, murder and rape, torture and imprisonment—these were dream representations of the crow and other anxieties Mama had to endure. Our guardian spirits would rescue Mama with a loud, cheerful ruckus.

At the time I still didn't think it was possible to visit another person's dreams. I mean, I couldn't even begin to invite somebody into mine. All I could do, at age fourteen, was to get Mikainaito to fly out the window. What he did outside I had no idea. So this Penelope Therapy seemed a big fantasy—even though I thought it could be great to actually invade another person's dreams.

But that night Mikainaito *did* appear in Mama's dreams. It was my first successful dream trip. And Mama was back in the apartment a week later. The place came alive for the first time since she'd gone into the hospital, and the following day the rental child office reopened. Katagiri usually never smiled, but on that day his face wrinkled up in a grin that wouldn't quit. Mama told me later that in her dream I painted the crow all sorts of gaudy colors and that I stuck newspaper, wire hangers, a teddy bear's head, and artificial flowers on it, turning it into some ludicrous peacock. The Penelope Therapy worked!

I couldn't believe it, of course. When she told me I was the only one who appeared in her dreams, I thought, wait a minute. I went to talk about it with Katagiri, who just laughed and couldn't be bothered. Mama said, why don't we try again tonight?

I didn't want my appearance in Mama's dream to end up a one-time fluke. She didn't just happen to see me in a dream; I had sent Mikainaito specifically to visit her. But maybe I was trying too hard. I couldn't fall asleep until late and got nowhere near her dreams.

I tried again several times, deciding before I went to sleep whose dreams I'd visit—Mama's or Katagiri's or Penelope's. But things weren't so easy.

It wasn't until three months later that I was able to refine my timing and get a much higher success rate. The trick was to send Mikainaito flying off just before the person woke up. That way there was a better chance of the dream being remembered. If the dream was forgotten, the me in the dreams vanished into thin air—I might as well not have bothered.

I began to train as a dream messenger seriously. I got into the Katagiri Meditation technique more than ever, and improved my mind control. Katagiri was happy that the meditation he'd invented was being put to other purposes. At first he might have thought the art of being a dream messenger kind of dumb, but later on his interest perked up.

"I'm impressed, Matthew," he said. "In Japan there was a famous priest named Myoe who reached nirvana in a dream; he supposedly used dreams for self-discipline. And there was that chemist—I forget his name—who discovered the structure of benzene in a dream. Anyway, the thing is to never abuse your power."

If I could master being a dream messenger, I thought, I'd have a free pass into the dreams of presidents and movie stars. I could woo girls in their dreams before I put the moves on. If I didn't like somebody, I could make them suffer. And I wouldn't stop at visiting other people's dreams—I'd invite them into mine. I could do what I wanted with them. Kill them, rape them, put a collar around them and lead them around.

But these were pipe dreams, the kind some good-for-nothing cartoon character might have, like Nobita in the *Doraemon* comics. They had nothing to do with the art of a dream messenger. If it's revenge you're after, why go to the trouble of dreaming? Scream at the ocean instead.

When I was eighteen, I awakened to the true value of being a dream messenger—the use of dreams to communicate with others.

One morning Penelope said to me: "Last night you were in my dream."

So after all that effort, I *had* become a dream messenger.

Mikainaito and Pinopino

Mikainaito, do you remember when you fell in love with Pinopino? You tried to hide it from me, but the truth came out at that marijuana party.

I was fifteen and I hadn't even smoked a cigarette before. The greenish-yellow leaves were still young—like me. And the grass was pretty good stuff, apparently.

Penelope had learned a clever way to smoke marijuana from a girl in her high school—for sure, no guy would ever come up with the idea of using a tampon for a pipe. She didn't use the tampon part itself, just the cardboard tube it comes in, the part you usually throw away. She made a hole about the size of your little finger at one end, covered it with aluminum foil, and pushed it down to form a depression. Then she made a tiny hole in the foil with the tip of her earring, laid the grass in it, lit up, and slowly inhaled the smoke.

It was embarrassing to be smoking dope out of that cardboard tampon tube. But the room filled with a pungent, sweet smell, and there we sat—me facing Penelope—wondering when that weird sensation we'd heard about would hit. Before too long, the world started to spin around like those giant teacups at amusement parks, with me at the center. Things at eye level floated by clear as crystal. And all the objects in the room began to vie for attention. The floor, the sofa, the bed, light stand, door, window, curtains—all those normally well-behaved things began to get rambunctious and shout out "Me! Me!" They quarreled, and the room turned into a battlefield. My mind was dragged into the fray, and I started to panic. The first symptom was a wave of acute aphasia.

"Hey, what's your name?" Penelope asked, checking to see what state I was in.

I was so stoned I couldn't answer. A silly laugh drooled out of my mouth and I managed only a few clumsy monosyllables.

Words broke apart, leaped out of order, went backwards, and ended up meaning something entirely different. Penelope repeated the question over and over. Finally I grasped what she was getting at and tried to answer, but my name wouldn't come out. I'd forgotten the names of my friends around me, too. Each person's name had cut itself loose from its owner and was swooping around the room. I felt like I had to catch my own name or I would end up nameless forever. Jostling up against each other in the cramped room, Penelope and I—and the others there, Eric and Pattie and Judith—sprawled out on the floor like dogs when all of a sudden my body felt like it was on fire. I looked at them in alarm, but all they did was grin at me.

Nearby lay the white tampon.

I was hot and wanted a shower to cool off. I stripped off my clothes. A minute later, though, I'd forgotten about the shower. Seeing me naked, Eric, the artist, asked me to crawl around while he scribbled on my back and stomach. Judith and Penelope joined in. The pens felt like worms squirming over my body. Eric twisted and bent and hit me to transform the canvas as he drew. Judith got slap-happy, and Penelope started pressing her nipples with her fingers. That's the way she called up her own alter ego, Pinopino. She must have decided to let Pinopino have some fun flying around the room. I did the same, and called you out, Mikainaito. The marijuana seemed to have a done a number on you, too. You weren't your usual self.

Somehow I managed to make it back to my own bed. It wasn't until the next morning that I washed off the graffiti on my body. That night, Mikainaito, was the first time I'd seen your face in two years, the first time since my bout with pneumonia.

Your face and body were exactly like mine, but you were covered over in a mist. I couldn't make out a clear outline—you were made out of clouds. You showed me how you flew through the air; a tail coming out of you like a comet. Every time you came close to crashing into a wall, I ducked my head. We shared the same eyes and mind, so I was like a flying comet, too. And then another comet joined us—Pinopino, darting out of Penelope. You chased her, she chased you, you formed a circle and tried to inhale each other. The circle gradually grew smaller, like Ouroborus, and ended up in a clump which just went poof! and disappeared.

At that instant, everything went black. But my mind was wide awake. I was cutting through the darkness, whizzing off somewhere at an incredible speed. The wind collided with my mind, hurting me. Out of the corners of my eyes I felt the pattern of the darkness changing. I could feel the touch of Penelope's body, her warmth and fragrance, so I wasn't afraid. Pinopino and Mikainaito had each entered halfway into the other's body. So half of me was Penelope and half of her was me.

It was a long trip. Pinopino and Mikainaito, joined like Siamese twins, eloped to some private place. Where, I did not know. Toward dawn, they arrived at a wilderness, pitted and bumpy, far beyond the horizon. If you looked closely, you could see it was the ruins of a city, covered in mud. They had traveled beyond the sun.

And here a little loving was the best cure for boredom.

A Contract

Touching Penelope became a drug for me. If I couldn't touch her, I shriveled up. Each time she went on assignment, I suffered withdrawal. I hung around my room like a mole that had surfaced in search of warmth. I squeezed a rubber ball, hugged my pillow, caressed my inner thighs, and roiled the air. On the days that Penelope returned, my biorhythms surged.

After that first time, I smoked marijuana pretty often, but Pinopino and Mikainaito never did an encore of their Siamese twin act. Their relationship had changed, and Penelope became someone I didn't know before. We were through playing house. She seemed more distant—no longer an older sister, but a woman.

Penelope was the same person as before, but the Penelope in my mind had become a steamy, sexy hooker. And just as I was being taken captive by Penelope the hooker, Penelope the elf was rushed to the battlefront.

Poor Penelope. Her beauty and intelligence were a burden she had to bear. More than any of the other rental children, she was the one whom Katagiri pinned his hopes on, the one whom he wanted to absorb his philosophy of life, completely. By the time she was fifteen, Penelope already knew with her body what Katagiri was getting at.

I hit a rebellious stage at eighteen, but Penelope remained the same. She was all business. She was Katagiri's masterpiece. She could marry into wealth or royalty, become a movie star or a stage actress, or turn spy for the government—it would make little difference; her special talents would always be put to full use. We were both rental children, but she was so refined, so bright, so relaxed that I couldn't help feeling second-rate next to her. And this sense of inferiority aroused my desire for her even more.

Mikainaito, do you remember when Penelope and I made our contract? That evening my pillow—my Penelope substitute—was cold as ice. I was hit by a sudden wave of anxiety, like the ground had opened up and I was about to plunge into hell. I realized that the day would come when Penelope would leave the rental child apartment and become somebody's woman. Boss bragged about her wherever he went, and several influential people had expressed interest. It wouldn't surprise me if she ended up being sold for an unheard-of price. I was frantic—I wanted to do something before it was too late. I knocked on her door.

"Come on in, Matthew," she said. "It's a full moon tonight, isn't it?"

Penelope sat in the dimly lit room, leaning against the wall and playing with a fan. Her fingernails, dusted with gold, glowed like fireflies. She was wearing a blue, strapless evening dress, and she looked like she was going to be whisked off to a fantasy ball at any moment. I watched, dumbfounded, as she waltzed around the room, then winked as she plopped down onto the bed. She said she was getting ready for a new job.

Which meant that this was a goodbye scene.

"Where are you going this time?" I asked.

"To the Roquentins'. The contract's for half a year, so I won't be seeing you for a while."

Roquentin was the retired prince of high fashion, a leader of New York high society. Penelope had been rented out as his daughter, to be tutor and older sister to his idiot son. The son, who had his father's name but not much else, was my age.

I was furious. Money had taken away *my* right to be Penelope's younger brother. But I didn't know how to vent my rage, let alone express my feelings or ask for the sympathy I craved. I prayed for a catastrophe. I was ready to die with Penelope on the spot.

My eyes darted around the room like a fly on its death flight. *Mikainaito, what did I look like then?* Penelope placed her hands on my forehead and asked me what the matter was. Her usual scent of lily of the valley and butter was so intense that I was overwhelmed. Nostalgia welled up in me, and I couldn't tell if it was really Penelope in front of me, or a vision of the two of us together. As if I were in fact facing the end, I was beset by a rush of memories—Penelope among them, of course. I wanted to cling to these memories.

"Penelope," I said, "I've come to say goodbye for the last time. I'm going to die. My love is unrequited."

Penelope burst out laughing. And I couldn't help smiling in embarrassment myself. I hadn't mean it to be a joke. I was serious: in the next chapter of my life, I'd be a dead man.

Of course, before I died, I dreamed of having sex with Penelope. I pushed her back on the bed and covered her lips and neck with piranha kisses. She kept on laughing. And little by little my loneliness and decision to kill myself faded.

"Oh dear, my dress is getting wrinkled," Penelope said.

Like a dog that'd been yelled at, I lay face-down on a corner of the bed.

"I'm going to wear this to the dance at the Demartins'. Look at the design—isn't it great?"

The sounds of clothing falling to the floor grazed my ears.

"Matthew, look at my body."

I looked up. Penelope stood naked before me, then walked over to the bed.

Mikainaito, that night changed me. I loved Penelope till my stomach muscles went into spasms. I explored every inch of her body with my fingers, my lips, my tongue. I whispered a hundred times how much I loved her, how much I'd miss her. I let the fragrance of her body seep into mine; I wanted to make her body a part of mine.

But I wouldn't be able to just knock on the door and visit her anymore. The only way to see her would be to open the door to my memory, to my dreams. There in a small room in my mind, behind veiled layers, I'd find Penelope. And I didn't think I could stand it.

"I want you to promise me one thing," Penelope said, tapping me on the cheek. It was near dawn and I was just drifting off to sleep. "You might love me, but don't think you can make me yours alone. That isn't the kind of love I want. That would be narrow-minded, using love as collateral. Maybe we've stopped being brother and sister, but we haven't turned into ordinary lovers. You know I love you, Matthew. I think you, more than anybody else, can understand the sort of love I feel."

"What sort of love is that?" I asked. "Doesn't love mean always wanting to be with someone?"

"No. That's not the kind of love I want. I want to love, and be loved, by lots of people. People I haven't even met yet. Whores trade love for money; well, I want to trade love for love. The kind of love I want means buying with your body and heart what you can't buy with money."

"What you mean is you want to sleep with lots of different men."

"Maybe, but that's only a part of it," she said. "I want to offer to as many people as possible what I'm capable of. It's like, you know, curiosity—reaching out to take in as much as you can. You have twice as much curiosity as the average person, so you should be able to understand what I mean."

At the time I thought she meant this: Two people who love each other the most have to keep on having affairs. Love isn't something just between two people, but something you both scatter in all directions. Yet the two of you keep special ties.

Penelope continued: "Matthew, three years from now let's make love again. That way we'll know how much each of us has changed. In three years you'll be as old as I am now."

Three years is too long, I said. How could I live without her that long? I wanted only Penelope, and without her, I'd be suffering withdrawal symptoms of desire by the next month.

"I'm not asking you to to stop having sex," Penelope said. "Quite the opposite. You should fall in love with other women—and men, too. That's the rule of our love. Got it? I'll see you in three years."

After this night, Penelope made a point of ignoring me. *Mikainaito, I know it seems like a joke now, but at the time I wanted to marry her.* I wanted to run away with her and settle down in some small college town. Ithaca, New York—you know, where Cornell is—would be nice, I thought. I was serious, but she doused ice water on my dreams.

"Are you kidding?" Penelope said. "When you can put up with loneliness, *then* you can suggest that. A spoiled boy who can't stand a little loneliness and nihilism doesn't have the right to love anybody."

In the Chinese legend, the star lovers—Vega, the weaver, and Altair, the herdsman—at least get to meet every seventh of July.

Once a year has got to be better than once every three years.

Oh well, if things went well, I could still end up marrying Penelope, couldn't I?

At least, that's what I thought at the time.

For the next three years I saw Penelope only in my dreams. She showed up any number of times. *And I sent you, Mikainaito, flying out the window to visit her dreams.* Every time she showed up, she was changed. But even if she was someone else's girl, in dreams she was all mine.

More than ten years have passed since we made our contract. When you reach eighteen, you graduate from the rental child business. Penelope left our apartment and headed west. I went to college.

But three years later, as promised, she came to see me. Her boyfriend was a German water polo player. Her body was tanned and taut, and when we were in bed together, I thought maybe Tarzan had lent me Jane for the weekend.

I graduated from college at age twenty-three and went to work in New York as a gofer. Penelope flew in from Paris to see me again. She'd done a complete turnaround in that three-year period, and was now a very elegant lady. She was the lover of a French composer, a guy whose kisses must have been something else. I could tell by the way she kissed me.

"Matthew," Penelope said, "you're still as innocent as ever. But you've gotten better at sex, I can say that. Keep up the good work. And make sure you enjoy yourself."

She was starting to remind me of Mama.

The last time I met Penelope was two years ago. We'd lost track of each other's whereabouts, but Katagiri put us in touch. I was already working in Tokyo, and I flew back to New York to see her. She'd just broken up with a Pakistani physicist, and stayed with me for a week. She was twenty-nine and had already created her own Penelope circle of contacts. I kidded her that by the next century she'd be the First Lady, but she could as easily end up president herself. She wasn't one woman anymore, but *many* women. An elf and a sorceress, a Venus and a whore, an older sister and a lover, orphan and mother, Joan of Arc and Carmen—all rolled into one. Penelope was every woman you could possibly imagine. In this world there is no man who can take them all on.

I could share a nostalgia for rental child days with Penelope no longer. She'd changed far too much, had known the world far too well. But fifty years from now, I'll still be in love with her.

PART
III

8

Primitive Man Arrives in Tokyo

A Tapir with Insomnia

Tetsuya Nishikaze. I'd never heard the name before. The guy was a rock singer, and his English was so terrible it was causing him grief. Singing in English is all the rage among Japanese rockers, but if your pronunciation makes the song sound like a Gregorian chant, you might as well hang it up.

Just when his manager was trying to figure out what to do, I showed up. A friend of mine is a friend of an acquaintance who's a childhood friend of Tetsuya's. The one who's my friend is a stockbroker, and we were having dinner while he filled me in on what was hot and what was not in the world of stocks and bonds. Anyhow, the friend of this guy, a scuba diving instructor who looked like he'd had one too many, happens to stroll into the restaurant. The two of them were college classmates and they hadn't seen each other in a few years.

For some reason, they got to talking about this Tetsuya character. The broker's friend had heard the gossip from a childhood friend of the rock star: That Tetsuya had a bad back and a cock that hooked to the right. That he had as many girls as he wanted and had orgies once a week. And that recently he'd started making it with men. According to this friend, Tetsuya wanted to do everything other big rock stars did; if he kept it up, he'd end up like Sid Vicious and kill his girlfriend and die of an overdose. Trouble was, this friend said, it'd never happen—rock stars, you see, don't OD in Japan.

I like to believe unexpected encounters happen because of some invisible bond. But actually there aren't bonds so much as walls between people. Friends scratch at a wall until a hole opens up and they catch a glimpse of each other. When they get tired of looking, they plug the hole up again.

Of course, what you see depends on where you make the hole. So even after the wall's plugged up, you want to scratch out a new hole. I'm looking at the other guy's knees, for instance, while he's got a glimpse of my back. This way you get the illusion that people can undergo a metamorphosis. Maybe this illusion is the closest thing to reality. It happens when friends understand each other through their bodies. They grow closer and more erotic with each other. Ordinary friends die and are reborn as friends.

Bonds aren't there to begin with—you have to create them. Take any two people. Before there are bonds, what comes between them is meaning. Create bonds, and meaning disappears. And friends are born. Friends resemble you more than any lover or relative. Friends show you how decent you can be—and how mean you can be. The person who's interchangeable with you—that's what I mean by friend.

Tetsuya and I never became friends. When I first met him, he was afraid of the kind of loneliness that comes when your closest friends start to think the only reason they want to know you is because they can get something out of it. The only person who could cure that loneliness was a stranger from halfway around the world, because what Tetsuya wanted was to win over somebody who just happened to come by, and turn him into a loyal retainer. The kind of person he could always count on.

Anyway, this friend of a friend of a friend put it to me this way: "I heard this rocker's looking for someone to teach him

English. He's a star and he thinks the world revolves around him, so if he doesn't like you he'll spray you with a fire extinguisher. Literally, at first. So far four tutors have gotten the spray treatment. Want to give it a try? The pay's great. Teaching English is only part of the job. You gotta run errands for him, too."

I didn't have any other work lined up then, and I thought it wouldn't hurt to meet the guy. A little voyeurism on my part, perhaps. Tetsuya Nishikaze. Nishikaze—"west wind." A phony name if I ever heard one.

I owned two suits. On the day of the interview I wore the one which looked expensive but wasn't—in case he pulled the fire-extinguisher trick on me. In my little room, as I pressed the suit, I couldn't keep from my habit of ringing the numbers through my head: I was going to earn five hundred yen for every wrinkle I ironed.

At the production office, I waited about five minutes and then the star appeared, led by his manager. Hands in the pockets of his pants, collar of leather jacket turned up—hiding his face, Tetsuya made a deliberate show of plunking himself down roughly on the sofa. He was trying very hard not to make eye contact.

"Hi, I'm Matthew Katagiri," I said, using the name I use on my driver's license and credit cards. Most people assume it's my real name.

"Matthew?" The name bothered him. He still didn't look at me directly.

"Are you half or something?" the manager asked.

A hard question, because there are so many possible answers.

"No, as you can see, I'm Japanese. I lived a long time in New York so I took a name that's easy for Americans to pronounce."

"What was your name before you changed it?"

"Machio. Machio Okamoto."

A lie. I was never Machio. Though, it was true, plenty of Japanese misheard Matthew as Machio.

"*Machio?*"

The manager was convinced, but Tetsuya seemed to have his doubts. Sunk back deep in the couch, he played with something in his pocket. A key, maybe.

"English makes me wanna puke," he muttered, head down. His chin was tucked in unnaturally, as if he didn't want people to see his Adam's apple. I suddenly saw how timid he was. An awkward silence followed. Of the three of us there, Tetsuya seemed the most scared of this silence.

"Where's the fire extinguisher?" I said.

I'd seen his leg twitching and I could guess what was going to happen next: To break the silence, Tetsuya was going to get up slowly, then go for the fire extinguisher. But in response to my question, he bared his Adam's apple and looked me straight in the face. A faint smile danced around the corners of his lips.

"I like fire extinguishers," he said with a slightly high voice. "I use them a lot in my concerts. If I'm a little on edge I might use up three of them."

"Must be fun," I said.

"Not really."

He reminded me of a tapir with insomnia; maybe, like the tapir in legend, he'd gobbled up too many nightmares. It took great effort for him to look straight at me.

"I'm an idiot," he said.

He might well be. But he'd worked hard to become one. Most people thought he was an idiot, and nothing more. But you had to understand the process which led to that. And that's what a professional friend was good at.

"What kind of idiot are you?" I asked.

"An idiot's an idiot. You're an idiot, too."

It was going to take some time to explain what Tetsuya meant, so it was decided that I would come to his place the next day to hear the explanation.

"Do It! Violate It!"

In Nishi-Azabu in the middle of Tokyo, there's a temple of the Sodo Zen sect called Hase-dera. Every day young monks, oblivious to what's around them, practice *za-zen*. One building in the temple compound houses a white statue of the Kannon goddess of mercy wearing a goofy face.

Just behind the cage for the Kannon statue stands a slim, tall castlelike structure, its outside walls covered entirely with mirrors, as if to keep anyone from seeing in. The mirrored walls reflect everything around them: the grimy highway running through Tokyo and the mass of buildings beyond; the clouds perpetually over the city; Tokyo Tower looking like it'd seen better days; the crows that'd flown over from the Imperial Palace; the darkness that brings on nightmares for every person in the city. And slicing through that darkness was the wind.

The people who lived behind these mirrored walls were the eccentric—and supereccentric—rich. The sort of rich who could be arrested by the police tomorrow or, if not, be killed on the streets or go broke or insane. Tetsuya's apartment was on the west side of the building, on the eighth floor. I visited him three times a week, always late at night.

The first week he was tense and confused. He glared at me cruelly one minute, and in the next became boyish and brought me a beer. He didn't know what to talk about, so he filled in the silences with tongue cluckings, slurps of beer, and *enka* records.

"Where should we start?" I asked. "With English songs?"

I tried to act cool and collected, a lump of unconcern, but I was on my guard. Silence made Tetsuya violent. His beady eyes were calm, sleepy, but always ready to attack. The eyes of a lion. Move a millimeter, and he'd catch it. When silence passed between the two of us, you could see his lion eyes take over, and he'd be scrutinizing me—this oddity from the other side of the world. Then in an instant the lion eyes would be gone and he'd be soft and gentle again, a little fidgety, clumsily trying to fill in the gaps of silence.

It took courage for Tetsuya to let me, a total stranger, into his place. The mirrored castle might hold back the scorn of the outside world, but it was not without a price. The price was loneliness. Even if you tried to drown your isolation with money, the loneliness would remain, your body filled with a sludge-like fatigue. To rid yourself of the sludge, to feel alive, you needed the help of a stranger. Your heart had to dance a strip-tease before that stranger. The problem was, if you couldn't communicate with this stranger, you risked embarrassment on top of your loneliness. As he sat watching me, Tetsuya feared this the most.

He had a weird way of drinking. He'd take a six-pack of beer from the refrigerator, pop open all the bottles at once, and give each bottle a girl's name. He'd take each bottle in his hands, whispering its name to it—Rumiko or Kaoru or Miyuki or Midori or Sadako or Ayako—then pour the beer down his gullet. When I took a bottle he'd just started to drink—Miyuki, for instance—and pour some in a glass, he'd give a running commentary on how she tasted better than Sadako, and so on. After drinking all six girls, the screws round his eyes got loose and out came a tirade of slack-jawed complaints, mixed in with some sad laughter or an irritated cluck of the tongue.

It was like I was in a bar in a port town. I was the sailor who just came into port, and he was the singer in the bar. A singer who liked to collar sailors and spill out his life story.

"If I was a plain jerk that'd be OK," he began, "but I'm a jerk from the sticks. And not the usual kind of sticks—I'm talking backwoods like you wouldn't believe. I was born in a sugarcane field, on a tiny island surrounded by the sea. The nearest land was four hundred kilometers away. Nobody even thinks Minami Daito Island is a part of Japan. If that itty-bitty chunk of rock disappeared, do you think anybody on the mainland

would notice? Nobody even comes to the island out of curiosity.
The only visitors are guys from the government, the weather bu-
reau, and the tax office. Forget about big-city girls. All we get
are typhoons, and you start to look forward to them. I used to
think of them as a kind of vehicle that could take me outta there.
Either that or something that could carry the whole island away.
If you grew up like that, where typhoons are the only thing you
can look forward to, you would understand what I mean.
There's no new blood from the outside, so you can't expect anybody born there to be very bright. And short legs like mine are
part of the deal. Everybody on that island has short legs."

"They're not that short," I said. "Nobody's gonna say 'Hey,
stand up—oh, you *are* standing up.' Your legs are long enough."

"No, I've got the shortest legs of any rock 'n' roller. You know,
on Minami Daito, there's a dog with short legs that mainlanders
call a *nanto*, a south islander. But there's no such breed as *nanto*.
A *nanto* is a mongrel, brought over from the mainland. Since
then, the *nanto* on the island have chosen not to breed with dogs
from the mainland, so they're pure. Pure-bred mongrels! I'm
talking incest here. Big surprise their legs're so short."

Tetsuya talked with a strange conviction. Naturally the
whole thing was a delusion, an offshoot of his inferiority complex. But this delusion had a weird realism to it. And that's what
made it funny. The girl he married, without a doubt, would be
one of those long-stemmed females. And his short-legged family
line could end then and there.

"Did you know that typhoons are female?" he kept going on.
"They all have these glamorous foreign names—Ruth, Helen,
Nancy. Every autumn I start getting itchy to go back to the island. You know why? 'Cause I love typhoons, that's why. When
I was a kid I used to sumo wrestle with them. I'd draw a circle
on the ground and get in a clinch with the blasts of wind. When
the wind was in the *yokozuna* class, it could send me flying a
couple of meters. This was wind that blew down palm trees.

When typhoons hit, the island shook like it was having an earth-quake. Everytime I feel an earthquake in this apartment, I think of the typhoons back home."

So the island boy was knocked around by typhoons that were female. Kind of ridiculous when you think about it. The picture that came to mind was short-legged Tetsuya being bounced around by some gigantic woman basketball player.

"I used to yell into the wind," he said. "That's how I first trained my voice. Do you know 'Typhoon Rock'? That was my first song. Really sold. Made me a star overnight. I became a typhoon myself."

Tetsuya sang it for me, slapping the table in time.

> Here you are, cutting 'cross the sky,
> The queen of destruction, in an opera from hell.
> You twist your body with gales and waves,
> Holding the town in your embrace,
>   then smashing it down.
> Do it! Violate it!
> Do it! Violate it!
>
> Your love is a whirlpool
>   that sucks everything down—
>   and drives it crazy.

The words and melody and the way Tetsuya sang—it was all about sex. It was the perfect song for him.

Sometimes Tetsuya'd give me small doses of his past. But never without a few burps from an *awamori*-and-7-Up cocktail. Officially I was his English tutor, and so at first I sang sixties' hits with him, trying to teach him some sweaty English pronun-ciation. But after three tries we gave up. My main job was to be his drinking buddy.

"Hey—Happy Birthday!" I'd say to him.

I said this a lot to Tetsuya. He didn't just have one birthday, you see. He said he'd been born more than a hundred times, that he often got the feeling that the day was his birthday.

What an easygoing guy, Mikainaito muttered to me. *The exact opposite of us.*

Mikainaito was right, of course. Neither he nor I has a birthday because no one can prove which day we were born on. For the sake of convenience, Katagiri decided my birthday was April 1st, knowing full well it was April Fools' Day, but many times the day came and went without even me remembering.

"How about some champagne?" I said. "We ought to celebrate. Tell me—what birthday is it today?"

"Today's the day I was reborn a rock singer," Tetsuya said. "It's been a long time since I felt like celebrating that. People don't have any idea how their lives're gonna turn out, do they? If I hadn't slept with this one woman, I'd probably still be a bum crawling in back alleys. I knew, absolutely, I had to sleep with her. She was this old broad with varicose veins. Not the usual kind of woman I'd sleep with, even if she asked. But she was my big chance and I couldn't let it pass. She was the director of this artist promotion company. I would've done anything to please her—and I did. I went with her everywhere. The empress of Japan can't hold a candle to a director, let me tell you. She's also the one who gave me my stage name. She told me my real name sucked. You know what my real name is? Masayoshi Warusato. You wanna laugh, be my guest. *Masayoshi*—justice; *warusato*—bad village. I was supposed to be a fighter for justice in a bad village. Fact is, a lot of people have that last name in Okinawa. Wanna make something of it?"

I couldn't hold back the laughter, even if it might be rude. After all, didn't "justice" and "bad" cancel each other out? If this guy fit his name, he was hopeless. His parents must have been pretty soused to give him a name like that. The lady was right: The name would be a bust in rock 'n' roll. When you start a new life, the first thing you need is a new name.

"When I got to Tokyo," he continued, "man, I didn't know

where to turn. I found myself staring at the sky. But it was like a haze over everything, a deadening feeling, kind of. Two or three days of that, and I was ready to look at the girls on the street. I was working road construction and I watched the girls going by all the time. I felt like I was screwing them, just by looking at them; I had a hard-on twenty-four hours a day. After work, instead of going to some yakitori stand with the other guys, I'd take a bath and change clothes and go someplace where the sharp-looking girls hung out. I'd see a fox and I'd tail her—to discos, bars, expensive apartments—everywhere she went. I'd latch on and never let her out of my sight. Sometimes I'd run into some hood and I'd have to disappear, but sometimes I'd get lucky and end up in a love hotel with the girl. That's how I got used to life in Tokyo. My world was turned upside down, but sleeping around helped straighten me out. Every time I slept with someone, things started to open up a little. I got the feeling that something good was going to happen."

So Masayoshi Warusato was still alive and well in Tetsuya Nishikaze.

What a sentimental guy, I whispered to Mikainaito.

"How'd you repay that director of the promotion company, the one who helped make you a star?" I asked.

"Her? She died. Cancer of the uterus."

"Do you remember the day she died?" I asked.

"I don't celebrate things like that. It'd make my drinks turn sour. Best thing to do with the dead is leave 'em alone."

The Desert Island

Tetsuya had a heavy beard. Every morning he'd shave until his chin was blue; by evening it was sandpaper all over again The soil on his face was as good as fertilized. Through his loose-fitting shirt, you could see his chest hair, which reminded you of the frizzy hair blacks have. A bush of hair like scrub in a desert, or like lichen at the foot of a volcano. His body hair was probably like plantlife on Minami Daito. The kind of sticky grass and vines that cling to anything. And every time Tetsuya turned, you were hit by a blast of body odor, like grass soaked in alcohol.

Wrestling with typhoons and working in the cane fields had made Tetsuya as muscular as a Caribbean boxer. Despite the muscles, though, you wouldn't call him butch. I mean, I was aware of the masculine side of him, but when I looked at Tetsuya I saw muscles slapped onto an insecure girl. Even when he struck someone, Tetsuya wasn't very macho—he hit them because he was starved for love. He didn't feel loneliness with his mind; he felt it with his body. Each sinew and muscle in his body strained for warm contact. He was always assessing the affections of anyone he was intimate with, and he took the slightest hesitation as a sign of betrayal. Yet, with all his strength, he wanted to prove he wasn't lonely.

I'm not like that. I can be alone any time. I can change from stranger to friend, from friend to brother, from brother back to stranger. A nonentity on an endless journey, selling my time and affection to the people I meet—that's me. In my line of work, the one thing you got to get used to is being alone.

But not Tetsuya. If he didn't have someone around to boost his confidence and comfort him, he couldn't go on living. He was like the orphan island in the Pacific he grew up on: It couldn't survive alone. Cut off supply routes from Okinawa and the rest of Japan, it'd be a deserted island in a day. Somehow that fear had seeped into every pore of Tetsuya's body.

Minami Daito was an uninhabited island discovered by a Russian admiral and visited later by the Black Ships. In the beginning of the century, twenty brave pioneers, led by an enterprising adventurer from Hajijo Island, came over by ship and settled at the base of the steep cliffs of the island. They were its first inhabitants. They burned the virgin forests of palm trees and planted sugarcane. The island ended up being one large sugarcane plantation, run by a sugar company. And to islanders, the president of the company was more important than the emperor. Their home was less a part of Japan than an island with sugarcane growing on it. The people on it weren't so much Japanese as migrant workers cultivating the fields.

Drink was the only amusement they had. Considering the number of people, the number of bars was extraordinary. Young and old caroused until two or three in the morning. They spent all their money on booze. They didn't bother to build new homes, for if they did they'd be flattened by typhoons. There was no one to show off for, and no point to buying a Mercedes.

The inhabitants of the island were like children raised in the wild. Their hearts beat to the rhythm of the waves, and they were as sensitive as sea gulls to changes in the drift of the clouds and shifts in the wind. They saw the same people every day, and they pretended to laugh at stories they'd heard a dozen times before.

Tetsuya liked scuba diving, but for him it was not a matter of recreation. The ocean provided him dinner. He speared sea bream and he tore shellfish from the sea bottom. He ate his catch the way a shark would—seasoned with only the salt of the ocean.

On land the biggest treat was goat meat. Red peppers were crushed into soy sauce, and the goat meat dipped into that. "Man, that's good," Tetsuya said, smacking his lips.

Once in Tokyo, Tetsuya was forced to become like everybody else in Tokyo. He'd never ridden a train before. The food in restaurants was new to him. Names made no sense. He was always lost. He didn't know how to find a place to stay, so he got some cardboard and made his bed near the coin lockers in a train station. The next day a guy who was dealing paint thinner and who had staked out the same spot for himself chased him away. That was when Tetsuya realized he was a bum.

He found a master who tutored him in the art of life as a bum. He found out where the cheap flophouses were, learned how to ride the trains, how to land a day-labor job, and what kind of pay and treatment to expect. Road construction work was good, since it didn't matter where you were from. You might have your share of masculine pride, or you might feel inferior because you were a wild child from a lonely island with dreams of making it in the big city, but all these distinctions were meaningless. Everything melted away in the exhaustion of physical labor.

Away from work, he was amazed to find that nothing around him had the slightest connection with him. Not the well-dressed girls, or the slope-shouldered office workers with briefcases under their arms, or the taxis and cars waiting at the intersections, or the dogs pawing through the discarded umbrellas and scraps of food in the garbage cans, or the ambulance sirens wailing in the distance, or the cigarette smoke trailing behind him.

Everything was backing away from him. Drunk on *awamori*, Tetsuya told me he wanted to go back to the island. But he couldn't, not until his purification ritual was over.

"Purification ritual?"

A mysterious look came over him. "I knocked up one of my cousins," he explained. "The island's a small place, so I had to leave. I was an idiot. The girl went to Naha to get an abortion. I was eighteen."

So Tetsuya came to Tokyo to get rid of his excess energy. It sounded like one of those stormy, ancient Japanese tales you hear recited to music. But all I could think of was whether the child would've had short legs.

"Now you understand what kind of idiot I am," he went on. "When I was on the island I acted like a jerk, and as a result, the world opened up for me. If I stayed on the island the rest of my life, I could've lived like the sugarcane. But living in Tokyo, the bigger fool you are, the richer you get. I earned my money by being a bigger idiot than anybody else."

In the capital city of illusion and amnesia, that was the thing: Be an idiot. It was Tetsuya's way of resisting the city. It was also why Tetsuya—in Tokyo, where he was like an amphetamine for kids with paralyzed brains—became a star.

Despite what happened later, Tetsuya loved Tokyo. He was

an adaptable creature and was able to hide his past in the city. In that way he was like me—the way I used to be, that is— which made me curious about what his dreams were like. I started to lay the groundwork so I could peep in on them. I began by telling him about my own dreams. And whenever we talked I'd ask him whether he dreamed of flying or falling, whether he had the same dream over and over. I persuaded him to talk about his dreams before they faded away.

His dreams were violent. That was a surprise. He was constantly killing people—and bragging about it.

"In my dream the other day, " he said, "you and I tortured that idiot prime minister—what's his name?—till he croaked. Know what his dying words were? 'Aarggh!'"

And again: "Man that was a great dream. I beat up Mike Tyson in a street fight. Know how I knocked him over? I stuck my fingers up his nose, twirled him around, and kicked him in the nuts. Damn shame I didn't get any prize money."

And again: "Last night I dreamed I was flying low over Tokyo. I opened the door of the plane and smashed all the people below with a club. Like that video game where you smash these moles on the head whenever they pop up."

And again: "I saw the Virgin Mary in a dream. It must mean I'm going to perform a miracle and wind up a hero. To do that, I have to destroy Tokyo. You know, man, I really dig Pol Pot. The guy who destroyed all the cities, sent everybody back to the farms. What he did was idiotic. Something just as idiotic's gotta be done in Tokyo. And I'm just the guy to do it."

I couldn't tell how much was dream, how much he really believed. Other than the emotion to destroy, I couldn't read a thing from his dreams.

Frustration City

That night a low pressure area hung over Tokyo. The streets were so soaked you couldn't miss stepping in puddles. People went scurrying home, the wet neon streets no longer beckoning, themselves lost in thought.

No Man's Land was another story, though. The place was boiling with excitement over Tetsuya's concert. It was the perfect place to get rid of excess energy.

I'd never been to a concert of Tetsuya's before. There were no tables or chairs. The floor and walls were covered with sheets of black plastic. The agitation of the crowd enveloped you, and it was hot as hell. Voices were shrill and got even louder as people danced, wildly, sweat from their bodies spraying out like a sprinkler.

One girl was dressed in black from head to foot, her face painted red. Another had jewelry everywhere—on her neck, arms, ankles, in addition to a sash of chains, all jangling to the beat of the drum. Another was a tropical parrot, her hair plastered down and dyed seven colors. There was a bodybuilder showing off his muscles, while others around him did push-ups and sit-ups. A group against the wall were passing around a Vicks inhaler probably filled with amphetamines, while a girl exhausted by the music sat collapsed against the wall, her blouse open. Two guys were feeling her up, their hands on her breasts and up her crotch.

On stage stood Tetsuya—his right pant leg torn off, a tuxedo jacket with no right sleeve flung over him, topped off with a World War I Prussian Army helmet. The helmet was topped with a Japanese flag, and he wore a volleyball kneepad on his right leg. The guitarist wore sweat-soaked Nehru pajamas, the bassist a black schoolboy uniform with a high collar, the drummer a loincloth.

"Let the party begin!" Tetsuya yelled to the crowd. "Last week I had a dream. The Virgin Mary came to me. She put her arm around my shoulder. And she said to me, 'You will perform a miracle!' And the miracle I will perform is to bring revolution in Japan! But I can't do it alone. I need your help. I need your help to wake Japan up!"

The place was packed with Tetsuya wannabes. When Tetsuya spoke, they listened.

"So come and get it!" he screamed. He stuck a shovel into a
large cardboard box, and out flew ice.

"Whoever's standing next to you, stick it down their
clothes!" Tetsuya shouted as he shoveled out the ice. After some
initial confusion, the crowd got into it. They scooped up the ice
and shoved it down people's pants. They rubbed it on their heads,
stuck it in their mouths, flung it at each other. Tetsuya lifted the
box of ice above his head, and with a scream tossed the ice out
into the audience.

"All right, let's 'Typhoon Rock'!"

Tetsuya's band of followers went wild. Tetsuya's voice shot to
a frantic pitch, as the drumbeat became a whip, lashing bodies.

My ears were ringing and I began to back away. Just then a
warm hand brushed my back. I didn't know anybody there well
enough to trade ice rubs, but I turned around anyway and was
met with a white face. It was a heavyset girl with red hair and
green eyes.

"Hi!" she said, smiling. In the din of the music I couldn't
catch what else she was saying. I cupped my hands around my
ears, shook my head, and motioned with my chin over to the
hallway leading to the toilets.

A skinny guy stood in front of the rest room cooling off his
head with ice wrapped in a handkerchief.

"Fuckin' asshole!" he spat out. He was really pissed off about
something.

You could hear someone puking his guts out inside the rest
room.

"Hi, I'm Cindy."

She stuck out her hand and I shook it.

"I'm Matthew. How you doing?"

"Really wild, isn't it? What a trip! How come you're not getting into it? What's the matter? You seem so down. Come on!
Why don't you show me your palm?"

"Can you read palms?" I asked.

I guess she was doing her best to inject a little energy into me. *Mikainaito, I heard once that the quickest way to get to know someone was to read their palm. It's not so hard. All you have to do is learn a couple of simple rules and you wouldn't be far off the track.* Cindy drew my palm close to her as her heavy breasts bounced without letup under her blouse.

"You're a very clever man," she began, "but people misunderstand you. What I mean is, you have a lot of enemies."

"Really? Where? In Japan? In my mind? Or here tonight?"

"Everywhere you are," she said. "But never mind. You have more friends than enemies. I can guarantee it."

She nodded in agreement with herself, and rested her hand on my shoulder. Her enormous breasts were overpowering. Suddenly I felt like slipping some ice down her deep cleavage.

"Typhoon Rock" over with, Tetsuya let out a piercing whoop. What was he trying to imitate? The giant bats of his home island? A low growl answered him. Fingernails scratched across frosted glass—maybe a girl's scream. The howl of a wolf echoed hollowly through the hall. Was the world coming to an end?

"Let's get out of here," I said.

Cindy gave me a look that said "in this rain?" I dangled the car keys in front of her. "I want to find out whether you're friend or foe," I said.

Outside No Man's Land, fans who hadn't been able to get into the club milled around. Girls stood flattened against the wall to keep out of the rain, as guys, dripping wet, cruised by, as wary of each other as the girls they wanted to pick up.

Tetsuya's car—a Mustang which Tetsuya'd driven through a ring of fire in his Yumenoshima concert, earning him the name "The Daredevil"—was parked in the lot outside the stage entrance. It was surrounded by thugs on motorcycles, guys who were supposed to be Tetsuya's bodyguards. But after the concert, Tetsuya would be off carousing with members of his fan club, the Shinjuku Pearl Harbor, and wouldn't be back before dawn. So I was on my own time until then.

Who knows, maybe they were some of the thugs who beat me up in the park. The cheap hoods, they were only allowed to touch the steering wheel when they cleaned out the ashtray.

"Could you move the bikes out of the way?" I said. "I wanna take the car outta here."

"What?!!" A guy, completely soaked, his hair plastered down like seaweed, lumbered up to us. A big guy, the kind you wouldn't want to have any disagreements with.

Smiling out of the left side of my mouth, I twirled the keys around like a propeller. Cindy said hi to the bewildered guards around us.

"I need to take the Mustang so I can take this girl for a drive," I told him. "You know, you get too wet, you're gonna go bald."

"Oh . . ."

The guy wasn't too bright, though his voice was loud enough. He signaled to the gang, and they slowly got their bikes out of the way. We got in the car. I started the engine and called the seaweed man over.

"What's your name, man?" I asked.

"Me? Yuki Kurihara."

"OK, Yuki, I'm going to make a right turn so you go out in the road and give me the all-clear, " I told him. "I'll tell Tetsuya you're cool."

The big guy perked right up. He stopped traffic going the other way and waved me out into the road. I knew why. If Tetsuya remembered some bodyguard's name, he might invite the guy to an orgy. In fact, there probably was going to be one tonight. Tetsuya was sultan of his very own harem.

Mikainaito, Tetsuya doesn't need me. He's the charismatic leader of a lot of frustrated people, and I'm just a humble dream messenger. After I go to sleep, would you go visit Tetsuya's dreams for me? Let him have the sequel to the dream he had before. The oracle in that dream might change him.

Sure, Mikainaito replied. *But the guy's just as crude in his dreams as he is when he's awake.*

The Whirring Jagged Edge

It feels so good! *Slam.* Ahh! *Bam!* Suck me! *Ahhh!!!*

Cindy had stamina that wouldn't quit. We'd been going at it for almost an hour, and I was about to keel over. But my cock, maybe out of a sense of duty, or greed—or maybe inertia—continued to make the earth shake for her without drooping or shooting.

Finally, after another twenty-five minutes, dripping with sweat, I got out of bed and went to get a drink of water in the bathroom. My legs were as wobbly as a newborn colt.

Mikainaito, the sap's sucked right out of me.

Serves you right. Now it's your turn for a nightmare.

When I returned to the bed, Cindy looked at me with sleepy eyes and whispered: "Come into my dreams and fuck me again."

I put on my underpants, lay face down on the bed and waited for my weary body to get comfortable. My back his trampoline, Mikainaito bounced up and down.

Dream messengers live through dreams. In dreams they think, they worry, learn, have visions of the future. In dreams they take their shattered selves and piece them together again. They cure sickness in dreams, die in dreams, and wake to be reborn.

"Sweet dreams."

Thanks, Cindy. You have a good one, too.

> All around the world is white—
> A snowy winter woods.
> I'm in the hollow
> of a huge tree, keeping out of the cold.
> I chew on acorns
> that squirrels have stored for winter.

Sorry about that, squirrels.
And I'm humming.
Silence wrapped in silence.
Snow falls from a branch,
like an explosion in the distance,
its echo swallowed by snow.
Again, silence wrapped in silence.
I listen hard, but again—nothing.
But now, in the stillness, something new.
Step by step, trampling the silence, someone
draws near.
From a crack in the tree,
I see a lumberjack, chain saw in hand.
        (Tetsuya! What's he doing here?)
Without hesitation
he steps up to the tree where I hide
and crudely
        (the guy is crude)
starts the chain saw
aiming it
right at my side.
Stop! Save it for your rock 'n' roll!
But my shouts are drowned
by the chain saw roar.
I suck in my gut, frantic,
and twist my body,
sawdust flying, filling eyes and mouth,
that whirring jagged edge,
a centimeter,
now five millimeters, from my side . . .

I sleep.
My eyes closed, I sleep,
but plainly I see the room.
Noiselessly the door opens—

enter man with red mask,
who glares at me.
It is—
Tetsuya.
In his hand a wrench.
My chest has sprouted a bolt.
Nut fit to the bolt,
tightened with his fingers,
tickles—
Until,
wrench to my chest, he
twists.
Tickle turns to pain—
No breath,
Ribs snap,
Tetsuya twists
the wrench again and again,
as hard as he can.

Before flames ten feet high,
Tetsuya and I play paper-scissors-rock.
Loser gets burned;
Best of three.
But I know a surefire way to win.
Your turn to die, pal.
First rock, then paper, last scissors—
In this order and I win.
First rock, I win.
Then paper—
but my hand sticks—
fist fixed,
No paper, no scissors.
Tetsuya—
I lose.
"The fire—go on," he says.

I step, first one, then another, as
anger, like flames, shoots up, singes my mouth.
And he kicks me in the back.

Before me, Cindy's sleeping face.
Matthew—you still alive?
You took your time, Mikainaito.
Matthew, you've got to get away from Tetsuya. The guy's deranged. There's murder in him, everywhere he turns. Those dreams are proof enough.

After I saw Cindy off, I returned to Tetsuya's apartment. I wanted to find out where his head was at.

I found him, legs set apart, standing in front of a full-length mirror. He was in full military dress, a samurai sword at his side; he'd found the getup somewhere along the line, maybe used it for one of his concerts.

"Where'd you go yesterday?" he shouted.

"No place special."

"You used my Mustang to slip out with a girl, didn't you? Now, of all times." He grabbed me by the collar and stared deep into my eyes. His own eyes were bloodshot as a drunk turtle's. Something must have happened after the concert.

"From now on, you're one of my bodyguards, y'hear!" he said.

"What if I say no?"

"Then you're an asshole."

"Let me try to guess what you're thinking," I said. "You want to destroy something."

Tetsuya's eyes turned cold, he grabbed me even harder by the collar and sent me flying.

"Shut up, ya idiot!"

"What happened? Talk to me."

Tetsuya unsheathed his samurai sword and thrust the tip up against my nose. He looked possessed.

"You'll find out soon enough," he said. "Tomorrow I'm gonna be a hero. God gave me the word to destroy Tokyo. The only way to save this pig capital is to butcher it. I'll destroy Tokyo all right. And you're gonna be one of my followers, right? Make up your mind."

His beady eyes glared at me.

"I was your friend," I said, "but I'll be damned if I'll be one of your bootlicking flunkies. Something's wrong with you, man. You want to act crazy? Do it on stage." I had some hate left over from those nightmares and wasn't being very cool.

Tetsuya swung his sword, cutting through my sleeve and slicing my upper arm. Blood trickled down my arm and dripped onto the rug.

"Anyone in my way gets offed!" he threatened.

He'd finally gone over the edge. I grabbed a clock and heaved it at him. In the instant that he flinched to avoid it, I made a dash for the door. I ran to a phone booth and called an ambulance. I had only a flesh wound, but I couldn't very well walk around in a bloody shirt.

All the hatred Tetsuya had in his dreams was coming to a head. He'd gone berserk. By tomorrow, Tetsuya was either going to be locked up in jail or bouncing around a rubber room.

I didn't think Tetsuya would try any more nonsense. I'd get his promotion company to foot the hospital bill. Whether I'd file criminal charges or not depended on negotiations with his manager. I figured a million and a half yen would be enough to keep me quiet about the whole affair. As far as he and I were concerned, that'd be all she wrote.

But things went from bad to worse. Two days later I was in Mariko the nympho's apartment. She was waiting for a facial pack to dry and switched on the TV. Who was there on the screen but Tetsuya. The announcer on the late night news put it this way:

"The rock singer Tetsuya Nishikaze and his group, who have

been holding the president of a real estate firm and three others hostage in a suite at the Palace Hotel, were arrested this evening at 10:23. As he was taken into custody, Nishikaze attacked the hostages with a samurai sword he was carrying, then cut his own carotid artery. Nishikaze is now in critical condition. The hostages suffered varying degrees of injury, while in the skirmish between police and Nishikaze's group, five other people were injured. Two are expected to be hospitalized for up to two months.

"Nishikaze's unusual list of demands included transformation of the Imperial Palace into a rock concert hall, the cessation of all real estate transactions in the Tokyo area, and the demolition of all the historic spots in the city."

"So the guy wanted to punish the land speculators, huh?" Mariko mused. "Too bad he didn't go after the president of *my* company. If you don't do something radical, Tokyo's never going to change." Clearly Mariko was on Tetsuya's side. Also, she wanted him to pull through because she wanted to sleep with him.

Some of Tetsuya's agitation must have rubbed off on me, because ever since I split, I'd been on edge and unable to sleep. I thought sex with Mariko might calm me down, so in a roundabout way, I suppose, Mariko's wish was coming true. Of course, I didn't say a word about the arm wound and my own connection with her hero for the day.

Despite what happened, I don't think Tetsuya was really crazy. He was just obsessed with this kidnapping scheme. But why didn't he reveal his plans to me? I could have given him a lot of great ideas. Thing was, Tetsuya didn't want a friend—he just wanted a lackey.

Like Mariko, I didn't want him to die—but for a different reason. After his heroics were forgotten, I wanted to see what this former rock star with a scar on his neck did next in the way of idiotic tricks. Then I'd offer to help. As a friend.

So I ended up unable to communicate with Tetsuya via

dreams after all. He remained an outsider who didn't want any part of my attempts to understand him. Still, I don't want this scar on my arm to be a mark of hatred. I prefer to think of it as a lesson I learned. The lesson that if you judge people by your own standards, you risk getting burned.

Next time around I'll be his real friend. I swore this to Tetsuya, as he stood at the brink of death.

9

In Search of Karma

A Mud-Eating Worm

In a week's time Kubi's nose hairs had sprouted a couple of millimeters. He settled on a daily quota of a thousand passersby that he'd click off with his counter. He didn't have enough time to look at each person's face, but he did follow the eye-catching bodies of all the young girls. Occasionally a young man pulling a luggage cart would stroll by, but then it was clear the guy was headed for Hawaii or someplace like it. Kubi would yawn and let him pass. He was always on the lookout for an excuse to goof off.

It wasn't hard to click off a thousand people. He'd achieve his quota in the time it took to smoke a pack of cigarettes. On some days, students working on traffic counts would be doing the same thing, clicking away. On one occasion Kubi was grilled by some official-looking guy, and a couple of times he was evicted from his spot by a couple of guys selling cheap belts and bags, shirts, and stuffed animals, who claimed Kubi was trespassing. Four days before, even the police had gotten into the act, stopping him for questioning. In this underground passage of the station if you weren't a passerby, someone hawking wares, a station employee, a mendicant priest, or a student helping with the traffic census, you were suspect. As advertised, Tokyo was a safe place to be.

One girl was pretty weird. She stood in the shadows of a pillar, selling her poetry. A street poet, eh? Maybe not so bad a business. The next time the cops stopped him, Kubi would tell them he was a troubador and growl out a chanson for them. Pleased with himself, he bought a copy of the girl's poems for three hundred yen. At quitting time, though, when the crush of workers oozed out of the buildings like paste out of a tube, there was nowhere for even a single street poet to stand. At rush hour, the mendicant priests hightailed it back to their temples.

If only he could hand out hammers to the crowd and get them screaming "Destroy Tokyo! Destroy Tokyo!" the city'd be in ruins over night. And who would care if the city was destroyed? Of the people Kubi knew, maybe only Mrs. Amino. After all, she was the widow of a guy who got rich jacking up land prices.

Nope, the ones who'd suffer the most would be this very crowd steamrolling toward him. Imagining the mass of them—decked out in business suits, fussily picking their way through the debris—sent shivers down his spine. Only foreigners—those who'd come to Japan to make some money off the strong yen—would know what to do in the rubble of Tokyo.

A new business scheme then appeared before Kubi. He could suggest it to Mrs. Amino: She could use all the land she owned to create a bunch of independent countries. Each country would have its own government. You could have a gay republic, a democratic ladies tea party, a constitutional monarchy for computers, an anarchic state surrounded by walls, and while you're at it why not a country where decisions were made by fortune-tellers? People could join any country they wanted. Someone who failed to be the supreme ruler of the anarchic state, for instance, could seek asylum in the gay republic and find himself a pretty boy. People could have fun being diplomats or businessmen of one country, making and breaking relations with the others. Countries could bid for the services of the more talented, and people could advertise themselves and sell to the highest bidder.

Tokyo is a city where thinking and looking the same as everybody else is the norm. If you wanted to start a revolution here, you'd have to build several different countries inside the city. It was the only way not to end up with what you have now—Japanese doing their best to be like foreigners, and foreigners pretending to be Japanese. Everyone would be free to join whatever country they wanted. That freedom was the guiding principle of Kubi's fantasy.

Of course, as long as there wasn't a big earthquake or stock market crash or a revolt by farmers or salarymen, Kubi's plans remained at the comic-strip level. Still, he couldn't throw off his illusions of grandeur. He sighed drily, and his stomach growled.

Why not add some garlic to your sighs, Kubi asked himself.

The underground passage was divided by pillars into two lanes, and people flowed in opposite directions. Next to one pillar was a trash can, and next to it a mirror. As he walked toward his reflection in this mirror, Kubi suddenly realized how down and out he looked. Like a laborer who gets One-Cup Ozeki saké from a vending machine at the end of the day and gulps it down.

Kubi was thirty-seven. Dante wasn't the only one lost in a dark forest halfway down the path of life. Everyone after age thirty starts to think the same thing. In the dark forest an old gay devil grabs hold of you and sneers:

"You're no better than a worm in a putrid swamp. Learn to be a worm, and you'll learn to live and to love. Learn to like growing old. Belief in self is a fantasy. Youth means a weak stomach. Eat, eat the foul mud of your putrid swamp. Do not hesitate. And wait. For death, or a market crash. Or the Big One."

Kubi sought out comfort in a bar, eager for a cure for his depression. Amid the odor of raw fish and fried food, he nursed his beer and listened.   In between the slurps and clinking glasses, he heard another sound, a chorus of *"Shigata ga nai! What can you do?"* There were as many voices repeating this refrain as there were people in the bar.   And everyone had the look of exhaustion.   It made Kubi sick.

Before him he saw the entire country, Japan, millions of people, drinking, spewing out their complaints, their misery and jealousy and fatigue enveloping them like mist.

. . . rotten things at work the boss is a pain my husband is cheating on me why go to school just to get picked on better locked up in a Zen temple him or my career? what do you think? I miss him got to be better men around how is one supposed to act gross-looking but helpless office girls falling all over I'm a much better actress but do I ever get a good part? the manager must be plotting against me how could that hack win? . . .

Excreting what they couldn't swallow, the crowd consumed more calories than was good for them.   Was this a black mass? Was this *normal*? Kubi yearned to be carried along by a megalomaniac who had the power to make the world spin all by himself.   The sort of mania to save the world!

The next day, and the next, Kubi was a wandering mole in the underground passage.   He sat through a porno double feature, lost five thousand yen at pachinko, hunted for his old novels at Kinokuniya, and squandered time, finally ending up back underground. Like birds of a feather, Kubi found himself standing quietly beside a guy selling mass-produced paintings and muttering to himself in Spanish. Kubi offered him a cigarette and asked him in English where he was from. "Mexico," the guy replied in Japanese. A friendly sort, always smiling, but whose eyes behind frameless glasses didn't miss a trick. His voice was nasal, as if he had some chronic nose infection, and the spot below his nose was chapped. In trilling Japanese he recited his own litany of complaints:

"What person with any class would ever want to hang these

miserable paintings in their house? They look custom-made for a motel in the sticks. It makes me sick people think *I* painted them. To put food on the table fifteen years ago, 'poor foreigners' bought bananas in Shimonoseki and sold them in Pusan. Today if you want money, the thing to be is a 'weird *gaijin*.' TV's full of them—flip to any channel, you'll see. I can hardly wait to quit this bullshit and become 'weird,' too. I can sing and dance. I'm strong and young and not bad in bed. I could use the yen."

"You're telling it to the wrong guy, " Kubi said.

Enrique was his name, and he was built like a middleweight boxer. He seemed pretty quick on the uptake, too. He'd been in Tokyo almost two years, his head deep in the Japanese language. His girlfriend was a model; naturally she spoke the language. He pulled out her picture to show Kubi. He lived off her, but she was sure he was going to score big one day soon. He hated the special treatment English-speaking foreigners got. Latins had rhythm; Latins knew how to live; Japanese could learn a thing or two from Latins; Japanese could learn to lighten up. After all, depression makes you tone deaf.

Which Kubi knew firsthand: When he was in the throes of depression, he couldn't dance a step.

Enter the Heart of Darkness and See the World

Every other day Kubi returned to Kamakura to massage Mrs. Amino's legs and report on his progress. And every day Mrs. Amino received a faxed message from Maiko in New York.

Maiko had also sent a photo of Matthew taken four years before. "So we're finally getting down to the real detective work," Mrs. Amino said. "Kubi, I want you to play the hardboiled detective, as if this were the movies. Walk around town, show people the photo, and ask them if they've ever seen him. You're no fool, so I'm sure you'll know where to go."

Biting back a few choice mutterings, Kubi said, "I'll get a fortune-teller to tell me where he is."

"While you're at it have him tell *your* future," Mrs. Amino retorted. "But make sure he's the kind who gives only good news. If you find one, I want to meet him."

Mrs. Amino would stop at nothing to find her son. The commander-in-chief of operations has to be sure of herself. Even bad dreams had to be interpreted to her advantage.

"Suppose your son's involved in something shady?" Kubi asked. "Could you turn a blind eye to that?"

As always, he couldn't resist pulling her leg while he massaged it. But Mrs. Amino, wrapped in her porcupinelike fur coat, had an answer ready:

"Don't forget I'm one of the idle rich," she said, very gently, "and if I have the resources to keep a mentally depressed monkey as a pet, I'm sure I can look after a son with a criminal record."

"You're calling me a mentally depressed monkey?"

"Well, what would you prefer? A pig with a persecution complex? Kubi, you missed your chance at a noble suicide, so why not go out and live? Discover reality. If that doesn't work out, I'll be more than happy to help you end it all." Mrs. Amino could act as his second. When he made a muddle of disemboweling himself, she would slice his head off but she'd leave it hanging by a thread. His head wouldn't hit the floor, it'd dangle loose, upside down on his chest, begging forgiveness.

To Kubi, Mrs. Amino's maliciousness was the crisp air of the high plains; it was more praise than scorn. He glanced around to be sure no one would see, then he buried his face in her bosom.

"Let *me* be your son!" he shouted.

Mrs. Amino's abuse was gratifying to Kubi. Sure, his self-respect went down the drain, but Mrs. Amino understood him. Anyway, there's always uncertainty in a master-slave relationship. Kubi had no idea what would become of him after Mrs. Amino freed him. Freed slaves begin life anew, full of hope—at least according to Jesus. In the real world, however, things didn't work out so nicely. Slaves take pride in their masters and don't mind some of the master's authority rubbing off.

In fact, Kubi was afraid of losing his master. Whenever it was that Matthew was located, Kubi would be set free. It occurred to him, finally, that this business of playing detective was training for that time. Of course, these neat analogies weren't quite right, especially since he wasn't really a slave.

But if not slave, then what was he? He had sold himself to escape his loans. But whether Kubi was son, husband, or secretary was up to Mrs. Amino; there was no contract that spelled out the details. And this, Kubi decided, he hated.

Best he check out the fortune-tellers after all.

At the station Kubi bounded up the stairs to catch a train just pulling in. He sat down to catch his breath, and as he did, childhood memories shot through the surface like dolphins.

When he was twelve, Kubi begged to see a *yuta* shamaness in the southern islands. He was so set on it, his father used his summer vacation to fly to Amami Oshima with his son. There Kubi spoke at length with three *yuta*. He wanted to learn about his past lives, and each shamaness provided him with a different answer.

The first *yuta* was the oldest, and her toothless mouth looked like the opening to the world beyond. What that mouth told Kubi was that in his previous life he was a blind Zen monk. The monk had first knocked on the gates of the temple at age thirteen, and for the next fifteen years underwent ascetic training under Master Reigan. Even when his parents were dying, the monk persisted in his training and did not return home. But enlightenment eluded him. After his master died, the monk took a lone pilgrimage through the provinces. He fell victim to plague, suffered from high fever, and collapsed alongside the road, where a samurai found him. He was carried to a dilapidated temple, where, after four days and four nights in deep sleep, the monk regained consciousness, only to find that never again would he see the light of this world. But he was happy to be blind, for in a dream he had finally gained enlightenment.

"Enter the heart of darkness, and you see the world." This is what he told the samurai who rescued him.

This temple was without a head priest, so the monk took the position. After that time, he was called Master Muyu—Master Sleepwalk.

The second *yuta*, as emaciated as a dried branch, was closer to Kubi's image of a poverty-stricken shamaness. In a raspy voice she revealed the crime Kubi had committed in his previous life.

Two hundred years before, Kubi murdered his wife when she got in the way of his rise to glory. He buried her body in a bamboo grove, where it remained. He spread the rumor that she'd been spirited away and managed to escape karmic retribution. He rose to become the retainer of a prominent feudal lord, and lived a long life, dying at age seventy. To atone for his crime, Kubi could never marry. It scared the pants off twelve-year-old Kubi.

The third *yuta* was fat and loud, and the few teeth she had were all gold. She radiated a calming energy, which made her so popular her home was always full of clients. Like patients at a dentist's office, clients wrote their names on a list at the door and waited their turn. Compared to this *yuta*, the other two shamanesses were destitute, weary, and not that healthy either, and they often turned people away. The third *yuta* picked up the slack.

Studying Kubi's face, she said:

"The karma from your previous life makes you fated always to be running away. This has its good side as well as its bad."

Perhaps because of her sonorous, booming voice, or her eyes brimming with confidence, the twelve-year-old Kubi believed that indeed that was his fate.

"In your past life you were a fugitive Heike warrior," the third *yuta* continued. "You fled from one mountain village to the next, the Genji pursuers always hot on your heels. But you survived and made your way to the Asian mainland. You married a Mongolian woman and fathered three sons, one of whom became a soldier of the Mongolian Empire during the reign of Kublai Khan. When the Mongols invaded Europe, this son fathered a child by an Italian woman. That child later became an interpreter for both the Mongols and the Europeans. The two sons who remained in Mongolia grew up and fell in love with the same woman. They quarreled, and the younger brother, who was bigger, ended up murdering the older brother. The woman they fought over, however, loved the older brother and was carrying his child. The younger brother took good care of the child, never knowing it was not his. And when this child grew up, he, too, became a soldier.

"By that child's time a powerful karma brought your spirit back to Japan. The Mongols had founded the great Yüan dynasty and were intent on conquering Japan. So the fugitive Heike warrior who had fled to Mongolia returned to his homeland in the spirit of his grandchild to attack it. A typhoon intervened, however, and this grandchild found himself washed ashore at Shimonoseki, barely escaping with his life. After this experience he became Japanese. He was your ancestor."

What a stormy adventure! In his previous life Kubi had become his own ancestor?

With three past lives to shoulder, Kubi spent the rest of that summer in a nightmare. Afraid to sleep, he stayed up late at night watching TV. The programming over, Kubi stared at the flickering test patterns on the screen, and in the TV picture tube he began to see his own past incarnations. He became frantic. This continued for three consecutive days, when, exhausted, he suffered a nervous breakdown before finally falling asleep.

Kubi's worried father took him to a psychiatrist who used hypnotism to rid Kubi of his fears. It's all a lie, the shrink told him, your being a murderer, a blind man, and a fugitive Heike warrior in your previous life. The idea of previous lives is a recidivist notion, a holdover from the pre-scientific age. You are the product of your father and mother, the shrink said, and before you were born you were like the air, invisible.

The hypnotism freed Kubi from his fears, but he was unable to forget the tales that the gold-toothed shamaness had spun. He believed that he really was fated to be on the run. Believing in karma is no different from believing in genetics, Kubi resolved, so he opted for the more concrete of the two—the *yuta's* story.

Either One Is Possible

But was there a fortune-teller in all Tokyo who radiated energy like that gold-toothed shamaness? An obnoxious street-corner fanatic wasn't enough. Nor was someone who happily told you what you wanted to hear. No, what Kubi wanted was a few words that would help point the way and give him some perspective on why he was doing what he was doing.

He began his search outside the east exit of Shinjuku Station, where a row of palm readers had set up business along the main street. A group of young women surrounded a middle-aged female fortune-teller. Wherever people gather a magnetic field is formed, and Kubi felt the pull.

The fortune-teller turned out to be Shinjuku Mama, who was pretty well known as a counselor of young girls. She sat at her candlelit table as these girls, lumps of worry, sobbed and nodded at her advice. Each session would end with Mama rising and patting the girls on their shoulders and spouting homilies like "Suffering now will help you in the future," or "People always start to hate life at your age," or "I've felt exactly the same way myself."

It was clear why Shinjuku Mama was so popular, but Kubi was too embarrassed to join the line himself with all those young girls standing there. Instead, he walked up to a fortune-teller sitting a few stalls away, alone and without clients.

"Can you predict something for me?" Kubi began. "I don't want just to be cheered up or anything either." Kubi's words were deliberately gruff so as to hide his discomfort. He sat on the folding stool and plopped his hand down on the table.

Stifling a yawn, the baby-faced fortune-teller put down the book he'd been reading. "What do you want me to predict?" he asked, his manner not quite inspiring confidence. In fact, the guy was the exact opposite of Shinjuku Mama.

"I'm looking for a person and I want to know if I'm going to find him. And if I'm going to find him, I want a clue about how I'm supposed to find him," Kubi began. Then realizing that the whereabouts of another person were not likely to be written in his palm, Kubi said, "What I mean is, please tell me what will happen to me in the near future."

The fortune-teller pulled out a computer keyboard from under his table. He asked Kubi his date of birth and punched the data in.

"A computerized fortune-teller, eh?" Kubi remarked.

As if he could predict Kubi's next question, the man explained, "I don't want people to get the wrong idea about me, so I'm out here looking like every other fortune-teller. I really will read your palm, though. Put your hand right here, please."

The man next pulled out a plastic board that was also attached to the keyboard. It seemed to be some kind of adaptor for inputting palm reading. The fortune-teller's gaze was directed down at his feet. Leaning over, Kubi saw the computer display set down on the pavement like some discarded junk.

"The program is called PRP," the man continued. "The Palm Reading Program. A guy I know at Berkeley sent it to me for this part-time job."

"Do you yourself know how to read palms?" Kubi asked.

"No, I just read the display."

Kubi was disappointed by the man's indifference, but the fortune-teller's hands were quick as they typed in the information he provided.

"You are confused at present." The fortune began with these words. Kubi decided to hear the man out, and nodded silently. Nothing could be more ridiculous than getting angry at a fortune-teller.

"A person will come to solve your confusion."

This was what Kubi'd been waiting to hear. Maybe this fortune-teller was OK, after all.

"You sure? When?"

"It's not good to rush things."

"So what *should* I do?" Kubi asked.

"Continue as you have been, don't think so deeply about things, and everything will work out."

"Is this person who will solve my confusion a man or a woman?"

"Either one is possible."

"When I meet that person, how will it change me?"

"You'll become free."

Kubi did not ask anything else. Fortune-tellers had their limits. Believe them too much and you turn into Macbeth.

Kubi paid his two thousand yen and hurried away. What he had to do now was wait.

Gas tank on the yacht empty, no wind at sea. OK, he thought, but I've got as much money as I need. This Matthew guy's nowhere in Tokyo. And I've been free all along.

That's Weird!

Kubi always carried the photo of Matthew/Masao inside his jacket pocket, but he never needed to take it out. The photo had become a poster glued to one wall of the living room in his brain. When he walked the streets of the city, drank coffee, had curry rice in a stand-up diner, the poster danced at the edge of his sight. Various Matthews, who seemed to resemble *the* Matthew, appeared and disappeared. Kubi followed each one a few dozen yards, just to be sure they weren't the one.

Kubi was convinced that Matthew didn't exist, even as he nurtured the hope that one day he'd turn around and there Matthew would be, right in front of him. Kubi had made the rounds of English-language and Japanese-language schools. He'd visited the editorial offices of the magazine Matthew once worked at. In each case, he came up empty-handed. Matthew remained, as before, a shadow in the shape of a person.

Of the fifty-some people Kubi talked with, though, two had known Matthew. One worked in the office of an English conversation school and had lived for a year in New York three years earlier. She and Matthew used to talk about life over there. Matthew knew the entire geography of Manhattan by heart, she said, and he wasn't too bad at figuring out the labyrinth of Tokyo either. In his dreams apparently, sometimes a back street in Greenwich Village and a part of Tokyo got jumbled together, and he'd find himself lost. Matthew had quit teaching at the school two years earlier. They'd talked twice since then, but he didn't say what he was doing now.

The other was a reporter for the same magazine Matthew had worked for. He had run into Matthew on the street a couple times in the last six months. The first time was in Shinjuku—Matthew was with the rock star Tetsuya Nishikaze, and he told the reporter with a laugh that Nishikaze had hired him as a "friend." The second time Matthew had bags under his eyes, was unshaven and gaunt. They'd exchanged just a few words. The reporter chuckled: Matthew looked like he was screwing too much.

So, thought Kubi, maybe Matthew really *did* exist. But tracing him was only getting more difficult. Matthew was beginning to look like a hustler or a henchman. Certainly, he was doing nothing respectable.

Suppose someone was looking for himself—Kubi, that is. An old girlfriend, say. After he gave up writing novels, Kubi's life had been less than ordinary. Boiling up a pot of coincidences, as he liked to put it, he'd ended up Mrs. Amino's human yo-yo. To track him down would be no mean feat. Matthew's life had been equally haphazard.

At that moment, Kubi felt an unexpected closeness to Matthew.

Two weeks after starting his detective stint, Kubi was sitting in one of his favorite restaurants, eating steamed *gyoza* and washing them down with Chinese wine. He was enjoying a pleasant absentmindedness when all at once a list of questions he wanted to ask Matthew popped into his woozy brain:

How many people have you slept with?

How many people do you meet in one day?

What kind of food do you like?

How many people do you hate so much that even killing them would be too good for them?

This morning, after you woke up, who did you call first?

What do you do when you're by yourself?

What's the biggest mistake you've ever made?

Have you ever met the devil?

What were you in your previous life?

Do you have any chronic illnesses?

Is there a song on your lips and the sun in your heart?

Kubi mulled these questions over, giving his own answers as he went along. Unlike him, Matthew was free to do as he pleased. Matthew wasn't paranoid like him. Nobody felt sorry for Matthew. Everybody liked Matthew. Matthew could sleep with anyone, and his cock would never let him down.

At the table next to Kubi sat a young couple flirting with each other. A university-aged boy was blowing into his girlfriend's ear. The girl, probably still in high school, wriggled and laughed hysterically and pounded him on his shoulder.

"How can you make such a joke?" she said.

"OK, OK, sorry," he answered. "To apologize, how 'bout I do this?" Staring seriously into the girl's eyes, he sent a wordless message to her, and then he stuck out his tongue and licked the tip of his nose.

"Now be serious," the girl said. "Are you going to marry me or not?"

At their age? Marriage? Apparently the boy had gotten the girl pregnant. The guy was good-looking enough, but his eyes flitted around like a fly. Maybe he knew how to please a girl, but when a decision had to be made he'd buzz off. The girl, on the other hand, seemed as calm as a Buddha on a lotus petal. Only her mouth was restless as she stuffed herself with one delicacy after another.

Kubi felt like he was peeping into an open bedroom. But to this young couple, he was as good as invisible.

"Stop stuffing yourself," the boy said.

"When I'm worried, I get hungry," the girl answered, pouting.

"Forget about eating. Let's go somewhere."

"I don't mind going with you," the girl said to her boyfriend, "but you've got to make a decision today. Before it's too late."

"OK, OK, I will, I will."

The girl set down her chopsticks and, closing her eyes, brought her face close to her boyfriend's lips. After a glance in Kubi's direction, and with a resigned look, he kissed her temple.

"Do you love me?" she asked.

"Umm—a lot."

"Then you have to tell me."

The girl's audacity set the boy back a bit. Kubi guessed the two had started out as pupil and tutor.

"I love you. That's why I want to go," the boy said and stood up. For a brief moment, the face of this boy—for whom the world might normally be a joke—seemed already etched with middle-aged exhaustion.

Kubi had the sudden urge to follow them. They were like a boring TV show he couldn't switch off. He had to find out how it ended.

Kubi rushed over to the cash register, but as luck would have it, he found himself behind a group of five people trying to figure out how much each owed. By the time he got out of the restaurant, the young couple was gone. Kubi wet a finger in his mouth and held it up to gauge which way the wind was blowing. And off he set walking downwind.

Plunging into the bowels of Kabuki-cho in pursuit, Kubi ended up at the fountain next to the Shinjuku Koma Theater. When he was a teenager, Kubi frequented the movie theaters and pubs here. He'd buy marijuana and take it home to smoke, a little at a time, getting all worked up over Beethoven's Grand Fugue.

Meandering through the crowds of young kids, their faces wistful, Kubi was struck by how superficial and timid they seemed. Born in Disneyland, raised in Harajuku, and nurtured on McDonald's—they were hanging out in this playground for the pubescent. They didn't have a lot of cash, but they knew how to make two thousand yen last till morning. Look innocent and latch onto some dirty old man—soon you'd be eating a good meal, having a few drinks, and heading for a Disneyland with a bed.

Dressed in jeans and polo shirt, linen sweater thrown over his shoulders, Kubi felt like an older brother to these kids. If a young girl wanted to talk, he wouldn't mind lending an ear. More than losing his wallet, what he feared was losing his sense of adventure. If a runaway wanted some fun, why he was just the middle-aged guy to give it to her.

He circled the fountain, but the young couple from the restaurant was nowhere in sight. What caught his attention instead was two girls, runaways probably, who were standing at the entrance to a video game center and carefully eyeing each passerby.

Kubi pretended to check his wristwatch as he walked into the game center. "What do you think we should do?" he overheard one of the girls saying. He slipped a thousand-yen note into the change machine and was collecting his ten one-hundred-yen coins when the two girls passed by. One had long hair and a tiny rump. She wore a knit dress and was a little pigeon-toed. The other was on the plump side and looked good in her culottes, though her stockings had a run.

The two girls wasted no time getting down to work. The plump one struck up a conversation with a young man in a navy blue suit. He was playing a game that required him to hold a machine gun.

"Excuse me. Can you tell us which direction the station's in? We're kind of lost."

The young man started to explain, but the girl's expression suggested she had something else in mind.

"What are you doing later?" she asked coyly. "We don't know Shinjuku very well. You wouldn't mind if we tagged along, would you?"

At that point, a friend of the young man came by. Negotiations were soon concluded, and the four departed.

Kubi was left standing alone, wondering if he'd lost in a game of musical chairs. He walked out of the game center and once again circled the fountain. He'd been locked out of Shinjuku, and he felt like sulking. He walked on when suddenly he was hit by the vision of a girl in a miniskirt and a black visored cap gliding past him. Kubi counted to four, then hung a U-turn and took off after her. He was in search of an aura, and this girl had it.

The girl's legs, wrapped in black stockings with a butterfly pattern, slid through the air. You don't see legs like those everyday, Kubi growled, his penis twitching. Karma had brought them together——those legs and his cock.

The legs headed at a fair clip down a street lined with love hotels, a section of the city where phony magnificence and bad taste were in a dead heat. Kubi couldn't believe she had legitimate business in a sleazy area like this, but he couldn't be certain, not having seen her face.

The girl's footsteps echoed louder and louder. Oh, to be stepped on by those high heels . . . Kubi quivered at the thought. He would cling tight to those calves! Such a feeling of . . . grace!

The girl slowed her pace and came to a halt. She glanced around, then turned and headed straight toward Kubi. He flinched for a second, thinking he'd been found out, but quickly recovered and stared into her face. Kubi grew tense. It was like he'd never seen a girl before, like he'd forgotten how to walk.

"Excuse me. Do you speak English?" the girl asked.

"*Mmmmmmay* I help you?" Kubi could only stutter. All this while he'd thought the girl was Japanese.

"I'm looking for a cheap hotel," she continued. "My friend told me there were a lot of small hotels around here. Could you recommend one to me?"

Scratching his temple, Kubi tried to explain in a hodgepodge of Japanese-laced English and hand gestures. "These are hotels for love," he told her. "You cannot go in by yourself. Once you go in, you cannot leave unless you check out."

"Wow!" the girl said. "Every hotel is only for couples who wanna make love? Weird! I wanna try it."

"What you mean?" Kubi's face grew unexpectedly serious before he pasted a smile back on. Oh, to touch those calves . . . This was the chance he wanted.

"I'm exhausted," the girl said. "I want some sleep. Why did I come here anyway? I don't know. It's all my friend's fault. She thought I was arriving tomorrow. She had to be somewhere tonight and all I've got is two thousand yen."

"I see. OK, let's go to hotel."

A weird sort of karma sprang up again between her private troubles and Kubi's obsession with her beautiful legs, a karma which lured the two of them in the direction of the Hotel Norwegian Wood. Beyond the automatic door with the shade drawn an electronic board listed vacancies and price. You pushed the button for the room you wanted. Looking for the cheapest as he scanned the rules and regulations, Kubi explained what kind of rooms were available.

In one you could sleep with a bunch of Mickey Mouse dolls, in another you could sing *karaoke*. One room was set up as a torture chamber, one had a surround stereophonic system and BodySonic bed, and one had a small swimming pool. One was set up like a church. And another had white sand strewn around.

"Which do you decide?" he asked.

The church.

As they rode the elevator to the fifth floor, the girl introduced herself. Her name was Samantha, she'd just arrived from San Francisco, her friend's apartment was in Shin-Okubo, and her luggage was in a locker at Shinjuku Station.

In church, Samantha removed her shoes, then immediately started to slide her stockings off. With those legs so close to him Kubi almost forgot to breathe. It was like it was his first time, and he couldn't look her straight in the eyes.

"I want to take a shower," Samantha said. "Why don't you stay for a couple of minutes."

"If you do not mind I massage your calves?"

"That's all? Such a gentleman," Samantha smiled.

Samantha, clad only in her underwear, disappeared into the bathroom, and before long there was the sound of running water.

Alone, Kubi surveyed the premises. The church was complete with a canopied bed. At the head of the bed was a plywood altar. Below the crucifix were two condoms, Kleenex, and a Bible. There were three buttons—one for the piped-in music, one for the bed vibrator, and one for a light that projected a stained-glass Pietà on to the canopy—so that Jesus and the Virgin Mary could peer down at the passion below. Man, Kubi said to himself, shaking his head, this is what you call *taste*.

"I'm so tired," Samantha groaned as she returned to the room, wearing a bathrobe and a towel around her hair. She sighed and plopped herself facedown on the bed.

Kubi gingerly reached out for the calves of his dreams. Touching them was like dipping his fingers in cool fondue. His fingers wandered from the back of her knees down to her ankles. Samantha giggled, her face deep in the pillow.

She must know I'm hard, Kubi realized, and quickly pulled his hands away as she turned and gazed at him. Her bathrobe fell open. She was a brunette, but really she was blonde. Kubi blushed, uncertain what to do next. Cupping her hands behind her head, she cooly awaited further developments.

"How much do you cost?" Kubi asked. His pants were getting so tight he had to figure out a way of easing the tension.

"I'm free. Because I like you."

"You mean you are not prostitute?" he said, surprised. "I am sorry. I did not know."

"That's OK. I knew you were following me. Why?"

"Because you are so beautiful," Kubi blurted out. Everything had been so simple. Boil up a potful of coincidences and that's what you get—her legs teasing his cock. Things work out that way sometimes. He stuck his hand out and shook her hand. "I am Kubi. I love you." And then he kissed her.

Kubi had never had sex like *that* before. Samantha sucked his cock with her beer-chilled mouth while he licked her clitoris with the tip of his beer-chilled tongue. Panting, she ordered him to suck her breasts, hard, to bite her shoulder. He parted her thick blonde bush and began drilling operations, as Samantha shoved her mouth against his, gasping. Air was forced out as they pressed their stomachs together. Their bodies dripped with sweat, and their hot breath made their cheeks glow. Her breasts, tan line visible, flattened and spread out against Kubi's chest.

Samantha then draped her legs over Kubi's shoulders, and he licked, bit, and caressed them, until the lower half of his body turned to gel and he felt his ejaculation being sucked into her. If something doesn't hold me down, she squealed, I'm going to float off into space, and she clung to him feverishly even after he'd come. His semen ran down her thighs, soaked into the sheet, and hardened into shards of transparent mica.

Kubi sat silently, drinking beer, as Samantha rattled on. Her words had that special rhythm you find only in young California girls.

"You're the first Japanese man I've ever slept with," she said. "With you it was gentle, sort of weird. Not like with Terry. He's the best. Oh, Terry, I'm so sorry. But you looked so sad, Kubi. But Terry's Terry, you know. Always flirting. He says he'll fall apart without me, but I know better. He didn't want me to come to Tokyo. He said Japanese men were perverts and who knows what could happen to me. But this hotel's pretty nice. There aren't any places like this in San Francisco. Tokyo lovers are lucky. Terry and I always have to do it at home when our parents aren't around. But I like doing it in wide open spaces. We do it in Golden Gate Park sometimes. Car sex I can live without. One time we were really getting into it and the car started to roll forward. The parking brake wasn't set. Terry grabbed the steering wheel and got the car to stop by crashing into a pile of garbage. God, I'm sleepy. What a weird night. I wonder what'll happen tomorrow."

What indeed, Kubi thought. He was exhausted, too, and soon fell fast asleep.

The next morning Kubi woke to a door shutting; Samantha had just left. He couldn't very well chase after her in the nude, so he let her go. She'd left a short note on the table:

So long. And thanks for investing ¥20,000 in me.
Samantha

That was precisely the amount missing from his wallet, but Kubi found he wasn't upset. If you considered it philanthropy for a runaway, he thought, there was nothing odd about it. He had mortgaged his life to pay his debts only to be playing Daddy Warbucks to some passing waif. But it wasn't a bad feeling—really.

In the old days when he was dreaming up his ship of fools, Kubi had secreted more hormones than he needed, and he got so horny he couldn't stand it. There was no time to be choosy about a partner, so he'd get a call girl or pick up somebody he passed on the street. Any. girl friendly enough to talk to him would soon find herself in bed with him, naked and limp with pleasure. Ah, spraying his sperm around—that was the Kubi of old.

And Samantha had revived that confidence he thought was gone forever.

10

Raphael

WEDNESDAY:

My energy meter had just about hit zero, so I took a few deep snorts from the portable oxygen inhaler I bought at Tokyu Hands and downed a handful of vitamins. Time to rebuild myself in a dream.

THURSDAY:

I've definitely caught a cold. Temperature 39°C. I felt like I died four times. I dreamed I was licked to death by a bunch of frogs, and jumped out of bed. I feel so lonely I really do want to die.

FRIDAY:

I cancelled all three jobs I had for today. And ordered out for some eel.

SATURDAY:

A phone call from Raphael. He said he saw me in his dream and I looked so wasted I couldn't even stand up. He rode a Shinkansen bullet train to the depths of the Amazon to gather herbal medicines.

A Beauty in Male Attire

What I've wanted most since I came to Tokyo is a friend whose dreams I could visit, and who could visit mine. A couple of friends appeared in my dreams, but a mental gap still kept us apart. Communicating through dreams was beyond our grasp. The most these friends could do was report back to me how I'd been in their dream the night before, or how they'd dreamed we had sex. I wanted something more intimate.

I wanted the kind of relationship where we play the lead role in each other's dreams, exchange prophecies, give each other advice. The kind of relationship where we travel freely back and forth between reality and dream.

What I wanted was another Penelope. No matter how far away from me she is, we still can send signals through our dreams. We may be apart, but we'll never be strangers again.

The closest I've come to a true dream friend since coming to Tokyo is Raphael Zacs.

The first time I met Raphael was two years ago, on a wintry day. The kind of day when you could be sure it was going to snow. I couldn't get a taxi because of the weather, and wound up drinking till late in a gay bar. That's where I met him.

My life was a real mess then. Just like the economy has its up and down cycles, my life goes through its own booms and busts. Right now it's pulling out of recession and heading for better times, but back then I was in the middle of the Great Depression. I was working at several jobs simultaneously, and my unemployment rate had topped 50 percent. I was desperate enough to consider working at a gay bar, and for several days I'd been making the rounds, checking them out. Raphael was one of the other customers. We sat at the L-shaped counter. There were others at the bar, but Raphael kept his eyes fixed on me and the bartender.

"Two handsome guys like you here—must be my lucky day,"
the bartender grinned.

He was one of those muscular guys, at least six-foot-three,
maybe 200 pounds. He challenged Raphael and me to an arm-
wrestling match. If he lost, he'd eat our bill for the evening. If
he won, we had to let him kiss us. I knew I didn't stand a chance,
even before we started. I was down in a flash, and he gave me a
good wet one. Raphael wasn't much larger than me, but he put
up a hell of a fight, his face turning bright red as he held out for
over a minute. But in the end he lost, too.

"Such *sweet* lips you guys have!"

The bartender couldn't have been happier. Next Raphael and
I were supposed to arm wrestle, and we were trying to figure
out what the bet should be. At first we thought we'd bet our
jackets, but, egged on by others at the bar, the thing started to
get out of hand. The loser has to strip completely, or the loser
has to let the winner tickle him as much as he wants. Nope, that
wasn't enough. It was finally decided that the loser would have
to spend one whole day as the winner's slave.

I thought I was stronger than Raphael, but after my match
with the bartender I wasn't so sure. But it was over before I
knew it: For the next twenty-four hours Raphael was to be my
slave.

Raphael's Japanese was charming and good, but mine was
better. So in a way I guess it made sense that he was the slave
and me the master.

After we left the gay bar, Raphael did his best to keep his end
of the bargain, though it was supposed to be a joke. Being a
slave for even one day is pretty embarrassing. I know how it
feels because most of my jobs have me playing if not slave then
something close to it. I couldn't figure out what kind of orders
to give him.

In this case, it was the slave who was superior to the master,
since Raphael ended up teaching me how to act. I was not supposed to lift a finger. We wandered around silent, snowy Shin-

juku until past four in the morning, Raphael brushing the snow off my shoulders, reminding me to watch my step, and opening the doors to the other bars we stopped in. At each bar he listened happily as I babbled on about everything from recent dreams I'd had to the story of my life. He was an easy person to talk to—a lot like Mikainaito. Warming to the task, I ended up the good-for-nothing hero of every tale I spun. By the time I stopped talking it was past five A.M., and I was so plastered I really *did* need his help. That's how relaxed he made me feel.

Raphael got us on the third train of the morning and delivered us safely to my apartment. Despite my personal recession, I was still living in a nice two-room place on the ninth floor of an expensive building, a place I'd rented in my boom days. I was planning to pick a sunny day the following month to move out.

I slept in my own bed, and Raphael sacked out in a sleeping bag. I woke up past noon to the smell of toast and coffee, but after I crawled out of bed I felt like my dream had gone into a second feature. My breath was taken away, so beautiful was the vision that stood before me. Here was a beauty woman in male attire. Wait a second—here was a gay man looking fabulous in women's clothes. At a time like this, it wasn't important which. Raphael was absolutely gorgeous.

When I was a teenager, in my fantasies about marrying Penelope, I imagined something like the scene before me now. Penelope posing as the housewife pouring out coffee. We'd have only one cup, which we'd take turns drinking from.

So with this memory of Penelope, and with my mouth agape, I looked more carefully at the picture Raphael cut. Bright red-and-white-check apron over black tights, pink lipstick, light purple eyeshadow, marine blue mascara, and foundation that couldn't quite hide the traces of his beard—all blended together very weirdly, particularly under the doleful influence of my hangover.

"Good morning, my dear Matthew," Raphael greeted me with a little curtsy like a prima donna taking a curtain call.

My knees threatened to give out on me on the spot. His little joke really knocked me out, and I said the first thing that popped into mind: "Why don't we live together!"

If he lived with me and shared the rent, I wouldn't have to move. But there was more to it than that. I had the clear sense that if anyone could pull me out of my recession, Raphael was the one. Not just in the economic sense either. I knew his friendship would help me in all kinds of ways. It was his eyes that told me that. And I trusted my hunches. The eyes tell more than the mouth, and Raphael's eyes were a lot more eloquent than his Japanese.

We cooked a *nabe* stew that day, joking and jabbing at each other as we ate. Raphael told me his life story. He spoke in English about his life up to his arrival in Tokyo, then switched to Japanese. His stories had me spellbound, and he had a million of them. I couldn't possibly retell the tales he told me, but there was one that really impressed me:

Ever since he was twelve or thirteen and got interested in sex, Raphael knew what type of person he was interested in.

"I love Oriental men," he said. "I don't know why. I don't think I'm hung up on exoticism. It's a totally physical thing."

His story started in August 1970, in New York. Raphael, shy and friendless, was a big fan of chamber music. During summer vacation he'd check out the listings in *The New York Times* and *The New Yorker* for free concerts, and then he'd go hear the music in the square in front of the Met or the garden at MOMA or go to the chamber music series Juilliard students put on. You'd think there couldn't be more than one kid in New York who'd attend three free concerts back to back in a single day. But in actual fact there was: Raphael and another boy Raphael spotted for the first time in the garden at MOMA. After that Raphael often caught sight of the boy at concerts, and at each event Raphael would always look to see if he was there.

One day Raphael was at a chamber orchestra concert given on a special stage at Lincoln Center, but he did not see the other boy. During intermission he combed the entire area for him. It turned out the boy was doing exactly the same thing, and when they saw each other, they shook hands and introduced themselves like it was the most natural thing in the world. The boy was a second-generation Chinese named Peter Lin. His father ran a movie theater in Chinatown, and his family seemed to be fairly well off. Peter studied the violin and kung fu and wanted to be a composer.

Since Raphael was little, his parents had insisted that he grow up to be a lawyer, doctor, or musician, so, at the least, what the two boys had in common was chamber music. What they were really looking for, however, was someone they could open up to about the urges swelling within them. Raphael had no interest in girls. He was pretty certain he was gay, but he needed someone else in order to know for sure.

The two boys became fast friends. The following week, alone in the shower after they'd gone swimming, they kissed. Neither of them initiated the act—it was more a magnetism that drew them together.

They spent almost all their free time together; they compared their skin complexion, noting the difference in color and texture. Because of kung fu, Peter's body was taut and firm. His movements were agile, and the shy smile that grazed his boyish face from time to time sent shivers up and down Raphael's spine. But they refrained from having sex with each other. It was fun enough to enjoy a cultural encounter, to grow more aware of their Chinese and Jewish backgrounds.

But a year and a half later, the necessary evil of youth was upon them. Peter's family was moving to San Francisco, Peter of course was going with them, it was time to say goodbye. As their farewell gesture—and as a way to remember their love for each other—the two boys decided to spend the night together. So in a twin room of a cheap, twenty-dollar-a-night hotel in Philadelphia, Peter and Raphael tasted the delights of sex for the first time in their lives.

A year and a half later, Raphael discovered another beautiful Oriental body, this time on the movie screen—Bruce Lee. In Raphael's mind, Bruce Lee and Peter Lin fused into one image, and ever since then the only men Raphael approached were Oriental.

Raphael did a little kung fu imitation, and added: "I like them because they're strong. White people get beat up too easily. Only Orientals are welcome in my bed."

We talked far into the night. Raphael remembered everything I'd rattled on about in my drunken stupor. We agreed it was strange we'd never run across each other in New York. Being in Tokyo had made Raphael more aware than ever of the New York inside him, and I knew what he meant. If it weren't for New York, we'd never be leading the kind of lives we were. We were different types, but both of us were messenger boys fashioned by the Big Apple.

For example, Raphael had met a Chinese boy and discovered he was gay, in the same way that Katagiri's teachings and my attempts to win Penelope had opened my eyes to who I really am—a rental child, a professional friend. Just as Raphael had joined the gay community in New York and found his mission in life, through being a rental child I'd learned my own way of living in the world. Raphael and I were on the same wavelength. And now we were friends.

Raphael and I found out we were leading the same kind of lives. A gay man who was hot for Oriental men and a messenger of dreams. We wandered in and out of people's lives, constructed pipelines, and fed into other minds with conversation and sex.

A little after one o'clock in the morning, Raphael challenged me to an arm-wrestling match. We bet the same thing as the night before—that the loser would be slave to the winner and do anything he was commanded to.

It was no contest.

"Don't tell me you lost on purpose last night," I said.

He held my hand and smiled, "I wanted to seduce you."

I'd been had. Following my master's orders, I started to take off my clothes.

After I met Raphael, my luck started to turn around. The telephone started ringing off the hook with more jobs than I could handle. People wanted me to interpret their dreams, they wanted me for long or short terms as a lover, they were willing to pay big for English lessons, there was even an offer to accompany someone on a trip to Africa. They were all jobs that put my talents to good use. Some of them Raphael had set me on to. The spider web of contacts he'd spun over Tokyo was alive and well. The gay network is nothing to look down on.

Raphael and I called each other to check in every once in a while, but we didn't see each other very often. We did talk about living together, but seeing as how our minds were already linked, what was the point? We promised to meet at least once every six months, and that if one of us got into a jam, we could depend on the other. Raphael visits my dreams all the time. And Mikainaito reports that Raphael's dreams aren't a bad place at all to hang out.

Sometimes the illusion hits me that I've known Raphael all my life. Where in the world does this nostalgia come from?

11

The Tale of the Heike; Taro Urashima's View of History

"Now there's a Heike face if I ever saw one!"

Kubi was seated on a bench in Miyashita Park in Shibuya, sipping a beer and reading a sports paper. He glanced up from an article about the Hawaiian sumo wrestler Konishiki's win over Chiyonofuji and found himself staring at a shady-looking, middle-aged bum.

"Heike?" Kubi asked. "You mean the Heike that the Genji destroyed?"

"You know of any other?"

"Who are you anyway?"

"Miyashita Park's own Taro Urashima. Taro Miyashita for short."

Kubi, who had nothing better to do, decided to go along with the joke and offered the bum his can of beer. The bum accepted it with pleasure and settled in alongside Kubi on the park bench. He was silent for a while, watching the wind blow through the trees, tuning in to the sounds around him. He took a slug of the beer and then stared so intently at Kubi's face you'd think he was about to sketch it.

"Yep," he said. "The more I look at you, the more Heike you look."

"What are you talking about? What are you—some sort of shaman?"

"I am a hermit-wizard, I think."

Hermit-wizard—the word called to mind the Akutagawa story "Toshishun," where a young Chinese man is tested by a wizard deep in the mountains. Kubi imagined a hermit exactly like Yoda in *Star Wars*. "If you're a hermit-wizard," Kubi said, "I suppose you can fly and make yourself invisible?"

A smile came to Taro Urashima's lips as he tipped back more beer. "Bums are a species of invisible men. Nobody notices us, right? And flying is a cinch. My spirit takes the shape of a gourd and zips off all over the place. But if you want to see the body fly, you should try leaping off a skyscraper. I guarantee you'll fly!"

The bum wasn't so dumb.

Kubi changed gears to tone down his cynicism and offered him a cigarette.

Smoke curled out of the bum's nose as he spoke. His voice was throaty: "Imagine—two descendants of the Heike running across each other like this. It must be karma or something."

Karma? To Kubi, the whole thing was spooky. First that *yuta* in Amami talking about him being a fugitive Heike in a previous life—now this bum saying pretty much the same thing.

"What is a Heike face supposed to look like?" Kubi asked.

"Our faces are completely different, but there is one thing in common. Neither has a nationality."

"What do you mean, they don't have a nationality?"

"I bet people often don't think you're Japanese, right? You have the kind of face that has all sorts of races mixed in."

Come to think of it, . . . Kubi knew he was being taken in by the bum's glibness, but there *was* some truth to what he was saying. When he traveled the Silk Road through central Asia, people thought he was an Uzbek, and when he was in Mongolia they thought he was from Shanghai. When he was in Shanghai, a student from Tibet addressed him in Tibetan. In New York people thought he was Mexican and spoke to him in Spanish, and in Berlin people were positive he was a Turk.

"In a Eurasian face," Taro Urashima went on, "you can always make out the two different races, but a face without a nationality isn't so clear-cut."

"OK, but what's the connection between a face without a nationality and a Heike face?"

"Fair question," Taro Urashima answered. "As you know, the Heike were destroyed 800 years ago, but don't for a second believe that every single Heike was wiped out. They—*our* ancestors, that is—became criminals and merchants, farmers and hunters; some of them even became retainers of the Genji or the Hojo clan, the ones who held the real power. That's how they survived. To say they were all exterminated is a bald-faced lie. History is a fiction that cares only about appearances. 'The Heike were destroyed'—that's what they want you to believe. And actually it was better for the Heike who survived that people believed it. That way they weren't bothered and could live in peace. Naturally, survivors of the Heike never opened their mouths about their real identity. They disguised and transformed themselves—that's how they survived."

"Eight hundred years ago, huh? So what number generation would the two of us be?"

"About the thirtieth, I guess," Taro Urashima replied.

"Well, to tell you the truth, an Amami shamaness once told me that in a previous life I was a Heike fugitive," Kubi said, and proceeded to recount the story the *yuta* had told him.

"Very interesting," Taro Urashima said, "but that's the way it should be. At the battle of Dannoura, the Heike sank with the seaweed, but they didn't all end up as crabs, which people like to believe are the angry ghosts of the clan. No, the Heike who died were reincarnated as many things. And the Heike who survived were reborn, too. That was their fate. The Heike weren't destroyed; they were reborn."

Taro Urashima repeated the last line several times as if driving home a point: He was proud to be a Heike. This pride was infectious, and Kubi himself grew excited, carried away by the prospect of solving the crazy riddle of his previous life.

"You're a very perceptive person," Taro Urashima said, "and, I tell you, that's rare. If you can't find someone to understand you, the world can get pretty lonely. Hey, what do you say we move along? Looks like rain." He finished off the remaining drops of beer and motioned to Kubi to come along.

But hadn't the weather report said sun going to clouds? Oh well, by Kubi's watch it was five o'clock. Any minute now, Tokyo would be jammed with a mass of angry faces elbowing each other out of the way. The streets get so violent that a tourist who didn't know better would think a revolution had broken out. But politics is the last thing on anybody's mind. Work lets out at five, and that's when the pubs open.

Kubi followed Taro Urashima into a bar on the fifth floor of a building in Dogenzaka. It had the name of Kachikachi Yama, catered to a mostly youngish crowd, and it was Taro Urashima's favorite pub. They toasted each other over a couple of beers, and then, as they snacked on *nikomi* stew, Taro Urashima told Kubi the following story: Kubi felt like he was listening to a sermon on board a ship.

There are all types of Japanese, Taro Urashima began, but 90 percent of them are peasant stock. Once in a great while, you run across a Heike. Before their defeat, the Heike commanded all the strategic routes along the Inland Sea. They were the Japanese version of Venetian merchants who built this enormous network for trade. Hermes, the god of commerce, was their guardian deity, and their plan was to create a commercial nation with Japanese spread throughout the world. But the Heike hopes were crushed by a race of farmers and the special malice found in communities bound together by rice cultivation. If the Heike dream of a commercial nation had been successful, who knows—the Japanese might have ended up like the Jews or the overseas Chinese with a network spread all over the globe.

Taro Urashima was really packing the food and drink away. Baked potatoes, deep-fried loach, tomato salad, octopus sashimi—he ordered one after another and washed all of it down with beer and sake. Everything he ingested was mixed into a stew in his belly and coughed back up as these tales he spun.

"Like I said, as far as the Heike were concerned," Taro Urashima went on, "Japan disappeared eight hundred years ago. The sea has been their home ever since. Like the Flying Dutchman. In China there was a group of people known as Chinese Jews. They were revolutionaries, scholars, doctors, capitalists, actors, activists. Whether they really had Jewish blood in them or not I don't know, but they were active and brilliant as Jews are, so I guess bloodline didn't matter—you could say they were Jewish. But the Heike were more like Chinese commoners. They were descended from the Emperor Kammu's line and there wasn't a drop of Jewish blood in them, you can be sure of that. But they were Jewish all the same. Do you understand what I'm saying?"

"I think so," Kubi replied. "I—yes, I understand exactly what you're saying."

Taro Urashima's words were like a meat cleaver pounding, and Kubi nodded, entranced by the rhythm.

"I have a dream that the Heike will unite again," Taro went on. "The problem is the Heike, unlike the Jews, have no sense of identity. Even if a person is a Heike descendant or a Heike reincarnated into something else, it's hard for him to believe that's what he is. That's pretty sad, don't you think? But I guess it stands to reason—the Heike have been hiding their identity for so long that some Heike brothers are content being peasants. But my point is this: It is the fate of the Heike to move about freely in the information network of Tokyo. Descendants of the Heike must understand this before any dialogue can exist between them."

Taro Urashima laid his chopsticks down and loosened his belt. Kubi noticed for the first time that he had gray eyes. The eyes of a man whose heart is a desert.

"Taro," Kubi asked, "when did you realize you were a Heike? You're just a bum, aren't you?"

Taro Urashima laughed. He gazed out the window. The darkness of evening was pasted against the glass, reflecting their two faces clearly. A few seconds later their floating faces were wet with rain. Rain, yes, rain, after all.

"Do you remember the summer of 1977?" Taro Urashima asked. "When it rained for twenty-two straight days?"

Yes, Kubi remembered that summer. It was the summer that his mania worsened, driving him into depression. He was having an affair with a married woman. Or to be more precise, he was having an affair with this particular married woman whose legs he was obsessed with. Keiko was her name. She had been a sprinter in high school, and she would visit Kubi on her way home from shopping—a little adventure in a humdrum life. After sex she would put her shopping bag into the basket of her bike and pedal home, having sucked up Kubi's rootless energy like a vampire. But day after day of rain, the voice of the housewife droning on combined with the twisted pride of a novelist whose work didn't sell was all he needed to plunge into depression.

"I wasn't in Japan then," Taro Urashima said. "I was training to be a mountain ascetic. I've never told anybody this, but I was once a member of the Japanese Red Army. One faction of the Red Army is made up of Heike descendants. I was in the international section. I wanted to import a revolutionary army from either South America or the Middle East. Japanese can't lead a revolution by themselves even if they wanted to, so I was going to rely on professionals. But my comrades were convinced they could 'transform Japan' themselves. I was pretty carefree about the whole thing. Who knew what would happen to the Red Army. Or Japan for that matter. I never imagined we'd end up on the side of the Palestinians, though I did want to be friends with them. I'm a dyed-in-the-wool Heike, so I can't think about people in units such as race or nation. All I can think about is myself. So just before the Asama Sanso Incident—you know, the business where the Red Army shot it out with the police—I split and went to New York. Then I went to Central America and then I went to the Middle East and then I settled down in India. And this was when an oracle in a dream told me I was a descendant of the Heike. I don't really understand it myself."

Taro Urashima tapped the back of his head and laughed up-roariously. He'd worked up quite a sweat over his own spiel.

"Japan is so rich now," he continued, "but you know, they're all serfs, from top to bottom. No need to distinguish rich from poor. They're all serfs. My mission is to pull a few Heike descendants from out of the mob of peasants. I'm really happy we met. It was worth staking out Miyashita Park."

Everything seems so clear now, Kubi thought. There was no need to agonize. Taro Urashima had used his intuition to dig up descendants of the Heike; Kubi would do the same thing—for different purposes, of course. Nor would he have to focus his energies on finding Matthew. Matthew was faceless. With the help of Taro, he could produce an up-and-coming Heike descendant and offer him to Mrs. Amino as her long lost son. She wouldn't know the difference. Everything was an act anyway. The reunion of mother and child separated for twenty-five years—talk about dramatic!

"Taro," Kubi said, "I'll be in touch soon. I need your help. I want you to introduce me to some fellow descendants of the Heike." He wrote Mrs. Amino's Kamakura address and phone number on a book of matches and handed it over to Taro together with a ten-thousand-yen note.

"Whenever you feel like it," Kubi said, "give me a call."

Taro Urashima frowned when he saw the address. He made a few nasty comments about the Genji, who, after all, had had their headquarters in Kamakura. But he soon calmed down and grinned.

Taro Urashima gave Kubi his number, too. Which turned out to be the number of the pay phone in Miyashita Park.

12

A Gentle Heretic; It's No Good to Suffer Alone

For Kubi, Samantha was Lady Luck herself, Taro Urashima the Mountain Sage. Kubi was on a roll. On the battlefield things might be different, but here on the streets luck isn't something you save up. You use it or you lose it.

He decided to stretch it. First, at the pachinko parlors and then at the race track. He was in the red for forty thousand yen before he knew what hit him. Luck had its preferences. He spent the next two days rethinking his luck, and on the third day it came to him. He would:

Follow someone—anyone!

In a flash, Kubi was a changed man. No longer a half-baked detective on a mission for Mrs. Amino, he became a salesman minus the wares, with a salesman's impeccable manners and friendly smile. One night with Samantha had turned Tokyo into Hamelin, with Pied Pipers strolling down the streets, Kubi a rat trailing behind.

Every day he followed ten people—age, sex, nationality, and appearance irrelevant. The sound of the flute—that aura—was all that mattered. Like a moth drawn to a light, a cockroach to leftover food, Kubi leaped after people who gave off that primal energy. Who knows—in the next moment a catch like Samantha might materialize in an alley. That possibility put spring into Kubi's stride. He was on a runway, ready to soar up over the valley of depression. He would fly from the Ginza, where he was, and land in Roppongi. But he settled on walking to Shinbashi, where he took a leak in a pachinko parlor; then he started chasing a bus to Shibuya.

Once he actually got his legs moving, however, Kubi's sides began to ache. He could barely lift his feet off the ground. The only running his body knew was running from one bar to the next. True, his house arrest by his rheumatic patron could also be blamed. He wasn't, in any case, ready to be an object of derision for anyone looking on, so at Toranomon Kubi ground to a halt.

It was already past 8:30 in the evening. The black Porsche that he'd passed a bit before was inching its way through the snarl of traffic, threatening to overtake him. But the light at the intersection turned red, and the car had to stop. Kubi was the tortoise to the Porsche's Achilles. Yo! Achilles!

Kubi began a slow trot. When the light changed, he stuck out his thumb. But the Porsche, its engine revved up in irritation, zipped by him before having to stop in traffic again fifty meters down the road.

An empty taxi came by, and Kubi clammered aboard. "Follow that Porsche," he told the driver.

"Are you a detective, sir?"

The driver had a bald spot like a Franciscan friar and an imperturbable voice to match. Kubi slipped him a five-thousand-yen note and told him to keep about a hundred meters behind his quarry.

"Thank you, sir, but I'm afraid it will be difficult today," the driver said. "It's Friday, and you know how traffic in Roppongi can be."

"He's going to Shinjuku," Kubi muttered, very hard-boiled.

It was a hunch, but sure enough the Porsche passed from Tameike to Yotsuya, then sped down Yasukuni Avenue in the direction of Shinjuku.

"Detective, what crime did the suspect perpetrate?"

"He ignored me."

"I beg your pardon?"

At the traffic light before Hanazono Shrine, the Porsche was stopped at a red light. Kubi asked the driver to speed up and pull off ahead.

He jumped out of the taxi, and when the traffic light turned green again, he was ready: waiting for the Porsche with both thumbs stuck out. It hadn't occurred to him that the Porsche might be *yakuza*. But it wouldn't have mattered even if it were—Achilles passed him by stonefaced.

Hey! Kubi wanted to yell. There's nothing ahead. It's the edge of a cliff! The end of the world! Achilles! Come back!!

Kubi had a sinking, hollow feeling. He was also starved, but he didn't want to eat alone. So, instead, he plunged into the sea of people. He felt like he was walking on a ship, or a sand dune. The air was damp, like near the ocean, stinging his lungs with each breath. His chest was heavy, but from the waist down he was light as styrofoam, and he staggered as he felt himself pulled along. The way you feel when you're out of shape. Kubi couldn't care less where his feet took him; before too long he'd know where he was going.

Faces, FACES, *faces*—all of them unhappy. Kubi decided that he would check the throats of each passerby for vampire teeth marks. Anybody whose throat had been bitten would be his partner for dinner.

"Got a match?"

It was a man's voice from behind, and it startled him. Instinctively Kubi grabbed his head in his hands and assumed a defensive, diagonal stance, as if he were taking on an assailant.

"How about a lighter?" the man tried again.

His skin was brightly lit by the neon sign of a bar. He was Caucasian. But what struck Kubi more was how the man's eyes sparkled, and the way he held himself.

"Are you alone?" Kubi asked in English, thinking, even as he uttered the words, what difference did it make. Kubi offered him his lighter. The man brought his face to the flame.

"Yes, I am."

"Do you speak Japanese?"

"Uh-huh," Raphael said, switching to Kubi's language. "I don't have anything to do right now, and I wondered if you wouldn't mind me joining you? You seem like you have time on your hands, too."

Kubi had been looking at people in front of himself; it had never occurred to him to look *behind*. Ironic how a person trying to follow someone should be followed himself. But what the hell—hanging out with this handsome white guy couldn't do any harm. Kubi suggested dinner. He didn't even ask the guy's name. Everything happened so fast.

They popped inside a bar nearby, checked out the menu written on the plastic board, ordered one of everything, and clinked beer mugs. The fellow's name, it turned out, was Raphael Zacs.

When the conversation lagged, Kubi took over. He told Raphael the story of his life: his hibernation, his success, his boredom, his work stoppage, his megalomania, the tanker of his dreams, his failure, his debt, his buy-out, his depression, his slavery to the rich widow.

Of all the above, Raphael wanted to know about the tanker, so Kubi started again. He told Raphael the fantasy of his floating stateless city, his gigantic ship of fools. "On sunny days people on shore would see this mirage on the horizon. At night, the mirage would glow, like Tokyo itself at sea. The sky would be filled with fireworks. Steadily, the mirage would approach the shore and someone would say, 'Hey, let's get on board!'"

Raphael's face betrayed no humor as he listened to this fairy tale. He sucked on his little finger, lost in thought, and finally said, "Very interesting. It'd be cheaper than a space shuttle. Sounds good to me."

Encouraged, Kubi went on: "On that mirage, there would be a university, a bank, a casino, a place to worship. A pasture and rice fields, too—not too big, of course—and a heliport and a dock. Anybody could come on board, anybody could leave."

"Like Noah's ark, huh? Noah's Ark, Inc."

"Once things get going, it'll turn a profit. At least according to my calculations."

"Where's the tanker now?" Raphael asked.

Munching on conger eels, Kubi thought: Where the hell *was* the tanker? "If it's still around, it's somewhere outside Tokyo Bay, waiting for its place in the *Guinness Book of Records* as the world's biggest piece of garbage. It costs too much to salvage, and it's not worth sinking."

"If I met you three years ago," Raphael said, "I could have helped with this project."

Well, you couldn't ask for a more considerate guy than Raphael. Raphael also never let Kubi's glass go empty. When Kubi dropped his chopsticks, Raphael asked the waiter to bring a new pair; he even pulled them apart for Kubi. And when the yakitori came, he suggested that Kubi have some first.

"You eat, too," Kubi urged.

Raphael, his eyes fixed on Kubi, smiled without showing his teeth.

Kubi, not knowing where to look, turned to the plate of food before him.

Suddenly the earth shook. It was an earthquake, and Raphael was as shaken as if the quake had taken place inside his own body. He grabbed Kubi's arm and covered his head. The shaking stopped soon enough. It wasn't the Big One.

"If a little quake like that scares you," Kubi smiled, "you won't last long on board a tanker."

Raphael didn't want even to consider the idea that the earth might tremble. And he was not amused when Kubi noted that with continents floating on a layer of magma like tankers on the sea, it'd be strange if they *didn't* quiver every now and then.

"So," Kubi said, "what are you doing in Tokyo anyway?"

Raphael's eyes roved over Kubi's face. "Well, I'm gay," he answered.

"I see . . ."

Now that he mentioned it, it seemed pretty obvious.

"Were you scared of AIDS? Is that why you came running to Tokyo?" Kubi asked.

A malicious question, perhaps, but it didn't faze Raphael.

"I don't have AIDS," he replied. "And I can prove it."

"No need for that. Your word's good enough for me."

Raphael sniffed twice and shook his head.

"Do you hate gay men? Do you want to back away?"

"No, I think you're a very nice person," Kubi replied.

"Thank you."

Kubi placed his hand on Raphael's shoulder as Raphael looked away.

"So why are you here?" Kubi asked. "You have to be in Tokyo for a reason."

"If you want to know the truth, I guess I like Oriental men. Especially handsome Oriental men. I don't know why. I don't even know why I approached you—you're not that good looking . . ."

"*Thanks.*"

"But there is something about you. That's why I spoke to you. Anyway, I came to Tokyo because in New York the most talented artists and cultural leaders of the future are dying of AIDS, one after the other. I've lost three friends already. At this rate, gay men in New York are going to be extinct, and culture will disappear. Before that happens I decided the thing to do would be to move to a new world and keep gay culture going. Like when the Jews escaped from Egypt. The Japanese are rolling in money, and I want to show them how to put it to good use. Tokyo would be the second gay Babylon. Gay men would bring love to Tokyo."

No doubt Raphael had repeated the same message many times as he walked the streets in search of sponsors.

"AIDS is turning history backwards," he continued. "If you want to create culture, people have to mix together freely. But AIDS attacks the source of creativity. A cure needs to be found quickly; otherwise strangers will avoid each other and culture will go down the tubes."

"But what can *you* do?" Kubi asked.

"Well, I could help preserve gay culture by spreading a circle of love and friendship. Invite promising artists to Tokyo and be their sponsor—at least as much as I can."

Raphael's talk had gotten Kubi's mind going. Raphael could come in handy. Maybe he should introduce him to Mrs. Amino. She liked crazy guys like this, though the gay part might be a problem.

"Gay people have built up a network of love and friendship all over the world," Raphael went on. "I don't think it would be an exaggeration to say there is a gay network between America and Europe. I know a man who is so well connected he might as well have organized it. He knows gay people everywhere, so he was able to do some great things as an art promoter. Right now he's trying to open up the Tokyo market, and I'm working as a researcher for the project."

"Yeah, but when you say gay men in Tokyo," Kubi said, "the only thing I think of is gay bars. I have some gay friends, but they tell me it's rough being gay and living here. They're not the sort who can make a life by themselves, so they try to get noticed by important people—you know, directors and artists and poets—who are supposed to be gay, too, and they take it from there. Maybe gay isn't the right word for these people—they're more like the gay elite. Regular people like me couldn't get near them."

*   *   *

When Kubi was still writing novels, the *mama-san* of a gay bar told him the following history:

Long long ago, when the Puritans landed in America, they brought their sexual hang-ups with them. So now in the States there are still a lot of weak-kneed conservatives who make a big deal about virginity and chastity, even though everybody knows that the average age Americans lose their virginity at is thirteen or fourteen.

But before gay liberation, homosexuals lived in hiding. Changing partners one after the other, never seeing the same partner twice, getting into bed without even exchanging names—they could only dream about that kind of freedom. Ask a cultured, upper crust, secretly homosexual professor why he never got married and he couldn't say that he didn't like women. He had to keep Dr. Jekyll and Mr. Hyde strictly apart; the only way to indulge in Mr. Hyde's pleasures was to belong to a secret circle cut off from society. Come nighttime he'd change into social outcast, but with first light he'd be staunch defender of the status quo. To be homosexual and not have a guilty conscience, you needed a strong will, plus a fair amount of animosity toward society.

After World War II, the sugar daddy of the free world, America, entered its golden age. Still, homosexuals in America lived the same cursed existence as before, held prisoner by their Puritan blood.

But a new world was ready and waiting—Tokyo. Young American homosexuals visited GHQ-controlled Tokyo and were freed from feeling like outcasts. In the burned-out rubble of the city, among the black marketeers, whores, and bums, no such thing as social propriety existed. In the ruins, morality meant money and power. Puritanism had nothing to do with Japan, and homosexual love flourished.

With their pockets stuffed with dollars—the most powerful currency on earth—the American homosexual cruised the ruins in search of beautiful, young men. He'd find a pretty Toshiro

Mifune look-alike and give him a thousand yen to spend the night. He'd strip him, suck him, and then beg to get fucked. Lost in the fantasy that this beautiful, macho Japanese kid was a survivor of the kamikaze corps, the American would melt in ecstasy.

In the past, the gay bar that Kubi would sometimes stop in was a hangout for American homosexuals on a pilgrimage of sexual freedom. With the sexual revolution of the sixties, though, American gay men earned their place as citizens in their own country. Outcast homos were reborn as gay men, and people could talk casually about the old gay guy living next door. Gay liberation spread to Europe, but it never got as far as Japan. As the *mama-san* put it, "Gay life in Tokyo hasn't changed in thirty years. It cost me five million yen for my sex-change operation, and, believe me, it hasn't been easy getting my investment back."

So considering the present climate, Kubi had a hard time believing that Japan had this long tradition of tolerance for homosexuality. Ever since the end of the war when naive Japanese were tortured by the illusion that General MacArthur had raped their country—or wait, you could back up and say ever since the end of the shogunate when Perry led his Black Ships to port and the already-declining samurai were getting more effeminate by the day—Japanese men have been chasing after their lost manhood.

In a civilized world, though, the cult of masculinity is of no use. Muscles are only for show. The male body is not a tool for fighting but a vessel of love. So the myth of the male has risen again—in the gay world. Raphael may have taken his time getting there, but his point came down to this: If you want to talk about masculine appeal, the superior male is gay.

Kubi's thoughts were scrambling all over the place, first this way, then that, aided and abetted by Raphael's grand notions, which had been tossed in freely. When Kubi was in the throes of depression, the threads of thought wound up in a hopeless tangle. But when you're depressed, the best thing to do is to charge ahead. Forget about logic and rationality, just charge!

"Let me get this straight. You're telling me that the best thing a Japanese man can do is turn gay?" Kubi asked.

"You could say that."

Raphael's thoughts on gay culture stopped abruptly with that pronouncement. Kubi was hoping the topic of conversation would change when Raphael added, "Being gay isn't necessarily something you're born with. Even *you* could become gay. They're many artists in New York who've turned gay in order to break into the scene."

Had Raphael guessed what Kubi was thinking? "You want me to be gay?" Kubi asked meekly.

"It's no good to suffer alone."

Raphael's eyes shone on Kubi like a spotlight. Kubi's face grew itchy. He looked around, desperate for something to divert his attention.

"Do I look like I'm suffering?" Kubi asked, trying to make a joke out of it. He wanted to order another drink, but the bartender was nowhere to be seen.

"Love's pretty hard to find, right?" Raphael asked. "You're resigned to your loneliness. Your face looks like you're about to go off into the desert. It's not so hard to tell. If you don't do something about your depression, it'll get worse. You don't have to be alone, you know. I can show you a way out of suffering."

A person will come to solve your confusion. Isn't that what the fortune-teller said? Was Raphael that person? Switch off the brain and go with the flow.

Yet Raphael was gay. And when it came to things gay, Kubi was strictly amateur. Sure, he'd peeked over to the other side of the fence, but his body always remained on the straight and narrow. Something had held him back. It wasn't morality, it wasn't disgust with the male body, he didn't know what it was. But whenever he thought about gay sex, his own body stiffened and his butt muscles clenched.

Now it was Raphael's turn to lay a hand on Kubi's shoulders. Kubi didn't know how to react. Surely Raphael could sense his nervousness. He felt embarrassment, but couldn't say why. How do you shake off an invitation like this? This guy was getting in the mood, wasn't he?

"Relax!" Raphael said.

"Listen to me, OK?" Kubi began. "I used to be a terrorist. I targeted myself. When depression hit, this huge circus would start up in my head. Trumpets and drums, the crowd roaring and cheering, louder and louder. Then the crowd would go wild, stomping on my nerve endings and squeezing my blood vessels. You think somebody can act rational at a time like that? Then the crowd would swell, and the orgy would begin. I was scared that if I stayed still, the circus would get bigger and bigger then blow up in my brain. Depression is a form of terrorism, a coup d'état of delusions against the dictatorship of the brain. So I kept busy, at a pitch. I gulped down health tonics. And then I was in the nuthouse and then I ran around trying to get that tanker project going. I was a whole size bigger than I am now, and anything that got in my way had to watch out." Kubi spat out the words, ignoring Raphael, who seemed dumbfounded by these revelations.

Kubi had seen a frog cuisine show in Bangkok. Slits were made in the frog's skin, then they pinned it down and gave it the old electric shock. The frog leaped right out of its skin—like it was just a suit of clothes. Pretty horrible, but the thing Kubi got out of this show was how the frog endured the nonsense that was life. It put its life—or rather its skin—on the line. And this picture of the frog inspired him.

Kubi made up his mind. He paid the tab, and they left the bar. Raphael had no idea what was going on and had to hurry to keep up.

A five-minutes' walk took them beyond the bright lights of Shinjuku into a maze of narrow alleys and cramped houses. An old dog lay sprawled outside one dwelling without a care in the world. It stared in their direction, but didn't bark.

"I'll show you, too!" Kubi thought.

A sign on a telephone pole told them they were in Fuku-cho. The kind of place where once you got lost, you stayed lost. Just behind them the white sign of a *ryokan* was lit up, like it'd been waiting for them. Kubi felt the tension drain from him.

"Should I be the man?" he muttered hesitantly. "Or do we . . . ?"

Raphael clapped him on the shoulder. "Leave everything up to me," he laughed. Kubi would do as he was told.

The smell of new tatami brushed their noses as they entered their room. They sat in rattan chairs before a table with two tea cups, a tea pot, and a well-used thermos. The bedroom was behind the shoji. When couples first entered the premises, they were always a little standoffish to hide their embarrassment. A new topic was needed to keep the conversation going.

Raphael got a beer from the refrigerator and poured it into two glasses. At least *he* was going to be relaxed.

"I imagine you must have had a hard time getting used to Tokyo," Kubi began. He knew it was a stupid remark, but something was needed to break the silence.

"Yes, I guess so," Raphael answered. "No matter where I go, though, I can't take New York out of me. I feel like I'm always in two places at once. But I like Japanese men, so I can put up with Tokyo."

A gentle heretic if there ever was one, Kubi thought, wearily shrugging his neck and shoulders.

"Let me relax you," Raphael said, moving over to massage Kubi's shoulders and then his side. Raphael could have been a professional masseur, he was that good. At this rate, Kubi mused, he wouldn't mind lying back and letting breakfast, lunch, and dinner be served. For breakfast, *okayu* and *tsukemono*. Spaghetti pescatore for lunch. Lentil soup and an omelette with rice for dinner. That would be the menu; Raphael wouldn't have to be a genius to figure out he had a sensitive stomach.

"Can you cook?" Kubi asked.

"Of course. A couple of years ago I learned how to cook Japanese—stews, *soba* dip, even tempura."

So the two of them talked about food. Raphael said that his favorite food was *kamaboko*, fish cakes. Kubi said that if he could only eat one food for the rest of his life—like koalas could only eat eucalyptus leaves—it would be *zaru soba*—buckwheat noodles. For Raphael it was chicken soup. If you couldn't get your first choice? Raphael chose bagels, Kubi chose *onigiri*, riceballs.

"That's interesting," Raphael said. "My friend, the one who taught me to cook Japanese, he picked *onigiri* as his second choice, too."

"What was his first choice?"

"Pizza. The plain kind with just sauce and mozzarella."

Weird, Kubi thought. Though he supposed it made a kind of sense—you ate both pizza and *onigiri* with your hands. The guy could be extra coordinated!

"What's this friend of yours like?"

"Well, we live pretty similar lives. I earn my living teaching English conversation, and I'm always hunting for a good-looking man. Matthew's job is being a professional friend. He sells love and friendship."

For an instant, Raphael's Matthew and Kubi's Matthew remained as far apart as the North and South Poles. But then came the collision.

Fumbling with his wallet, Kubi pulled out the photo of Matthew he kept sandwiched between his phone card and his credit card. His heart was fluttery, his voice suddenly falsetto. "I've been searching for this person. He's the same Matthew you know, right? Do you know where he is?"

Raphael nodded, rather stunned himself.

A high-pitched whirring switched on inside Kubi's head.

Something began to spin around and heat up.

"How did you meet Matthew?"

"It was a snowy day, and we arm-wrestled in a gay bar."

And so Kubi recounted his tale of Mrs. Amino and the search for Matthew.

The story isn't supposed to develop this easily, Kubi thought. It's like a cheap detective novel. This is what they call "misuse of happenstance." Mrs. Amino's novel isn't supposed to be this simplistic. One of the characters, this former novelist in fact, was supposed to prove that Matthew didn't exist, wasn't he?

"Is Matthew gay, too?" Kubi asked.

"Matthew's bisexual," Raphael replied, laughing. "His clients aren't limited to men. Gay men have their own lifestyle, but Matthew could fit in very nicely."

Ah-hah! A bit of static mixed in with the simple plot of the novel. Kubi liked that.

"Have you ever slept with him?"

"A few times. He always cheers me up. Whenever I meet him, I remember what I'm supposed to be doing with my life. The last time I saw him was about six months ago. I'm sure his lifestyle hasn't changed—he's still busy racing from one place to the next. It's his job."

Kubi couldn't keep still. He started pacing like a remote-controlled toy jeep. Energy that had shriveled inside him suddenly swelled.

"Raphael, tell me more about Matthew, OK? I want to know everything."

Raphael started to unbutton his shirt. "If you want to know more about Matthew, then do what he does."

Kubi nodded slowly.

"I'm going to wash myself," Raphael said and went to the john.

"Okay, then I guess I'll just . . ."

Kubi went to take a shower. Lathering up his hair and scrubbing away the grime of depression, he suddenly heard the overture to *Carmen* burst forth in his head. His body began to move in time to the music.

In the next moment his thoughts had flown off to the tanker floating in Tokyo Bay. I'll charter a fishing boat. The tanker's a monster so it shouldn't be hard to spot. And probably rusty as hell. A shipbuilder would know how much it'll take to fix it.

"Raphael," Kubi called out, "come with me!"

PART
IV

13

Talks with Ghosts

But What Should I Wear ?

"I just met this Jewish guy named Raphael in Shinjuku, and we got on terrifically. He's gay, though—or maybe I should say *because* he's gay, he's a great guy, and I want to introduce him to you. He has this idea about making Tokyo into a center of gay culture and he's looking for a sponsor. How about meeting him and hearing what he has to say?"

Massaging his sponsor's calves, Kubi was making his obligatory report on his detective efforts.

"Gay people should do whatever they want to do," Mrs. Amino answered.

"But you should know that Raphael's life is a lot like Matthew's," Kubi said. "And he's just as good looking. Yeah, one night with Raphael has really opened my eyes. I feel like the whole world's opened up to me."

As Mrs. Amino's eyebrows twitched, Kubi went on, "I found out I get hard even when I do it with a guy."

"Hmph. I didn't know you were bisexual."

Mrs. Amino was neither surprised nor disgusted. She was cool about it, and didn't pursue the topic further. It never occurred to her that Kubi's one-night stand in a love hotel had ended up leading, of all things, right to Matthew's doorstep.

"Anyway," Kubi went on, "I'd really appreciate it if you'd meet my friend Raphael."

"I'm not in the mood right now," Mrs. Amino said. "I don't mind gay men, but then again I can't say they're my favorite people. And bisexuals, well, they're even worse, doing whatever they please. Now that you mention it, though, the role fits you perfectly. But here, I have something I'd like you to read."

Mrs. Amino had the maid bring in a stack of xeroxed papers. They constituted Katagiri's record of Matthew's youth that Maiko had sent from New York.

"I could never have imagined the kind of past my son has had," Mrs. Amino said. "I can't begin to picture what kind of man he's become. How am I supposed to act when I meet him? It's very frightening. Compared to him, you're easy to understand. I read this report, and I just don't know what to think."

Kubi decided to hold off telling Mrs. Amino what he'd learned—that he knew where Matthew lived and that in fact Matthew was bisexual, too. He couldn't bring himself to tell her this when she seemed worried enough as it was. Her breath smelled of booze. And it was only three in the afternoon.

"If Masao showed up now," she said, "I don't know how I'd handle it. I've got to prepare myself mentally. How should real mothers look? I know what you're thinking—you're wondering why get excited at this late date. But I can't help it. What kind of expression should I have when we first meet? What should I wear?"

"Just act like you would if you were meeting a complete stranger," Kubi said. For the time being that seemed the best answer.

I Am the World

At Narita, Maiko's passport, the red document that would allow her anywhere in the world except North Korea, was stamped ADMITTED. She zipped through customs, exited into the lobby, only to find her path blocked by a walking monument to bad taste—a man decked out in paisley shirt, red leather pants, purple muffler hanging to his waist, topped off with a black cowboy hat. She pushed her way past him just as the man's arm leaped out and grabbed her. Furious, she turned to face him, then burst out laughing.

His face was a little darker than she remembered, but it was unmistakable: It was Kubi. Reeking of cheap perfume, humming "The Sukiyaki Song" to her.

With Maiko rendered speechless, Kubi spoke up, his voice a little louder and higher pitched than she remembered. "Perhaps you will rethink your opinion of me. I'll get straight to the point: I've located our treasure."

"You've met Matthew?!" Maiko cried out.

Having traced his history so carefully, she now could not wait to meet him. Her head was full of a thousand Matthews—including, in a dream during her flight, Matthew as the chief steward assuring her the plane wouldn't crash because it was beyond the pull of gravity. His words had made her feel light as a feather.

"Let's talk about it in the car, shall we?"

A suitcase in each hand, Kubi bustled off to the car, the same Jaguar they'd taken on their visit to the prison. As Kubi placed Maiko's plastic duty-free shop bags on the back seat, he spied a bottle of twelve-year-old bourbon. "Hey, you remembered my brand!" he exclaimed.

It had not exactly been Maiko's intention.

"While I was waiting for your plane to land," Kubi began, "I walked all over the airport. If you think about it, it's pretty strange having a crummy airport like Narita as Japan's window to the world. And, oh yeah, I found this."

Kubi pulled out a crumpled piece of paper from his pocket and handed it to Maiko. It was an immigration form for foreigners entering Japan that someone had messed up and discarded.

> Name: AMELIA PELLION
> Nationality: PHILIPPINES
> Date of Birth: 16–8–1969
> Sex: FEMALE
> Address: 205 PHASIA BAGON SILANG,
>   CALOCAN CITY
> Occupation: DANCER
> Address in Japan: 502 SKY BLDG.,
>   3-28 FUKURO-CHO,
>   YASHIRO CITY,
>   KUMAMOTO PREFECTURE
> Passport Number: G 924419
> Flight Number: CX 504
> Purpose of Visit: DANCE

Probably the girl had thought better of what her purpose of visit should be. Kubi wouldn't have been the only one to guess the kind of dance she performed. Amelia took her clothes off, you could count on it. Her body was her working capital.

"A whole crowd of Filipino girls came out just before you did, and then this fat little guy wearing sunglasses led them out to a minivan. I bet they're nervous. Sure, it's a job, and they'll make money and they'll send it back home. Maybe some of them will do fine, maybe some of them will get cheated. But they don't even speak the language. This country's wall-to-wall Japanese—spaced-out and half-asleep. Somebody's gotta wake them up. If I had to put money on somebody to splash ice water on them, I'd put it on Matthew."

"Where is he? When can I meet him?" Maiko asked eagerly.

"Hold on," Kubi replied. "I'll show you where he lives. I found him by pure luck. If I relied on regular detective procedures, I never would've tracked him down. As you can imagine, Matthew has spider webs all over the place. You get caught in one corner of the web, you get to meet him. I mean it's not like he's running away. Now that I've located him, my job's finished."

"*What!?* You're going to miss the climax?"

"Grabbing Matthew and getting him to meet Mrs. Amino is *your* job. Just hang out near his place, and he'll show up soon enough. This is the chance you've been waiting for. I don't think Matthew's got a clue his mother's looking for him."

"Mrs. Amino must be excited."

"Haven't even told her yet. I mean, it's bound to throw both of them off when they meet—the orphan out in the storm and the mother waiting for him to come home. Somebody's got to keep things from getting out of hand—which is where you come in. What I think you should do is meet Matthew and explain the tough time his mother's had waiting for him all these years. I read that report on him; it's like her son became a heathen. No—not a heathen, a man from outer space, an alien. A real tear jerker of a story. Incidentally, old Mrs. Amino's going to free her slave pretty soon. The slave's picked up some confidence along the way, and he doesn't need his master. I mean, sure, I'd love to see this dramatic reunion of mother and son take place, but I hate these endings of stories. Even when I was writing, I could never end a story without boring myself stiff. Anyhow, I'm outta here."

For all that Kubi was saying, it was still hard for Maiko to believe the real Matthew was so close at hand. It was as if the hero of the novel she'd been engrossed in had leaped right out of the book.

Moreover, Kubi had gone through a complete transformation in the past month. Not just his clothes and voice—his face looked completely refreshed, as if he'd been exorcised. The arrogant but refined novelist was back. What happened?

What happened was during the last month Kubi'd been a regular Indiana Jones.

Tokyo was a city with rheumatism, where even the young played decrepit games, and adventure and ideals were fossils of the past. The point of life was to wear yourself out. At least that's what everybody thought, and Kubi had been no different. Someone needed to say out loud: "Hey! This is a bad dream!" But Kubi had woken up without this warning.

Kubi's depression went full circle, and he found himself back at square one. The young man who'd been an old geezer was now an infant again. Kubi had always been an outsider, cut off from events in the world. When he tried to participate in the world, there was always a steel door blocking his way. So his role became passive—to sit alone and listen to the complaints. Paranoia had a field day. But then came an astounding discovery: With only a slight push, the doors swung wide open. The stir of the world rushed at him now, the sound of his own high-pitched grumbling mixed in.

Nothing in particular had happened. Kubi had searched through Tokyo for one man—that was all. He'd boiled up a pot full of coincidences. To call it adventure or exploration was to say too much. It was killing time. The perpetual outsider Kubi leaped into the clamor of the world and the world wriggled up inside him. There was no longer a dichotomy of insider/outsider. Just the world.

What happened was Kubi had been watching countless passersby, and then he found himself curious about them. And finally affectionate toward them. For him, a man whose vocation it had been to sneer at everyone, even a vague feeling of affection was an event of epic proportions. Kubi had experienced firsthand the pleasures of offering up his body to the world. From the computer-programmed fortune-teller to the young couple at the Chinese restaurant to the runaway girls in Kabuki-cho, from Samantha of the lovely calves to Taro Urashima to Raphael Zacs, this had been Kubi's fresh experience with the world, and the world was now open to him.

There was no need to meet Matthew. Kubi knew the life he

led, the troubles he had, the people he loved. Even the food he liked. In the ups and downs of the past month Kubi—with his own body—had been living Matthew's life. And the lesson he had learned was this: *I am the world!*

"The important thing," Kubi said to Maiko, "Matthew's hide-out—you'll never guess where it is."

Maiko *was* surprised when she heard. It was only fifteen minutes from her place. Sugamo, Toshima ward, Tokyo, an apartment off Jizo Avenue, near Koshinzuka Station on the Ara-kawa Line. Maiko's job now was to phone him every other hour and then race over and nab him.

The Seal Building

Before she returned home, Maiko had Kubi take her to Matthew's front door. Kubi had been there several times, but never when Matthew was home.

The Seal Building—that was its name, and what a name. The owner probably had had one too many when he thought that one up. It was a four-story box of the roughest, unfinished concrete imaginable. On the mailbox for apartment 301 was the name Matthew, written in katakana on a slip of paper. A spiral steel stairwell led up to the third floor where a dimly lit hallway stretched out with rooms on either side, like a hospital. 301 was at the end of the hall. A pile of old newspapers lay outside 302, and from 303 weird one-quarter time music drifted out like a worm twisting around itself. Muslim music.

Maiko knocked on 301. She waited fifteen seconds and knocked again. Someone came out, but it was the guy next door. A tan face, eyebrows that grew together, and piercing eyes. A mustache over a row of yellowed teeth. At least he was smiling. The man stared at Maiko as if he was considering how to carve up his catch. Maiko felt the air getting thin, and she turned to Kubi for help.

"Hey, how's it going?" Kubi started in. Apparently, Kubi had met him before. The man stuck his hand out and introduced himself. His name was Aphmet and he was from Bangladesh. His hand was tanned, thick, and damp.

"Maiko, is it? You're beautiful. I can't take my eyes off you."

Aphmet wouldn't let go of her hand. Maiko's put-on smile faded.

"Matthew isn't here," Aphmet said. "I haven't seen him for a week. Why don't you come in and have some tea?"

"I think not," Maiko replied. "Maybe another time."

"Why not?"

"We have to be some place."

"It'll just take a minute."

It would have been more trouble to continue refusing, so Maiko and Kubi entered Aphmet's apartment. Cushions were scattered about the one large room; they sat on them and leaned against the wall. Next to the window was an old steel desk and folding bed; on the desk a computer, on the floor a boom box.

"Aphmet's going to be a computer technician," Kubi explained. "He's in grad school now. He'll be one of the elite when he goes back home. You wouldn't mind having a Japanese wife, right, Aphmet?"

With Aphmet in the kitchen, Maiko whispered to Kubi: "I don't like guys who come on so strong."

"What's the matter—you prefer Buddhists?"

"No, I don't dislike Muslims."

When the tea was ready, Maiko did her best to steer the conversation away from herself. Instead she asked about Matthew: what he did in his room, what kind of person he was, . . .

"Matthew and I often have tea together," Aphmet answered. "We talk in English. I don't know much about him. He's different from Muslims, Christians, Japanese. Different from Buddhists and Hindus, too. He talks to himself a lot. If you put your ear to the wall, you can hear him. It sounds like he's talking to someone, but he's all alone. I pray a lot myself, but it's not the same thing. Once I asked him what he was always mumbling about, and he said he talks in his sleep."

"What does he say?" Kubi asked.

"I don't know."

"Maybe he's talking on the phone? Or it's messages people left on his answering machine?"

"No. It's not the phone. He's talking by himself. To some invisible person."

"You mean a ghost?" Kubi asked.

"I don't believe in ghosts."

"Have you ever been in Matthew's room?"

"No. I've only looked in from the outside. He sleeps in a tent in the middle of the room."

Tent? Did he mean mosquito netting? But it wasn't even summer yet.

Aphmet didn't know what kind of work Matthew did either. It was clear that to him a person who came home just to talk to himself was nutty.

As Kubi and Maiko were leaving the Seal Building, Aphmet ran down the stairs and caught up with them. There was something he'd forgotten to tell them.

It was only toward the end of the story that they realized what he was getting at. This was his story:

One night Aphmet dreamed about running up a hill. From the top of the gentle slope, something was rolling down. When he looked closely, he realized it was naked women. As they rolled nearer to him, they picked up speed. He leaped out of their way; he couldn't have grabbed one if he wanted to. So he continued to run up the hill, as hard as he could.

Over tea one day, Aphmet told Matthew this dream. Matthew's response was this: The next time Aphmet had this dream, he should watch to see what happens to the women. And then Matthew added: I might show up in your dream, too.

A week later, after Aphmet had forgotten the dream, he had

the dream again. Which, strangely enough, Matthew was in. Aphmet remembered to watch what happened to the women. In a pond at the bottom of the hill, the naked women were frolicking about. Aphmet followed their lead, tumbled down the hill, and leaped into the pond with them.

The next morning, Aphmet awoke refreshed, his body alive with energy. And if that weren't enough, when he asked a girl he often saw on the train for a date, she was delighted. The dream had been a prophecy.

"So Matthew shows up in other people's dreams, eh?" Kubi said.

That's right, Maiko remembered, Matthew visits other people's dreams.

14

A Weird Job

Still Life by Caravaggio

The nine-day tour was over, and I finally had a couple of days off. What I needed was sleep, a deep sleep to filter out the junk clogging up my mind. For two days Matthew won't be here on the earth.

On Jizo Avenue they were having one of those three-times-a-month sidewalk sales. Somebody once called this part of Tokyo the old folks' Harajuku. Dried fish and Daruma dolls for sale, underpants, grilled eel livers, red pepper, suspicious-looking supernutrient medicines, Kintaro candies. And a ton more. I glanced at the stalls on both sides of the street as I headed back to my apartment. I wanted to avoid running into that busybody Aphmet. He acts as if I'm his personal spiritual physician. But I'm not going to analyze anybody's dreams for free. He's got his own god, right?

Mikainaito, when you run into Aphmet tell him that, OK? That he shouldn't pal around with heathens too much. Having me analyze his dreams is blasphemy to Allah. Tell him that!

I took the mail out of my mailbox. I'd only moved to this apartment two months ago, so most of the stuff was forwarded from my old place. I couldn't hear the usual music, so Aphmet had to be out. My room was damp and pleasantly musty. I opened the mail up right away. Among the credit card bills and mail-order announcements there was a postcard from Mama.

> Matthew,
> I hope you have an easy life. You have a natural talent to be good at anything you try. You also recognize life's various problems. But let me advise you, my sweet boy, be careful of the woman who wants to make you her son!
>
> Your Mother

On the back of the postcard was a Caravaggio still life. Mama likes Caravaggio. But what was this warning all about? Was she telling me not to cuddle up too close to Japanese girls?

I pulled the beer I'd bought from a vending machine out of my baby buggy and drank it as I played back my phone messages.

"Hi, Matthew, this is Cindy. How about coming over Tuesday? I wanna dance. Give me a call."

Tomorrow. Too early to think about dancing.

"Uh, . . . Nomura here. I appreciate your taking care of the matter we discussed. On Wednesday I was out drinking with you till morning."

Alibis for guys having affairs, three thousand yen a shot. No way I'd really go drinking with that jerk.

"This is Kyoko. How come you haven't called me? There's something I want to talk about. I'll be home today so stop by anytime."

Better heed Mama's warning and put Kyoko on hold.

"How are you, Matthew? This is Raphael. Nothing to say, really. No need to call me back. I had a dream about you. You were a flying bird. Somebody was trying to catch you."

Raphael—this is a surprise. Him I wouldn't mind getting together with. 'Cause we're dream buddies. A bird flying around, huh? Who's trying to catch me? I'll call Raphael later and find out.

"Good afternoon. My name is Maiko Rokujo. I heard about you from Mr. Katagiri in New York. I'm calling because I would like very much to meet you and talk. I'll call again, but just in case, my number is 94X-12XX. Thank you very much."

So polite, but her voice was so young. Wonder what's troubling her. Wonder what Katagiri told her. How did she track me down anyway? Katagiri and Mama don't know this address. What the hell, wait till tomorrow to worry.

I took a shower and got under my mosquito net. My own palace of dreams—my private system for filtering out mental impurity. And disconnected the phone. *Mikainaito, see you in fifteen hours, OK? I've had only about four hours' sleep a night the last nine days. I'm dying for some ZZZs.*

An Offbeat Backstroke

Matthew's message to callers on his answering machine was spoken in both Japanese and English, both saying the same thing: This is Matthew. I'm out now. Please leave a message.

For some reason Maiko was moved. So this is the voice that he whispers to himself. She'd rung his apartment dozens of times and his voice was virtually recorded into her ear, the slightest jog sending it into playback.

On Sunday Maiko went swimming, hoping to wash away the jet lag. She was doing laps in the 25-meter pool when she heard Matthew's voice underwater. In the next lane a guy was sending up sprays of water doing his own version of the backstroke—a breaststroke kick with a butterfly stroke, all done face up. Maiko was positive she'd heard Matthew's voice calling out her name. She raised her head to look around, but the only thing she saw was the spray of water from the offbeat backstroke.

After swimming 800 meters, Maiko languished in the sauna.

Her body buoyant, she called Mrs. Amino. As Kubi said, she was suffering a case of the nerves. You're the only one I can rely on, Mrs. Amino pleaded, hurry to Kamakura, *please*.

Maiko prepared for the trip, feeling her mission less business than sympathy. But before she took the Yokosuka line out to Kamakura, she dialed Matthew's number again. All she got was the forlorn sound of a phone ringing without end.

Mulling things over on the train, Maiko wondered if she should wait a bit before telling Mrs. Amino the news. But letting the paranoia build up wouldn't be so wise either. Perhaps it would be best that Mrs. Amino meet her son as soon as possible. Maiko would use the dentist's technique: Tell the patient you'll pull on a count of three; then do it on two.

Fifteen minutes later, though, as the train zipped past Tsurumi, another thought occurred to Maiko. Across from her sat a middle-aged factory worker and an old woman who could be his mother. Suppose the factory worker was one of those Japanese children abandoned in China at the end of the war, now grown up and united with his aged mother? Maiko had seen these touching reunions over and over on TV but had felt oddly untouched. It was the drama of politics and greed in these reunions that interested her more. For instance, if China was rich and Japan was poor, how many of these touching reunions would there be? Of course, some of these abandoned children could genuinely *want* to meet their real parents. But wasn't it more likely that most of these abandoned children had hopes of getting some money and freedom? Was that their right? What about their parents? Even if they weren't rich like Mrs. Amino, unless they had the economic means and psychological soundness, would they go searching for children they left behind forty years before?

Mrs. Amino's search for her son was a hobby. Did she realize this? Did it bother her? Well, fortunately it didn't matter—either way Matthew would be fine. Need to be businesslike about this. If Mrs. Amino wants to be preoccupied with meeting her son again and filling the blank in her past, so what? At the least, Matthew would end up financially secure. No point worrying about something nebulous like the bond between parent and child.

The train pulled into Ofuna as Maiko was resolving this conversation with herself, and the mother and son across from her exited. The old woman could barely walk, and Maiko found herself watching as the son gently helped her up the stairs. Above and behind them was the Ofuna Kannon, the goddess of mercy seeming a bit absentminded.

"The relationship between parent and child is not something you can put into words."

It might have been Maiko's mother who said this to her, a long time ago. Her mother, of course, had been both—daughter and mother. Yes, Maiko could stand to be more sensitive to Mrs. Amino's feelings after all. Besides, the time had come for Maiko to fulfill her role as mediator in the long-awaited reunion of mother and child.

Mrs. Amino looked as absentminded as the Kannon. But certainly not as silent—she was full of questions. She lay waiting for Maiko on the sofa in the living room, the curtains drawn, and as soon as Maiko entered the room, she asked, "Do you think Masao will be friendly?"

"I think so," Maiko replied.

The questions followed, one after another.

"What is his foster mother like?"

"She's . . . quite kind," Maiko answered vaguely. She felt sympathy, even respect, for Barbara. "She lost a child herself. People around her had the wrong idea about the rental children, but she overcame their suspicions. The kids all started out as strangers, but before long they trusted her. It takes a special person to accomplish that. And you're about to do the same, Mrs. Amino—build a relationship of trust with Matthew. You and Barbara, however, are very different people."

"Maiko, which one of us do you think is better for Masao—me or her?"

"I don't think you should be asking questions like that. Your roles are different and you shouldn't try to compare them."

"But one mother is enough, isn't it?"

"No, that's not true. Just as Matthew has two names, he also has two mothers. Come to think of it, since he was a rental child he probably has many more."

"Then what am I to him?"

Mrs. Amino was in turmoil. The pride she had at being Matthew's real mother waged war with the uncertainty of actually meeting him.

"You're Masao's real mother," Maiko said. "What more can you hope for?"

"I might be his real mother," Mrs. Amino said, "but as far as Masao's concerned I'm a stranger."

Maiko was stuck for a reply.

"Maybe I should have called off this search for him," Mrs. Amino went on. "It probably would have been better if we went to our graves as total strangers, unaware of each other."

"What are you so afraid of? Matthew isn't as odd as you think. I'm sure he'll be delighted to meet you. Just act like you did the first time you met Kubi."

"You know, I saw Masao," Mrs. Amino said. "It must have been a prophecy. I saw Masao in a dream. It means he'll show up soon."

This came as quite a surprise to Maiko. Matthew already in Mrs. Amino's dreams?

Without prompting, Mrs. Amino began:

She was somewhere, she didn't know where exactly, walking in a deserted bamboo forest, the wind hurrying her along. She wore a white dress, but it was muddied. The buttons at the top were ripped off, and one breast was hanging out. She didn't want anyone to see her in this state, but it was necessary for her to cross the bamboo forest to reach L.A. She had the terrifying feeling that someone was watching her. At that moment the bamboo in her path bent over and a huge bear leaped out. She wanted to run, but she could not move her body. Afraid that she would die, she struggled to wake from the dream, but someone grabbed her and held her fast, refusing to let her awaken. Let me go! she screamed, as a hand was clamped over her mouth. Then the man holding her down started to bark like a dog. Dejectedly, the bear retreated. Everything around her turned dark, and a feeling of happiness welled up within her. When the feeling passed, she was standing on the bank of a stream, a child on her back.

Maiko was sure the story continued, but the dream ended there.

"It was *Masao* on my back," Mrs. Amino declared. "It had to be. Even when I was dreaming, I was sure of it."

Matthew spends most of his life in dreams, Maiko reasoned. No, Matthew *is* a dream. Suddenly she was convinced—though how, no garden variety law of cause-and-effect could prove—that they had to hurry. There was not a minute to lose. They had to hurry and grab Matthew.

What Kind of Job Did You Have in Mind?

Early the next morning Maiko began ringing Matthew's apartment. She lost track of how many times she tried. She let the phone ring upwards of thirty times. She was convinced Matthew was at home; if he'd gone out his answering machine would be on. He had disconnected the phone.

She rushed over to the Seal Building. Matthew was on the verge of leaping from her imagination into the real world. A scene she envisioned taking place in ten—no eight—minutes replayed itself over and over: Matthew appearing behind the door of apartment 301.

But it didn't work out that way. When Maiko got to the building Matthew was on his way out. For an instant Maiko completely forgot how to speak. She quickly recovered and started to follow him, rehearsing a number of opening lines.

Matthew looked younger than in his pictures, and more dashing. He had on a mustard color jacket, moss green cotton pants, white sneakers, and a dark red scarf. And he walked quickly. He wasn't pulling his baby buggy with him, so maybe he was going on a date. He headed down Jizo Avenue toward the station.

He didn't know Maiko, but Maiko knew everything about him. The odd thought occurred to her that this was the way he used to be, as a child.

He went into the bank to use the ATM. Maiko halted in front of a fruit stand adjacent, scrutinizing the plums with one eye while keeping the other on Matthew. He was soon out of the bank and on his way again; then he stopped again, this time at an electric goods store, where he stared at something in the window, a vacuum cleaner perhaps. Maiko stopped as well—ten meters away, outside a bar that hadn't yet opened for business. When she looked up in the next instant, Matthew was gone. She ran. She dashed into an alley, but he had disappeared. She sensed someone behind her. Turning around, she found Matthew in front of her.

"Hi," he said.

Cold water suddenly flowed in her veins. Stuttering, she managed to say hello, too, but couldn't get out anything else. Matthew beamed broadly.

"I was going to eat some tempura soba. You're Maiko Rokujo, right?"

His intuition was unbelievable. Embarrassed by her feeble attempt to shadow him, Maiko blushed.

"Well, you see," she said. "I have a favor to ask."

"What kind of job do you have in mind?"

His reply was so quick Maiko was speechless for a moment again.

The Very Least I Can Do As a Good Son

"To get straight to the point," Maiko had said, "your real mother wants to see you."

Mikainaito, she was serious about this, but I was so surprised I almost laughed.

So you have a mother like everyone else, eh?

Looks like it. I don't know if I should feel relieved—or sad. I always thought that maybe I came from the gods—or the devil. But I guess that's the end of that.

Don't think that way. Maybe you used to be called Masao a long time ago, and popped out of the womb of some Japanese woman named Mika, but you're still Matthew. You just borrowed that woman's womb to give birth to yourself.

Mikainaito, you know, our friendship goes back even further than I thought. Even my real mother knew about you.

Maybe so, but are you really going to meet her?

Umm. Nice I didn't have to go to all the trouble of finding her myself.

But what's the point? For money?

To find out more about myself.

You know enough about yourself already. It's a little late in the day for anybody to teach you anything new.

A lot of people helped create the person I am today—Katagiri, Barbara, Penelope, my rental-child brothers and sisters. But not one of them shares my genes. I want to find out more about my prototype.

Come on. Don't get too serious about this.

Mikainaito, if I didn't have a real mother, would I exist? She's half of the team that made me. If it wasn't for her, neither of us would be here. I've been like some baby abandoned under a bridge or stuffed in a coin locker. I haven't known a thing about my real parents. Luckily, though, I didn't have any hang-ups about being abandoned. Katagiri saw to that. He taught me that abandoned kids could be saviors. Be proud of being abandoned, was his line. Play to your heart's content.

Mama taught us how to play, too. But my genes were constructed by my real parents when they had sex. Maybe they didn't teach me anything, but a lot of what I am today is thanks to them—my looks and my IQ anyway. Mikainaito, I'm curious, all right? It doesn't cost anything to meet her.

Yeah, but what would Mama think? Mama doesn't want your real mother to steal you away from her. Let me put it this way: Who are you going to choose? Mama, or your real mother?

To me they're both gods. One god gave birth to me, the other god raised me. It's not a question of choosing. Maiko said I was kidnapped by my father. I can feel that gap in my history growing right now, like a tumor. You know those posters in the bus terminals in Buffalo, Syracuse, Berkeley, El Paso? The ones with photos of kidnapped kids? In the past that I can't remember, I might have been on one of those posters. Seeing travelers off with a smile.

> *MASAO: LAST SEEN 1964*
> *EYES: BROWN   HAIR: BLACK*
> *HAS A VERTICAL LINE OF FOUR MOLES ON*
>   *HIS BUTTOCKS*
> *HAS ANOTHER SELF CALLED MIKAINAITO*

I think I finally understand, Mikainaito. All this time, the link between me and my real mother has been you. You're my alter ego between me and other people, and you played your role perfectly.

I know the phony story Katagiri concocted. A man was supposed to have brought me over one day. Poor kid, he said, both your parents were killed in a car wreck. Overnight you became an orphan. You used to be an unhappy orphan, but now you're a happy rental child. You don't remember anything about your real parents, he said, and that makes you luckier than the other rental children.

He was probably right. I had no idea of what a real mother is, so I didn't suffer the way real orphans would.

Maiko said my real mother's a rich widow, wealthy enough never to have to worry about money. Her life was screwed up by the man who kidnapped me—my real father—but after that she carved out a life for herself on her own. A regular Horatio Alger story.

"She always believed she'd be able to see you again," Maiko told me. "That's what kept her strong. She still has a clear image of you before you were stolen. She never forgot about you. But she's not in the best of health now and she spends most of her time in her home in Kamakura. If she could see you I'm sure she'll feel better. Think of what she did to track you down. She worried about you for twenty-five years. You're the only one left in the world who shares her blood."

Mikainaito, her words touched me. I wanted to thank my real mother for her secret prayers that kept me safe. But I'm curious about my father, too. I want to meet the guy who gobbled down the lives of a woman and child, and tell him this:

"Father! Here's some money. Use it to make a new life for yourself."

The very least I can do as a good son.

But what about being a good son to your mother?

"For the time being," Maiko told me, "please come and stay at Mrs. Amino's for a couple of days. Please—as a favor to me, the person she asked to find you. Mrs. Amino will have her own favors to ask, I'm sure. I'll leave that part up to the two of you."

I decided to go along with her. Mikainaito, I did catch it, you know —that look in her eyes. I know she likes me. She's beautiful. I wouldn't mind checking out her dreams from the inside.

What good will that do?

I don't know yet.

She seems kind of naive. She doesn't know squat about men.

I'm not going to deceive her.

What's going on here? Love at first sight?

Maybe. But what a weird job—meeting my own real mother.

15

The Desert Troubadour

A Handsome Young Lover

Matthew had been found.

No point in her sitting around, letting her mind race off in all directions. Especially since, before too long, Matthew, accompanied by Maiko, would be arriving at her doorstep. So Mrs. Amino called for a masseuse to work out the knots in her body. That would be Kubi's job ordinarily, but she'd had no word from him in the last four days.

After her massage, she stood before the mirror, carefully appraising, yet once again, the outfit she'd chosen after four hours of indecision—a dark green silk dress with amber necklace, ruby earrings and matching ruby ring. Deciding that white stockings were, after all, better than the black, she changed quickly, adding for a final decorative flourish a spider-shaped accessory on one ankle. It was just the thing to make her look more youthful. Next came her makeup. Rather than cover up her age, she worked to improve the luster of her skin. That was not to mean, however, that she shouldn't try to cover up the gray in her hair with some one-touch purple dye.

Finally, she tried on, one last time, the smile she'd been practicing since the night before.

It was then that the maid called out: "Miss Rokujo and the young master have arrived."

Twenty minutes early. "Coming," Mrs. Amino called back, giving her mouth a quick Listerine spritz.

Matthew wore a gray suit, a shirt with dark blue stripes, and a pink necktie. His hair was neatly parted on one side, his nose hairs trimmed. But detracting from what was otherwise a very pleasant appearance were squid tentacles of stray hair hanging down his forehead. As they waited for Mrs. Amino, he was clearly nervous, keeping up a steady dialogue with Mikainaito as he stared intently at Maiko. Something made him want to trust her.

Maiko felt his gaze at her temples. She would count to seven, then turn to look at him. But Matthew spoke up before she could.

"I forgot my toothbrush," he said.

Maiko laughed. "Don't worry. Everything's prepared for you." All Matthew needed was himself, but he had shown up pulling his baby carriage crammed full of things. "Enough to fill a house," he answered when she asked what was inside it.

There was the sound of approaching steps, one foot dragging. Then the brass doorknob turned and the fragrance of roses filled the room. The air in the spacious parlor swirled restlessly as Maiko and Matthew rose from the sofa to greet their hostess.

Mikainaito, that's the woman who gave birth to me twenty-eight years ago.

You're kidding. I don't see any resemblance. Everything's different, your eyes, nose, mouth, the shape of your face. You look more like Katagiri and Barbara.

"How do you do? I'm Matthew." Perhaps a strange way of greeting your mother.

"Masao," Mrs. Amino said, "we finally meet. You look well." The words came out exactly as she'd practiced. And she managed a natural smile, too. Matthew's handshake was firm, and he was bigger than Mrs. Amino had imagined, more filled out.

The three of them sat and were silent for a few seconds. No one knew who should speak first.

"Matthew . . . ," Maiko began, making certain both were listening, "Matthew isn't quite used to being called Masao yet."

"It doesn't matter what name you call me," Matthew intervened. "It doesn't change who I am. Like, take for instance—," he glanced around the room and slowly pointed at the chandelier, "—that chandelier. You could call it a whale, but it's still a chandelier."

You're so nervous you don't know what you're talking about. Come on, pal, buck up. You used to be a professional child, right?

This isn't as easy as I thought.

"Please let me call you Masao," Mrs. Amino said. "To me that's who you are. Masao."

"Of course, Mother."

A stupefied Maiko looked back and forth at the mother and son. Matthew nervously jiggled his foot.

"You're my mother, so that's what I'll call you," he went on, doing his best to convince himself. On the other hand, it still hadn't dawned on Mrs. Amino, by the looks of her, what in the world *mother* meant.

"It's amazing you could find me," Matthew chattered on. "I know we're both living in Tokyo, but still, trying to track down a guy who's been lost for twenty-five years—it could be like looking for one particular grain of sand in a desert. I mean, here I am alive and all, but you could have spent the rest of your life searching for somebody who didn't exist."

"I was positive you were still alive," Mrs. Amino said to Matthew. "Even if you were dead, I knew that if I was determined enough you'd come back to life."

"Is that right? Actually I *did* die once. Thanks for saving me."

"You're quite welcome," Mrs. Amino laughed.

"I've worked as the reincarnation of other people's dead children," Matthew said, "but I never expected to be the reincarnation of myself. I don't remember a thing about the time when I was Masao. Masao died, and he was born again as Matthew."

"But Masao and Matthew are the same person," Mrs. Amino insisted. "Mikainaito's proof of that. Thank god I remembered him. When you were three, you were always talking with him. He's still around, I presume?"

"Yes, he's still inside me."

To tell the truth, Mikainaito, I don't know when I first met you. You're the messenger of my consciousness—Katagiri taught me that. But even before I met him, I knew you. When I was three we were already pals.

Mrs. Amino looked at Maiko and half-whispered, "I imagine Mikainaito doesn't remember me, either."

Sorry. You got me. When I was three, the world was destroyed. And again at thirteen, and again at seventeen. Right now it's like we're in the Renaissance—for the fourth time around. Right, Matthew?

"I think as the two of you talk more," Maiko interrupted, "you'll find out where your memories overlap."

Only Mrs. Amino nodded at this. They could try to trace their past, try to find out what they shared, but expecting Matthew to dredge up memories of age three from the swamp of his unconscious was almost asking the impossible. For the time being, all that tied them together was a word: *Mikainaito*.

"I plan to do everything I can to help you," Mrs. Amino said.

Here it is, Matthew. Play your cards right.

"I'm really glad to hear that," Matthew answered, "but I'm on my own now, and have my own work—"

"Naturally you're free to do whatever you please," Mrs. Amino declared. "It's just that I—"

It was an awkward situation that Maiko thought best handled by being forthright and businesslike. If they negotiated as rental child and client, things would proceed smoothly. "Matthew," Maiko said, "Mrs. Amino is hoping to invest in your work."

"What are you asking me to do?" Matthew asked. "It's OK for me to live here as Mrs. Amino's son for a while, isn't it?"

Mikainaito, I feel like a rental child all over again. The only difference is, the client happens to be my real mother.

Mrs. Amino nodded. She had no idea what Matthew was thinking, but despite the ease with which he called her "Mother," she was sure a part of him didn't buy the idea at all. Perhaps she hadn't laid the proper groundwork, but she was determined to do whatever was necessary to make herself mother to Masao once again. Otherwise, she had nothing to look forward to but lonely old age.

If it boiled down to a choice between his real parent and the parents who raised him, Mrs. Amino understood that the smart money wasn't on her. His foster parents had had over twenty years to her three. She and Masao would have to start out like total strangers. But even total strangers have it easier than this.

"Mother, I'll do whatever I can," Matthew said.

What a cheery voice. But maybe a little cheeky besides.

"You must have gone through a lot, too," he continued.

The room prepared for Matthew was a regular luxury hotel suite. Natural light filtered in from the ceiling, and paneling made the place almost soundproof. It had been thoroughly cleaned, the sheets and bedspread were new, the bar was freshly stocked with whiskey and brandy. Only one thing in this room didn't belong. Matthew thought at first that it was a pair of old panties someone hadn't thrown away. But it turned out to be a dirty, flattened pillow with most of the stuffing gone.

At nine that evening, Mrs. Amino knocked on Matthew's door, photo album in hand. In answer to his question, she opened the album to a photograph of the same pillow, full of stuffing, next to a little boy.

"Everywhere you went you took your pillow," she said.

The way she put it, Matthew felt maybe he really had. He

looked at the other photos. He couldn't quite connect himself with the three-year-old Masao, but if Mrs. Amino said it was he, why not believe her? He presumed that the young woman carrying Masao was a young Mrs. Amino. But she could just as well have been a stranger.

"A pity photographs can't talk, " Mrs. Amino sighed. "They just lie there."

"If photos could talk," Matthew said, "you wouldn't be able to stand the racket. It's enough that real people talk and people in movies talk. And the people you see in dreams."

For a long time, in fact, Mrs. Amino had lived through these photographs—which she'd enlarged and superimposed on the mental images she had of Masao growing up. But photographs can be scary things, especially photographs of children. And looking at a photo when Mrs. Amino was depressed would produce the overwhelming feeling that he was dead. Immediately she'd be sure that he was quite alive, but that one part of her was killing him off. She would be vulnerable to every possibility imaginable: that the child might be living in the lap of luxury, or might be in an insane asylum, or, again, dead. In the nether world of delusions, Matthew had died any number of times, been reborn, been successful, been a failure.

Mrs. Amino turned to the last page of the album and pointed to a photo that had been crumpled up once then smoothed out again. "This is the man who kidnapped you," she said. "Do you remember him?"

The man had a scruffy growth of beard. Cigarette hanging out his lips, he had turned to squint at the camera. Did he think he was James Dean?

Matthew gazed at the photo, then said, "I've seen that face before."

"Do you remember him?" she asked.

"No," he replied, staring silently at the photo. Then he closed the album sharply and held her hand.

"I think he probably died a long time ago," Matthew said. "He wasn't alive when I was four, was he? But it was thanks to him dying that I was raised by some pretty wonderful people. You still hate him, don't you, Mother?"

"Yes, I do," Mrs. Amino said. "I still can't believe I was stupid enough to let him fool me like that."

"By the way, what's your blood type?" Matthew asked.

"O."

"Me, too."

So what? That doesn't prove you're parent and child. The world's full of type O's.

"Do you know your real birthday?" Mrs. Amino asked.

"I use April 1st. It's the day I first met Katagiri. As long as I don't have a real birthday, I'm four years old forever. What day did you gave birth to me, Mother? What's my official birthday?"

"February 13th."

"February 13th. Now I'll have two birthdays each year. Two isn't so many, really. I have a friend who has a birthday every three days. He's in a hospital now. When is your birthday?"

"April 17th," Mrs. Amino said.

"That's coming up soon. Do you remember the last day you saw me?"

"July 7th."

"The day Masao died."

From that day to the day Matthew was born, what was I? I wasn't Masao or Matthew. Where was I? What was I doing?

You weren't here on earth those nine months. Me, I was up in space, floating around.

"How about a drink?" Matthew asked. "What can I get you?"

Matthew decided to put that nine-month gap out of his mind, for the moment at least. He had no memory of it, and there wasn't anybody who did. For all intents and purposes that time didn't exist. A feeling of relief spread down to the soles of his feet, even as he felt like grabbing hold of Masao and pulling him close. But Masao was, on a conscious level, someone else. That the boy in the photos was really him would take convincing. It would have been more reasonable to suggest that Masao was his previous incarnation. But what if, say, Matthew's father showed up with proof that filled that nine-month gap? Would that turn Masao into Matthew?

*Matthew, forget about it. There've been three of you, as I see it: Masao up to the kidnapping, the child during the nine months with your father, then Matthew up until now. Nobody knows anything about the guy in the middle, so let him be. Just act the grown-up Masao. That's good enough for now. It's your *job*, remember.*

The next morning Mrs. Amino prepared breakfast herself. She hadn't touched a knife or frying pan in five years, but following the maid's instructions, she managed to cook up a decent batch of scrambled eggs with ham and tomato. Then she carried it out to the terrace and sat down across the table from Matthew.

"Did you sleep well?" she asked.

"Yes," Matthew answered as he dug into the eggs. "You know, I often wake up and can't figure out where I am, and the same thing happened this morning. I felt like somebody was next to me, and I ended up over by the edge of that king-sized bed. I had so many dreams. You were in one of them, Mother."

"What part did I play?"

"I was trying to climb up a wall and you were helping give me a boost. You lifted my legs up like this." Matthew turned both hands palm up.

"What was on the other side of the wall?"

"A nebula."

"A nebula? You mean like in outer space?"

"Right," said Matthew. "In the dream I thought that nebula was where I was born."

"Then what happened?"

"I was standing on top of the wall. I didn't know which way to go—whether I should jump into the nebula or return to the world I came from, where you were. Then I woke up."

"Which one did you want to choose?"

"I don't know. But the next time I have that dream I think I'll check out the nebula."

Matthew stared with his dewy eyes at his tomato juice, his thoughts dissolving in the thick, red liquid, which he then downed in one gulp. He couldn't sweep away one fact: He lied. In his dream it wasn't Mrs. Amino who gave him a lift. It was that bastard father of his. His father had pushed him up to the top of the wall, like he was doing the shot put, then poked him with a stick, trying to make him topple over to the other side.

Mikainaito, I was crying as I ran around on top of that wall, trying to get away from him. The nebula wasn't the place where I came from. It was a hell where all these terrible people battled to survive. I managed to keep my balance and escape. I ran until I couldn't see him anymore. And this is where I ended up.

The Pacific Ocean spread out below the terrace. The scenery was a blur, as if it were half-asleep. Even the sparrows' chirping sounded flat in the heavy air.

So his father still lay buried in the swampy bottom of Matthew's memory. In dreams, Matthew became a bottom feeder and dug into the mud. His father *had* taught him something. And was *still* trying to teach him something. It was the art of fending for yourself.

Mikainaito, before I met Katagiri, I was with that guy. He was always poking at me. Maybe I hated him. But what could I do? He was my father. The last time I saw him, he bought me a Coke and a hamburger at a coffee shop, and that was it—he was gone for good. Another Japanese guy took me on a long trip. And we ended up at Katagiri's.

After breakfast Mrs. Amino invited Matthew out for a walk. Her rheumatism had improved, and a stroll on the beach was possible. Matthew offered her his arm.

"This area is called Zaimokuza," she explained.

"I went swimming once at Yuigahama," Matthew said, "just down the road from here."

They walked on silently for a while, picking spots where the sand was firm. Windsurfers impatient for the season to get under way shivered as they came out of the water.

"I can't believe that thirty years ago I was on the other side of this ocean," Mrs. Amino said.

The sky was milky, the sun faded. In California the sun as usual sparkled, carefree. In New York the beginning of spring is the loveliest season of all. New Yorkers shed old skins for new. White people turn from reddish, pale gray to pink; blacks go from charcoal to the luster of a violin; Orientals shuck off their dried-up sand for gold. Warmed by the sun, the afternoon air collides with the coolness of the shadows, etching invisible patterns in the air. The season discovers shapes. Color and form come alive.

But in Tokyo in spring everything is dozing—the sun, the air, colors, shapes. Spring is when Matthew landed in Tokyo. And Tokyo had indeed nodded off.

"Mother, do you think you'll ever go back to the U.S.?"

Mrs. Amino shook her head. "I hate America, and I hate Japan, too. Here I feel like I'm living in a country inside my body. I think I understand pretty well what your foster father meant."

"Maiko happened to mention that you were a professional lover in Tokyo."

"What? Oh, you mean in Ginza. Yes, people used to say I was the most successful bar hostess of all."

So Mrs. Amino told Matthew the story of her past. The hard times she had after coming to Tokyo and starting life from scratch. Her struggle as a woman—from nothing to a Ginza bar to Motonobu Amino to *yakuza* wealth—and she did so with a wonderful sense of perspective. If she'd remained just mother to the son she adored, she never would have known this array of experiences. Perhaps now, her past seemed a mere backdrop to her child's growing up, but with Masao here, she felt satisfied, as if she'd finally gotten to the punch line.

For his part, Matthew was surprised at how his mother had laid everything she had on the line to begin a new life for herself, and he warmed to her. The two of them were mother and child, but there was another bond between them. The mother who'd found a new life in Tokyo, and Matthew, the refugee son seeking asylum in the same town, were like a master craftsman and apprentice. One the seasoned pro, the other a rookie new to the circuit.

Matthew tapped his mother on the shoulder. "You know," he said, "we're a lot alike."

From then on, their conversation never flagged. The Pacific Ocean lay beneath their feet.

Matthew explained how he worked as a professional friend and lover, while Mrs. Amino confessed her hobby of squandering the fortune left behind by her real estate tycoon husband. At this point the ideal parent-child relationship seemed to be this: Matthew would think of ways to use the money, and Mrs. Amino would provide it.

That night a proud Mrs. Amino took Matthew out to a gay bar she'd had occasion to visit a few times. She was eager to show off her son.

"Well, Mrs. Amino. What a surprise!" A vase of gorgeous roses lay arranged on the counter, and behind it, the kind of face that would make children burst into tears.

"What a handsome lover you have today, Mrs. Amino," the *mama-san* said. "I'm simply green with envy!"

"Don't be stupid," Mrs. Amino retorted, disappointed and pleased at the same time. "This is my son."

The *mama-san* managed a gulp of surprise but no more. Matthew was kind enough to explain.

"My mother decided when I was little that other families would raise me. So we hardly ever get to meet."

One way of looking at it, for sure. After a long, long voyage, the son has returned. Even though they lived apart, the reunited mother and son find out how much alike they are.

Three days passed in a hop, skip, and a jump. And the distance between mother and son shrank with each day. What came next, though, they hadn't a clue.

Mrs. Amino couldn't have been more taken with Matthew. Her expectations had been betrayed in a most pleasant way, for despite her initial worries, her son turned out to be the kind of young man everyone around him envied. With a twinge of jealousy of her own, she realized she had the Katagiris to thank.

Mother, Your Eyes Are Wet!

Maiko would be coming to see them in the afternoon. As they waited for her arrival, Matthew and Mrs. Amino spent the morning trading jokes and throwing back cocktails. They talked of many things, including Mrs. Amino's dream of Matthew barking like a dog to save her from the bear.

"It was Mikainaito," Matthew said. "At night when I sleep, he jumps three times on my body and leaps out. He drifts around the night sky like Songoku—that monkey hero of *Journey to the West* who floats on a cloud—and slips into the dreams of people who are thinking about me unconsciously. What did I look like?"

"I couldn't see you. You were behind me. But I was sure it was you."

"Next time you'll probably see all of me."

"Speaking of dreams," Mrs. Amino said, "these last three days have been one magnificent dream to me."

"It isn't over yet. In dreams and reality, there's always another installment."

"In dreams, too? Once you have a dream, isn't that it?"

"No," Matthew replied, "dreams are like TV dramas. You always feel like it's To Be Continued, and then you wake up. And then maybe a week, ten days later, you see the sequel. If dreams stop having new installments, the dreamer's as good as dead. Don't you think so?"

"Is it always like that for you?" Mrs. Amino asked.

"Yes. Because I live in dreams the same way I live in reality."

"I've dreamed about you as a three-year-old. You hadn't grown a bit. Like Oskar in *The Tin Drum*. I used to take your photo out of the album and pray to it that you'd appear in my dreams. Otherwise you'd be dead to me."

How many Matthews and Masaos had appeared and disappeared in her mind? Matthews and Masaos without bones, flesh, blood—or shadow, . . . It didn't matter now. Matthew was here—before her eyes. This was one Matthew who would not vanish, even when the sleeper awoke.

The railing on the terrace was dotted with sparrows, and Matthew stared blankly at them.

Mrs. Amino's eyes followed him as he daydreamed, sticking out his lower lip. It was a gesture that three-year-old Masao used to have, and suddenly the 9,000-plus days that had passed since he was taken from her evaporated. The face of the young man sitting beside her now was the face of her three-year-old son, clutching his pillow and about to cry.

This is my child, the realization came to her. I gave birth to him. He weighed 2,400 grams. He loved to play tag and dash from his parents. He ran naked in the dining room at bath time. He bawled uncontrollably when his pillow slip was removed for washing. Yes, this Matthew before me is the Masao of twenty-five years ago. He is my child.

"Masao!" she cried out.

"Hmm?" Matthew said and turned to face her. "Mother, your eyes are wet!"

It wasn't what Mrs. Amino wanted. She couldn't show such sentimentality—yet. The connection had been made, but they were still just pro and rookie. Don't rush things; don't frighten him off. Be natural. Take things nice and easy.

Maiko arrived, dressed in her favorite white dress and red high heels. Mrs. Amino hurriedly shifted emotional gears, as Matthew looked Maiko over from top to bottom, seeming to undress her with his eyes.

"What've you been up to?" he asked.

"Not much—just thinking about things," Maiko replied.

"Like what?"

"The future."

"Whose future?"

"The future of this mother and her son."

As well as her own, if the truth be told. With the happy ending to Mrs. Amino's search, Maiko had to consider her next move. Kubi, the other detective of the team, had already disappeared from the stage of Mrs. Amino's novel and was setting out to live a tale made just for him. He'd called and said he was proceeding with his "Movable Stateless City," sprinting around Tokyo soliciting funds.

"I failed before because, among other things, I tried to do everything myself," Kubi told her. "But now I have a partner, a guy who's bright and handsome—and most important, full of contacts. His name is Raphael Zacs. The tanker won't end up a ghost ship this time around. I'll be going over one of these days to ask old Mrs. Amino to dip into her pockets. Put in a good word for me, OK? I guarantee she'll double her money. I may start by asking the government for funds to house Vietnamese and Chinese refugees."

"Well—," Maiko didn't know how to continue. She could feel Matthew's gaze on her. Why was he watching her? When she turned in his direction, Matthew, with an innocent childishness, nodded at her.

"How have you enjoyed yourself these last three days?" Maiko finally asked.

Mrs. Amino stammered, "Well, I . . . uh . . . that is, . . . Masao says you always wake from dreams feeling there'll be a sequel. Well, that's how I feel. I'm hoping the relationship between parent and child has a sequel. I want him to stay here forever. With his foster parents' permission, I'd like to have his name entered in my family register. There'll be complications about nationality, I'm sure, but I would really like to take the steps for him to live here in Kamakura."

"In other words . . . ," Matthew began, then stopped. What he had been about to say was, you want me to be your adopted son, but how do you become the adopted son of your real mother? So instead, he said, " . . . you mean you want me to become Japanese and live here, just the two of us, all nice and cozy?"

"Yes."

"Sounds good," he said. "But I can't give you a definite answer right now. I need some time to think it over."

Matthew thought this a fair reply, but seeing Mrs. Amino's face cloud over, he quickly added: "I really like it here. And I want you to know I respect you, Mother, as a professional. Thanks to you, I've established an advance base in Tokyo."

"An advance base for what?" Maiko's nostrils twitched.

"For conquering the world, of course!" Matthew grinned, just like Chaplin in *The Dictator*.

"Why don't the two of you go for a drive?" Mrs. Amino winked at Maiko. Any further negotiations Maiko could surely handle.

You Don't Know How to Whistle?

"You really don't know how to whistle?!"

Maiko leaned toward the car, pursed her lips and blew out some air. Matthew was crouched beside her, changing the tire.

They hadn't planned on going far, but Matthew had driven the Jaguar along the coast and before they knew it, the sea was far behind and they were on a mountain road in Hakone. Ten minutes earlier, they'd run over a board with nails sticking out and had a flat.

"I'll show you how." Matthew stood up, whistled a one-octave, five-step scale, and even showed her how to make a sound while breathing in. "Let your breath out slowly, evenly. It works better if your lips are moist."

Maiko licked her lips as she was told to, and without warning Matthew's own lips were on hers, smothering her.

Taken aback, Maiko stared straight into his face, but Matthew avoided her eyes by turning his attention back to the flat.

Until they had to pull over, Maiko had been trying to persuade Matthew to live with Mrs. Amino. Mrs. Amino was very lonely; Kubi, who was company for her, had left as soon as Matthew was found; Mrs. Amino had no one else to depend on; Mrs. Amino would take good care of all financial matters. Consider her one of your patrons, Maiko said.

"There is a better way," Matthew responded. "Don't worry —it'll all work out. I'll stay at my mother's for at least a couple more days."

And then he changed the subject. He asked Maiko what her plans were. Now that the detective assignment was finished, wouldn't she need a new job? True, Mrs. Amino would help her find employment, but had she decided what she wanted to do?

No, she hadn't.

"Aha! That's why you look so depressed, " Matthew smiled. "Don't worry—that'll work out all right, too."

What could he be thinking? Matthew and his irrepressible optimism had been buddies for twenty-eight years. And that smile must have rubbed off from Barbara. It was the kind of smile that could turn toads into princes and make flowers bloom on barren branches.

Maiko suddenly wanted to upset the basket. Was there some

way to peel away his mask and get down to the man behind the smile? "Matthew, if your mother loved you not as a son but as a man, what would you do?"

It was a cruel question. This morning as she saw the two of them laughing together, Maiko hadn't failed to notice how much Mrs. Amino had changed in the past two days. A menial servant is a sharp judge, and accurate as well. But the question didn't faze him.

"It *has* thrown me for a loop," Matthew said, "suddenly finding myself with a mother. I feel like I'm in the middle of a play starring her and me, and I'm trying my best to play the son. When the play's over, she'll go back to being a woman. But it doesn't matter how much time passes—three days, a week, a year—Mrs. Amino will always be the mother I never thought existed. If you want me to think of her as a woman, not a mother, OK, I can handle it. Like, what if Elizabeth Taylor showed up and said she was my real mother? I saw her on TV the other day and she's still gorgeous. I'd want to sleep with her, even if she was my mother. Mrs. Amino's no Elizabeth Taylor, but that's not the point. The point is that she'll always play the role of my real mother. And for her, I'll always be her son brought back from the unknown."

"You're a very honest person," Maiko said, impressed.

Matthew was always honest. He was a former rental child, but this real parent and real child business wasn't the same. Being a rental child means being everyone's child, and no one's. But never just *one* person's.

"I've been thinking," Matthew said. "Mrs. Amino's still young for a widow. Instead of taking care of her beloved son, she could try to find a new lover. I could be her lover, but that wouldn't fly—she'd say we had to be mother and child. That's our relationship. Maybe I should say *contract*. But without a lover she'll just grow old. She used to be a hot Ginza hostess, so she knows how to use her body to live. She's found her son. Now she's got to find a lover."

"But what would you do if she did?" Maiko asked. "Leave her and go off somewhere?"

"Oh, I'll be in and out. I've got two little ideas I've been toying with. One of them I can't tell you about now. It's top secret."

"And the other one?"

Matthew tightened the final nut on the tire and started to lower the jack.

"Finished!" he exclaimed. "Good thing this didn't happen on the highway."

"So what's this other plan? Tell, me, Matthew-*san*."

"Just call me Matthew, Maiko. That's very important. Hey— I still have to teach you how to whistle."

"And while you're at it?"

"Honest Matthew will confess. What I mean is, I like you. You make me feel—I don't know—nostalgic."

"But Matthew," Maiko said, "you already have Penelope. She's the woman for you, right?"

"We only meet once every three years. That's our agreement. In the meantime we see each other in dreams. We have a dream contract. I want to make the same contract with you. I have a dream friend in Tokyo—Raphael—but still no dream girlfriend. Maiko, the first time I met you, I felt I needed you. I'm not sure why. Maybe Mikainaito picked up some strong vibes from you. When I'm with you, I feel like anything is possible."

"How do you go about making a dream contract?"

"I plant a seed from my consciousness in you. And you do the same in me. Why don't we go somewhere we can relax and think about what comes next, OK? Including *your* next step."

Coaxed on by the Jaguar, Maiko soon found herself in a room at a resort hotel on a hill. The scent of newly laundered sheets filled the room. Maiko practiced whistling. As soon as they entered the room, rain began to fall. Matthew stood watching the rain, then abruptly turned and lay down on the bed.

"Do you always take girls to hotel rooms like this?" Maiko asked.

"Only the ones who want to. I have my own likes and dis-likes when it comes to women, and my own set of rules."

"'The man who makes a million girls cry,' right?"

"'Fraid not. The one who always cries is me."

Maiko continued her whistling practice, but the air just slid past her lips without a sound. Tense your nostrils, Matthew told her; when she did, out came a plaintive sound.

"All *right*!" Matthew said. "Way to go. So the first goal was pretty easy."

"First goal? What's the second?"

"Come over here and sit down." Matthew patted the bed, urging Maiko to come to him. Tugged by his will, she peeled herself off the wall and walked toward the bed.

I'll Be Your Lover

(Only five days ago that I met you, Matthew—what a strange first meeting—there I was shadowing you, and a minute later we were saying hello like old friends—like childhood friends who hadn't seen each other in two years—and Kubi—what in-tuition, what luck—it's almost scary—tracking down one per-son in the middle of Tokyo, meeting this gay man named Ra-phael and then conquering his depression—on the trail of Matthew, Kubi said, he'd discovered a whole different Tokyo—while I went off to New York to meet your past, Matthew—your Boss looked so lonely—and poor Barbara, the one who loves you so much—without her there would have been no rental children—Katagiri, the refugee Japanese—laying his body on the line to survive, making his own religion, his own country—the kind of Japanese you'll never find in Japan—before going to New York I went to that jail—met the man who brought you to Tokyo—why did I take this job looking for Matthew?—because spending all my time with money made me sick, that's why—Mrs. Amino tempted me—please find my son, she said—every-thing started with these words—for the past three months my head's been filled with nothing but Matthew—why?—Matthew, you weren't supposed to really show up—you were supposed to stay a shadow—what was I trying to gain by looking for you? I feel empty—it's like everything worked out before anything really happened—my turn's over—Matthew will be gone some-day—and we'll all be phantoms again—it makes me sad—but it wasn't as if looking for you was why I took this on—bringing you and Mrs. Amino together—that wasn't my job—you're my Matthew now, too—I don't know why, yes, I'm attracted to you—I want to go wherever you go—I want to know more about you—I still haven't found *my* Matthew—all I've found is Mrs. Amino's son—my real job's barely begun—that's right—you're more interesting than money—but you're still a riddle—and my job is to solve the riddle—)

Matthew whispered in her ear: You were trying to get me—Maiko, we're in the middle of a desert—there's just the sand and the sun and us—no one else—there's nothing there to do but love each other—but if you left me alone, or if I left you alone—what would we do? we'd still continue to love each other—com-munication in dreams works best when you're alone in a desert—I'll send Mikainaito flying off to see you—leave the window to your dreams open so he can get in—he's made out of the same stuff as dreams—me, my lovers, my friends—we all have to love him, or else he'll disappear.

You make it sound like you're going to go away somewhere and just leave Mikainaito behind—stop talking like that—I want the *real* you here.

(*God, what gorgeous skin—Maiko's breathing harder—I can suck in her breath—reminds me of Penelope when she was still an elf—what a wonderful smell—the smell of Maiko's body, like butter wrapped in silk—because my mother searched for me, I can be here like this—be-cause I was a refugee in Tokyo, because I made a contract with Penelope and became a professional lover, because I was a rental child, because Katagiri trained me, because you, Mikainaito, are with me, because my real father kidnapped me, because my mother gave birth to me, because*

Tokyo and New York didn't get destroyed——here I am——I am here because of me——I've found a new elf——with lovely legs——and skin as fine as flower petals——even if I wander in the desert, I'll never stop wooing women——even if no one listens, I'll still sing a song of love——with a dried out throat I'll sing my song to love and friendship——'cause I am one happy-go-lucky guy.)

Ah, Matthew——I just don't know——I love you——but I'm not Penelope——I know, Maiko——but I need you——I need you too, Matthew (I want you)——I want to be like this forever.

(But you understand I sleep with guys, too?——I sleep with anyone, and flattery goes to my head——you should understand that——I'm a wandering merchant peddling platonic love, and sexual love, too——but Maiko, you're something more than a client——something more than just a lover——like Penelope——)

(Matthew comes in through my mouth——seeps down underneath my skin——no, stop——that's dangerous——Matthew's inside me——my whole body is filled with Matthew——)

Why do I feel like we've been lovers for a long time?——Matthew——who are you?

Matthew——please, no——I'll get——ah——don't stop——you're inside me——oh god——the air's getting heavy——kiss me——hold me tighter——(you feel like you're going to fly away——to an earth on the other side of the sun)

Don't worry, everything'll be OK, Maiko——'cause I love you——we'll be together even if we're apart——hold me tighter——I'll be your lover——Matthew, I love you——I'll never let you go——come with me——come inside of me!

16

Creation

A Happy Ending

"I have a little job to take care of, Mother. I was wondering if you could let me have some spending money?"

Matthew pocketed his pay and left Mrs. Amino's estate, dragging his baby carriage behind him.

Ever since the night at Hakone, he and Maiko had been like childhood sweethearts. "I'll be gone for a while," he told her, "but don't think I'm running away."

Maiko was his lover, he informed his mother.

Mrs. Amino was surprised at how quickly things had developed, but relieved, too, that they had gone generally according to script.

Two days passed, then three. Matthew still hadn't returned. He did call Maiko on the second day to say he loved her. "I'll send Mikainaito flying off to see you tonight," he said glibly. Maiko knew that Matthew was often gone on business for a week, but on the seventh day she began to worry.

Stopping by his apartment, she found his things gone. He's left me, she told herself matter-of-factly. Until now, she had refused to believe that the vows they'd made were just the whisperings of a one-night stand. And here, against evidence to the contrary, she couldn't fully accept even the notion that he may have jilted her—for the misery would be unbearable. Of course, Maiko never expected that they would marry and live at Mrs. Amino's. *That* would be too simple. And for Matthew, marriage would be the same as a prison sentence.

Maiko didn't want to be unrealistic, but she'd been on the verge of collapse. Matthew, for all his unpredictability, was a safe foothold that kept her from plunging into darkness. She couldn't tie him down, but at the least she wanted to know where he was.

Matthew has no home to return to, she reasoned. He met his real mother, but her house isn't his home. The only home he has is the next place he's headed for. But that's not entirely true. In his mind he *does* have a place to go back to—Penelope. Penelope is the only home Matthew has. And Maiko was completely overshadowed. Matthew, you are a jerk.

Had Matthew made the same kind of agreement with Maiko that he made with Penelope? Would he not show up for three years? That was asking a bit much. Did that mean they were to spend the next three years apart, playing around and having other lovers? Maiko felt conned. It meant she didn't even need to be his lover, didn't it? But . . . what if Mikainaito really *did* come back to visit her? Could she mean more to Matthew than Penelope?

Around the third week, a postcard arrived. A French stamp, postmarked Paris. Brushing aside her doubts, Maiko read Matthew's rather blunt explanation:

I dreamed of you today. I'm not sure where it was, but there were these crumbling pyramids. All the pyramids were made out of scrap, empty cans, junked cars. The air was heavy. Maybe gravity had gotten stronger. I was worn out. You were up among the garbage scrounging around for things we could use or eat.

And you know what you said to me?

"Matthew, dinner's ready."

Maiko, I have this job that's a pain in the butt I've got to take care of. It'll take a while to finish up. As soon as I can, I'll be back to see you.

That night Maiko had a dream. The marvelous feelings of that night at Hakone came flooding back. She was floating inside a spaceship free of gravity. She couldn't see Matthew, but she felt him holding her, caressing her. She felt something growing inside her. A sunflower.

A month passed and still Matthew didn't return. Maiko wondered if she'd have to start from scratch and look for him all over again; then he phoned:

Sorry I haven't stayed in touch. I'm in Beirut now, but I'll be back soon. Tomorrow this company's going to be paying my ransom. And then I'll be freed. I'm being held hostage, but I made a deal beforehand with the kidnappers so even if negotiations break down I won't be killed. When they get the ransom, I get 10 percent. I promised I'd do this job for them a long time ago so I couldn't back out of it. Who would ever think the hostage and the kidnappers were in cahoots? But once is enough. When I get back let's start something new. How about a rental child business in Tokyo? I'll ask my mother to help. We could invite Mama and Katagiri over as consultants. Don't worry—everything'll work out fine. Well, this call's getting expensive so I'd better hang up. Say hello to Mother.

Say hello to Mother *yourself*! Going to Beirut without a word, getting these Palestinian guerrillas to kidnap him. Was she supposed to *believe* this? No way! This was a bad joke. Or maybe a bad dream? Let this be a dream, please, because if it's not it's pretty hard to swallow. Always getting people in an uproar, that's Matthew. But was it really him on the phone? Maybe he'll be showing up any minute and she could tell him about this weird dream she was having. *Matthew, please, come back, soon.* Was he really in Beirut? . . .

Wait—she'd almost forgotten—Matthew lives in dreams. The real Matthew is not the one on the phone, or the one who wrote the postcard. The real Matthew is the one in her dreams.

Mikainaito, tell me—where is he? If I'm pregnant like I'm sure I am, what kind of future is the child going to have with a father like Matthew? Do rental children's kids become rental kids? Was Matthew serious about starting a rental child business in Tokyo? Would he become Katagiri? Would I become Barbara? Would Mrs. Amino be our sponsor? Can the comedy, Matthew.

On second thought, though, it does sound intriguing.

Mikainaito, tell him this: "I'm going to have your child. And I'm going to play to my heart's content, too. Like Kubi used to say, all you can do is boil up a pot full of coincidences and enjoy life as it comes."

This was one dream from which she didn't plan to wake.

Creation

Once I dreamed that I created the world. Since it was a dream, becoming a god was a cinch. In dreams anything can happen, and everything is real. Nothing is impossible. Only where there is gravity do certain things become impossible— and in dreams there is no gravity. To become a god, I became a perfect dream messenger, traveling beyond time and space. Only in dreams am I free.

It took me just three days to create the world.

DAY ONE:

The day Nothingness changed into Something.

A multicolored, starfish-shaped cloud was floating in the blackness of the universe. The cloud was created by the Big Bang at the same time as the universe, and it was packed tight with Nothingness. This was the womb which gave birth to Everything, and it is still somewhere out in the universe raining down meteors. Meteors smashed into each other, and that is how the Earth was made. Bits of junk were created at the same time, some flying off in all directions, some staying on the Earth. Some of this junk became the moon, some later on the living things of the Earth, the oceans, the air, the mountains and forests. When the Earth was first formed, though, these were still covered in flames, without form or name, neither dead nor alive, floating like the moon around the Earth.

In the afternoon of the first day, an unseen force began to act upon the Earth—an energy called gravity. The junk could not float in space any longer and poured down on the Earth's surface. Formless things took on shape, took on weight and size. Things that were the same became different, and became part of the Earth. Some things froze immediately, and others burned up. Some turned to gas and evaporated, some to solid rock; some became flowing water, or dissolved in water. Some things had a use, and some were useless.

DAY TWO:

The day things created out of Nothingness combined to create something new.

Water and rocks and thunder and air joined to make fish. Birds were created out of wind and air and clouds and soil. Animals that roamed the land were made out of soil and air and fire and rain. Humans were created from water and fish and birds and animals and insects and vegetation and light. Plants were born from the wind and fire and soil and rain.

There were ten varieties of things on the Earth. Water, stone, air, gravity, fire, soil, heat, light, time, and form. From early morning they banged one into the other, creating billions of invisible objects which swirled around the Earth. Whirlpools. These whirlpools became wind and rain and clouds and thunder, friction and explosions, seas and rivers, mountains and valleys, magnetism and electricity. These new moving objects multiplied one after the other, animating the Earth. Unheard-of things came into being. By the evening of the second day, the Earth was overflowing with countless varieties of things. The situation was getting out of hand, though—there were just too many things—so Wise Beings decided to put everything in order. These Wise Beings were one of the masterpieces born of Nothingness. Some people call them gods. A billion gods were born at once. Gods were wise because at any time they pleased, they could return to Nothingness.

The gods drew lines over the Earth. They gathered the fish in the oceans, people in cities, birds in the air, moles under ground, and pigs in styes. And they created death, so that everything, when its time was up, returned to Nothingness.

DAY THREE:

The day gravity goes nuts, and everything becomes free.

Gravity starts to work backwards, forming whirlpools, radiating every which way. The gods' order is shot to hell.

Children become birds and leave on trips, trees turn into missiles and shoot into the sky, stones dance through space like they're skipping on water. Birds change into moles, and cats stand up straight. Whales and dolphins climb trees, kangaroos return to the sea, elephants flap their ears like flying squirrels, dogs do handstands. Turtles spin around in place, oceans turn to clouds, mountains into valleys, rivers into tornadoes and flow up into the sky. The wind digs holes in the ground, and deserts turn into jungles. Old people lie clinging to the ground, deep-sea fish leap out of the water at blinding speed. Droopy eyes turn slanted, wall-eyes become crossed. The gods start fighting each other, the north and south poles turn into tropical paradises, the equator bids the Earth adieu and flies off to become like the rings of Saturn.

In the middle of the night everything sleeps, dreaming dreams of starfish-shaped, multicolored clouds.

We are still in the second day of creation. But the morning of the third day will surely come. People who hope to be a part of that world await the coming of the dawn. As long as we stay mired in the night of the second day, this sense of powerlessness and despair can never be wiped away. A rental child cannot remain forever innocent. As the night of the second day deepens, a realization hits him—he can become no one else; to try to do so is to struggle in vain. And with this newfound knowledge, as the morning of the third day breaks, the rental child will come into his own.

The world wasn't created according to some plan of an all-knowing, all-powerful god. It came about by accident, through the gods' wasted effort, through unprogrammed, free play. A million gods loved each other, hated each other, grew jealous, went insane, got sick, fought battles, formed conspiracies, were transformed, died and were reborn. And dreamed. And before anyone knew it, the world was born.

Until the evening of the third day, creation is not complete. On the morning of the third day, the rental child will join the gods at play. And the world will never be the same.